ANSEL ADAMS

ANSEL ADAMS

IN THE LANE COLLECTION

Karen E. Haas

Rebecca A. Senf

MFA PUBLICATIONS

a division of the Museum of Fine Arts, Boston

MFA PUBLICATIONS
a division of the Museum of Fine Arts, Boston
465 Huntington Avenue
Boston, Massachusetts 02115
www.mfa-publications.org

Published in conjunction with the exhibition "Ansel Adams," organized by the Museum of Fine Arts, Boston, from August 21 to December 31, 2005.

Generous support for this publication was provided by The Lane Collection Fund.

For a complete listing of MFA Publications, please contact the publisher at the address at left, or call 617 369 3438.

Cover illustrations: Ansel Adams, *Rain, Yosemite Valley, California,* about 1940 (front); *Dunes, Oceano, California,* about 1950 (back).

Endpapers: Detail of *Grass and Pool,* from *Portfolio III: Yosemite Valley,* 1959 (front); detail of *Sodium Sulphite Crystals,* 1962 (back).

Frontispiece: *Self-Portrait, Monument Valley, Utah,* 1958.

Unless otherwise noted, all illustrations were photographed by the Photo Studios, Museum of Fine Arts, Boston.

ISBN 0-87846-693-2 (hardcover)
ISBN 0-87846-694-0 (softcover)
Library of Congress Control Number: 2005926794

Edited by Sarah E. McGaughey and Emiko K. Usui
Copyedited by Dalia Geffen and Denise Bergman
Proofread by Dalia Geffen

Designed and produced by Cynthia Rockwell Randall
Printed at The Stinehour Press, Lunenburg, Vermont.

FIRST EDITION
Printed on acid-free paper

CONTENTS

DIRECTOR'S FOREWORD

THE MUSEUM OF FINE ARTS, BOSTON is proud to present the work
of Ansel Adams, one of the most highly regarded photographers
of the twentieth century. The quintessential photographer of the
American West, Adams was also an influential author, teacher, and
environmental activist. A tireless promoter of photography as a fine
art, he believed that "art is the affirmation of life."

The inspiring images that fill these pages are all drawn from
the collection of the late William H. Lane and his wife, Saundra.
The Lane Collection of American modernist photography is on
long-term loan to the Museum and encompasses the largest holding
of Adams' work in private hands. This catalogue, which is supported by The Lane Collection Fund, and the exhibition it accompanies
are the latest in a series of projects based on The Lane Collection
that have been organized over the past two decades by the MFA.
Others have been devoted to the work of Charles Sheeler and
Edward Weston.

None of these projects would have been possible without the
help and enthusiasm of Saundra Lane. Her generous public spirit
and longstanding commitment to art education inspire her to share
these important works with our visitors and to tour them for the
benefit of audiences worldwide. We are profoundly grateful.

A number of public institutions and private collectors have
generously lent additional objects to the exhibition, and we particularly want to thank Leo and Gabriella Beranek, Polaroid Corporation, the George Eastman House, the Bancroft Library, and the
Center for Creative Photography. These loans complement the rich
holdings of The Lane Collection and allow us to offer a complete
presentation of Adams' varied and dynamic photographic career.

MALCOLM ROGERS
Ann and Graham Gund Director
Museum of Fine Arts, Boston

Imogen Cunningham (1883–1976), *Ansel Adams, Yosemite Valley*, 1953. Gelatin
silver print, 25.4 x 20.3 cm (10 x 8 in.), The Lane Collection. Photograph courtesy
of The Imogen Cunningham Trust. © The Imogen Cunningham Trust.

ANSEL ADAMS, THE MUSEUM, AND THE ART OF PHOTOGRAPHY

THE MUSEUM OF FINE ARTS, BOSTON'S photography collection was initiated by Ansel Adams' mentor and role model, Alfred Stieglitz. In 1924 the Trustees accepted the gift of twenty-seven Stieglitz photographs on the recommendation of Stieglitz's friend, the MFA's extraordinary keeper of Indian Art, Ananda K. Coomaraswamy.

A second, larger donation of Stieglitz's photographs was received in 1950 from the artist Georgia O'Keeffe, the widow of the photographer and impresario of modern American art. These gifts were, as was undoubtedly intended, the seed from which the Museum's photography collection has grown. However, no purchases were made until 1967, when the Museum acquired works by Adams' friend Edward Weston from Boston's pioneering gallery of photography, the Carl Siembab Gallery. In retrospect, it is clear that the late 1960s and early 1970s was historically a time when many American art museums began to pursue more actively the acquisition of photographs.

The year 1967 was also when the Ansel Adams retrospective "The Eloquent Light" was shown at the Museum of Fine Arts. This, the first major photography exhibition to be held at the Museum, attracted much favorable attention and strong attendance, and inspired not only collectors Bill and Saundra Lane (see Karen Haas's essay "A Great Day for Photography" in this volume) but also the Museum itself. About the same time, director Perry Rathbone invited Ansel Adams and photo historian Beaumont Newhall (who had been involved with the organization of the exhibition) to meet with him, curator of prints and drawings Eleanor Sayre, and me to advise us on the collecting of photography. Needless to say, Adams and Newhall were in favor of the idea, and their distinguished presence blessed the beginnings of our acquisition program.

At this time, both Adams and the Museum were closely involved with Edwin Land's locally based Polaroid Corporation. In 1968 Adams gave the Museum photographs of our Old Kingdom Egyptian sculptures that he had made with experimental Polaroid negative material. The Museum's relationship with that company, undoubtedly fostered by Adams' guiding spirit, in 1972 resulted in a series of three purchase grants from the Polaroid Foundation, which we used to acquire work by classic and emerging photographers.

Adams and his associates continued to be an integral part of the collection's growth. In 1970 David H. McAlpin, a friend and collector of Adams' work, gave funds to purchase a group of platinum prints by the great British architectural photographer Frederick Evans. In 1974 we ordered prints of two expressive Adams landscapes, *Mono Lake* and *Frozen Lake and Cliffs, Kaweah Gap*, which the photographer kindly chose to donate to the collection. Starting in the 1970s, we began to receive gifts of fine Adams prints from one of the department's staunch supporters, Carolyn Rowland, who was a participant in Adams' second Yosemite workshop in 1941.

The culmination of all these initiatives occurred in 1977 and 1978, when the Museum acquired a significant group of photographs from the estate of Stieglitz's friend and protégé Paul Strand, and the Trustees agreed to change the name of the department to Prints, Drawings, and *Photographs*. For several decades, I served as the Museum's unofficial curator of photography. Hired in 1966 to work with old master prints, I was part of an early sixties generation attuned to multiple originals, whether contemporary prints or the art of photography. Today, Anne Havinga is curator of photographs and Karen Haas is curator of The Lane Collection. The Museum's collection has grown significantly, and The Lane Collection, as this exhibition so clearly demonstrates, continues to be a marvelously rich resource full of artistic surprises.

CLIFFORD S. ACKLEY
Chair, Prints, Drawings, and Photographs
Ruth and Carl Shapiro Curator of Prints and Drawings

ACKNOWLEDGMENTS

FIRST AND FOREMOST, we are deeply grateful to Saundra B. Lane for the continuing inspiration and support she has provided to the Department of Prints, Drawings, and Photographs over the years. Her passion for the work of her friend Ansel Adams has been a significant source of inspiration for this exhibition and catalogue, as well as for all those who have had the pleasure of working on it. We also owe thanks to Malcolm Rogers, Ann and Graham Gund Director of the Museum of Fine Arts, who has encouraged this project from its inception. Many members of the Museum staff gave of their time and talents, and the success of the exhibition and book are, in large part, due to their collective efforts. We gratefully acknowledge Clifford Ackley, Jennifer Bose, Keith Crippen, Elliot Davis, Gail English, Kena Frank, Kim French, Kerry Gaertner, Katie Getchell, Phil Getchell, Ann Ghormley, Kelly Gifford, Kerry Greaves, Dawn Griffin, Andy Haines, Anne Havinga, Greg Heins, Erica Hirshler, Paige Johnston, Jill Kennedy-Kernohan, Debra LaKind, Thomas Lang, Barbara Martin, David Mathews, William McAvoy, Terry McAweeney, Sarah McGaughey, Maureen Melton, Patrick Murphy, Janet O'Donoghue, Roy Perkinson, Mark Polizzotti, Cynthia Randall, Sue Reed, Jaime Roark, Katherine Sanderson, Rachel Saunders, Gilian Shallcross, Hao Sheng, Lois Solomon, Stephanie Stepanek, Emiko Usui, Tanya Uyeda, Gerald Ward, Jennifer Weissman, and John Woolf.

We are extremely appreciative of William Turnage, for sharing his recollections of Adams and his work. He, the Trustees, and Claudia Kishler of the Ansel Adams Publishing Rights Trust deserve special mention for making this project as a whole possible. We also extend our heartfelt thanks to the Adams family and, in particular, Jeanne, Michael, and Matthew Adams and Anne and Ken Helms.

For their generous assistance and support of our research, we are indebted to many individuals and institutions. We extend our warm thanks to Richard Aspenwind, Cultural Affairs Specialist of the Taos Pueblo; the staff at the Beinecke Library, Yale University, New Haven, Connecticut; Janice Braun, Special Collections Librarian, F. W. Olin Library, Mills College, Oakland, California; Thomas Carey, Librarian, San Francisco History Center of the San Francisco Public Library; Mariana Cook and Hans Kraus; Glenn Crosby, Curator, and Claudia Welsh, Manager, Ansel Adams Gallery, Yosemite, California; Susan Ehrens and Leland Rice; Patricia Farbman; Dave Forgang, Director, Barbara Beroza, Curator of Collections, Jim Snyder, Historian, and Linda Eade, Librarian, Yosemite Museum and Research Center, Yosemite Valley, California; Steve Henrickson, Curator of Collections, Alaska State Museum, Juneau, Alaska; Paul Hertzmann and Susan Herzig; Barbara Hitchcock, Curator, and Thomas Gustainis, Polaroid Collections, Waltham, Massachusetts; Lisa Hostetler, Research Associate, Metropolitan Museum of Art, New York; Stephen B. Jareckie, Photography Adviser to the Fitchburg Art Museum, Fitchburg, Massachusetts; Drew Heath Johnson, Curator of Photography, Oakland Museum of California; Chris Jones, Assistant Curator of Prints and Photographs, University of New Mexico Art Museum, Albuquerque; Deborah Martin Kao, Richard L. Menschel Curator of Photography, and Michelle Lamunière, Charles C. Cunningham Sr. Assistant Curator of Photography, Fogg Art Museum, Cambridge, Massachusetts; Richard Maack, Photography Editor, *Arizona Highways*, Phoenix, Arizona; Robert Mann of the Robert Mann Gallery, New York; Paul Martineau, Curatorial Assistant, Department of Photographs, J. Paul Getty Museum, Los Angeles, California; Estate of Sarah Sage McAlpin; Alison Nordström, Curator of Photographs, Joe Struble, Assistant Archivist, Photograph Collection, and Jiuan-jiuan Chen, Assistant Director for Conservation, George Eastman House, Rochester, New York; Ted Orland; Sandra S. Phillips, Senior Curator of Photography, and Erin Garcia, Curatorial Associate in the Department of Photography, San Francisco Museum of Modern Art; Dennis Reed; Alan Ross; Carolyn Rowland; Amy Rule, Archivist, Leslie Calmes, Archivist, Marcia Tiede, Curatorial Associate, and Denise Gosé, Rights and Reproductions at the Center for Creative Photography, Tucson, Arizona; Amy Scott, Curator of Visual Arts, Museum of the American West, Los Angeles, California; Andrew Smith and John Boland of the Andrew Smith Gallery, Santa Fe, New Mexico; John Sexton; Aaron Schmidt of the Boston Public Library Photograph

Collection; Kim Sichel, Art History Department Chair and Associate Professor, Boston University; Tom Southall, former Curator of Photography, High Museum, Atlanta, Georgia; Andrea Stillman; John Szarkowski, Director Emeritus of the Department of Photography at the Museum of Modern Art, New York; Blair D. Tarr, Museum Curator, Kansas State Historical Society, Topeka, Kansas; heirs of Willard Van Dyke; Leonard Vernon and his collection curator, Paul Duff; Jack von Euw, Curator of Pictorial Collections, Anthony Bliss, Curator, Rare Books and Literary Manuscripts, and Susan Snyder, Head of Public Services, Bancroft Library, Berkeley, California; Vivian Walworth; Jennifer Watts, Curator of Photographs, Jessica Todd Smith, Curator of American Art, and Genevieve Preston, Art Information Cataloguer, Huntington Library, Pasadena, California; Maggi Weston and Rod Dresser; Stephen and Mus White; Peter and Barbara Winkelstein; David L. Witt, Curator of the Harwood Museum, Taos, New Mexico; Don Worth; Steve Yates, Curator of Photography, and Joan Tafoya, Registrar, Museum of Fine Arts, Santa Fe, New Mexico; and Carl Zahn.

For their generosity in lending work to the exhibition, we are grateful to Charles Faulhaber, James D. Hart Director, Bancroft Library; Leo and Gabriella Beranek; Douglas R. Nickel, Director, Center for Creative Photography; Alison Nordström, Curator of Photographs, George Eastman House; Thomas W. Lentz, Director, Harvard University Art Museums; Barbara Hitchcock, Curator, Polaroid Collections; and Linda W. Bahm, Director, University of New Mexico Art Museum.

Most of all we want to thank Kate Harper for all of her help in managing this project through its critical last months; Mary Ellen Beaurain, Al Kaszniak, and Janet Senf for graciously hosting us in Tucson; and, last but not least, Jason Hollister and Greg Heins, for their unwavering humor and encouragement.

THE AUTHORS

Dedicated to
VIRGINIA BEST ADAMS
1904–2000
who quietly encouraged and
inspired all those who had the
privilege to know her
Saundra B. Lane

1. ALFRED STIEGLITZ AT AN AMERICAN PLACE, NEW YORK CITY, *ABOUT 1939*

ANSEL ADAMS: SEEKING A CENTER FOR PHOTOGRAPHY

ANSEL ADAMS NEVER IMAGINED in his early days as a photographer that he would one day become an "institution."[1] In his *Autobiography*, he wrote: "Without my awareness, I became famous. Relatively few really know me, but millions know the folk hero they think is me. I have apparently touched many people through my work, and this gives me great satisfaction."[2] Although he could not have foreseen it, Adams emerged as the first real photographer "superstar" in America in the late 1960s and early '70s, at a moment when the field was capturing the attention of a broad swath of the public, a number of fine art photography galleries were starting to open, and museums were beginning to seriously collect photography. His career spanned more than six decades, from the early 1920s until his death in 1984, and, as is often recounted, it produced tens of thousands of negatives, dozens of books, hundreds of exhibitions, and thousands of students. In 1979 *American Photographer* magazine hailed Adams as "Mr. Photography" and *Time* featured him on its cover; the following year, he was granted the Medal of Freedom, America's highest civilian honor, and a print of his most popular subject, *Moonrise, Hernandez, New Mexico*, sold at auction for $71,500, the highest price ever paid for a photograph at the time.[3]

Although there are many accounts of his awards and accomplishments as a successful landscape photographer and outspoken environmentalist, what they often overlook is the other Ansel Adams, the author, teacher, critic, curator, and tireless promoter of photography. Adams is frequently compared to his mentor, Alfred Stieglitz, whose fight for the recognition of photography as a fine art greatly inspired the younger man. Stieglitz was an important early advocate for the medium through the example of his own photography, the influential magazines he published, and the avant-garde exhibitions he presented in his various galleries. However, describing Stieglitz—as one writer has—as "the towering figure in American photography during the first half of this century" and Adams as "his equivalent during the second"[4] is deceptive, for it credits Adams only

with having assumed his role very late in his career. In fact, long before midcentury, Adams consciously took up the cause of photography and exported his own brand of proselytizing to the West Coast. He gradually gained confidence in his abilities as spokesperson for the field and spread his reach far beyond the San Francisco Bay Area that he called home.

The two men had very different characters, as their lengthy correspondence attests. Unlike Stieglitz, who by the 1930s was content to hang his gallery walls with the work of a select few and otherwise to avoid the larger public debate, Adams, a generation younger, took a much more democratic view. Harboring a long-standing belief that photography should be accessible to a broader audience, Adams set out to spread the word through exhibitions, publications, and teaching. He also came to believe in the fundamental importance of a "center for photography," a term that meant many different things to Adams, all of which had their roots in his formative experience at Stieglitz's New York gallery, An American Place. "The Place," as both men came to refer to it over time, grew in Adams' mind to symbolize his dream of a gathering place, an exhibition and education space, and a vehicle for promoting the idea of "straight," unmanipulated photography. The debate over the sharp-focus modernist photography that Stieglitz championed versus the more painterly, imitative pictorialism that amateur camera clubs promoted is so long over (and won) that it is easy to forget the passion it still inspired during the 1930s and '40s.[5]

When Adams went to New York City for the first time in 1933 and met Stieglitz at the gallery at Madison and Fifty-third, Adams had only recently given up his dream of becoming a concert pianist. He had been avidly photographing since 1916, when as a teenager he first visited Yosemite National Park with a brand-new Kodak Box Brownie camera, but it was only since the late 1920s that he had come to think of his hobby as a possible profession. He and his wife, Virginia, arrived in New York in late March at the height of the Depression; he was thirty-one years old, and she was pregnant with their first child. The initial encounter with Stieglitz began

2. NEW YORK CITY FROM THE BARBIZON PLAZA HOTEL, *ABOUT 1940*

badly, when the older man summarily dismissed him and told him to return with his work later in the day, obviously unimpressed by Adams' letter of introduction from a wealthy San Francisco patron. The situation improved only after Adams swallowed his pride and went back to meet with Stieglitz, who looked through his photographs twice without comment before pronouncing them some of the finest he had ever seen.[6]

Adams later claimed that what he gained from that 1933 meeting was an "affirmation of [his] approach" and the knowledge that he was "obviously on a good track,"[7] but it is clear that he came away from the experience with much more than that. Stieglitz was by then the *éminence grise* of the photography world and still a force to be reckoned with; Adams was the latest in a long line of photographers who had made the pilgrimage to show work to him. Friends Paul Strand and Charles Sheeler had preceded Adams in the 1910s, and Edward Weston made the cross-country trip in 1922.[8] The time spent at An American Place was pivotally important to Adams, and his vivid memories of it stayed with him long afterward. In a letter to Stieglitz written three years later, he described the gallery as a kind of sanctuary, like "a deep pool of clear water in a desert. . . . Whoever drinks from this pool will never be thirsty."[9]

In 1936 Stieglitz gave him a one-man exhibition at An American Place, which Adams maintained was the highlight of his artistic career. The forty-five prints in the show, carefully sequenced by Stieglitz and hung against cool gray walls in the austere space of the gallery, were a revelation to Adams, leaving him feeling as though he was seeing his own photographs for the first time.[10] In a letter to his assistant, he wrote: "The show was presented in a way that I can never describe. Not only were the prints hung in a visually perfect way, but the hanging actually psychoanalyzed me. The prints were never grouped to achieve culmination of effect or idea—but were related one to the other in such a way that both my strength and weakness were indicated."[11] For Stieglitz the show was a welcome opportunity to feature the work of a young photographer whom he admired, something he had not done in more than four years.[12]

Adams' exhibition, which ran from October 27 through November 25 of that year, included only a handful of his better-known western landscape views and was made up instead of close-ups, portraits, still lifes, and images of architectural and man-made

Fig. 1. Willard Van Dyke (American, 1906–1986), *Ansel Adams at 683 Brockhurst*, 1932. Gelatin silver print, 23.3 x 18.3 cm (9 3/16 x 7 3/16 in.). The Lane Collection. Photograph courtesy of The Willard Van Dyke Estate, © 2000, The Willard Van Dyke Estate.

3. SNOW ON TREES, YOSEMITE NATIONAL PARK, *ABOUT 1930*

subjects. The show was a critical, as well as financial, success for the young photographer, and Adams was greatly encouraged by the experience.[13] He corresponded with Stieglitz on his way back to San Francisco, writing, "My own work has suddenly become something new to me—new, and exciting as never before";[14] not long after, he wrote again: "I wonder if you can ever know what your showing my work has done for my whole direction in life?"[15] According to Adams, after the exhibition closed, he asked Stieglitz what he thought he should do next and what direction his new work should take. The older man simply replied: "I do not care what you do, provided you go beyond me."[16]

THE ANSEL ADAMS GALLERY

Although Stieglitz had not initially offered Adams an exhibition after their first meeting in 1933, his positive response to his work did inspire the younger man to show his photographs to Alma Reed, who owned the East Fifty-seventh Street Delphic Studios, one of the rare New York galleries regularly exhibiting photography during the 1930s.[17] Reed granted Adams a solo show later that year, and, beginning in November, he exhibited fifty of his photographs with her, selling eight prints for a total of $120 (which he apparently never received).[18] A glowing review of the show in the *New York Times* must have pleased him immensely: "Photography by Ansel Adams, a Californian, strikingly captures a world of poetic form. His lens has caught snow-laden branches in their delicate tracery; shells embedded in sandstone; great trees and cumulus clouds. It is masterly stuff."[19]

The first meeting with Stieglitz also motivated Adams to try his hand at starting his own gallery when he returned to California. Although those closest to him worried that he did not have the constitution for this type of work and that the general economic situation at the time was grim, Adams was determined to carry out his plan based on Stieglitz's An American Place, as there was nothing of its kind in San Francisco. Unlike Stieglitz, though, who had independent means, Adams was obliged to do portraits, magazine work, and advertising photography to support himself and his family.[20] Nevertheless, in the midst of all the freelance work, the birth of his first child, and his annual summer trek in Yosemite with the Sierra Club, Adams managed to open the Ansel Adams Gallery in September 1933. The simple, light-filled space was located downtown, at 166 Geary Street near Union Square, in what had previously been the Galerie Beaux Arts, a modernist paintings gallery. Adams

RIGHT: 4. LEAVES, MILLS COLLEGE, OAKLAND, CALIFORNIA, *ABOUT 1931*

envisioned his gallery as both an exhibition space and a studio, using the phrase "center for photography" for the first time when describing it to Stieglitz.[21] He hoped that not only would it draw the public in to see exhibitions, but also that it might have the practical outcome of bringing in additional commercial work and portrait commissions.[22]

The gallery's opening exhibition featured Adams' own photography and that of fellow members of f/64, a loosely knit group of northern California photographers who favored glossy printing papers and a straight, unmanipulated photographic style, rather than the pictorialist style then in vogue. The name of the group, which was founded in 1932, refers to the aperture setting that produces maximum sharpness and greatest depth of field with the large-format cameras they typically used. Included in the Adams Gallery show were f/64 members Edward Weston and his young son Brett, Willard Van Dyke, Imogen Cunningham, and Sonya Noskowiak, as well as Consuelo Kanaga, a like-minded San Francisco photographer who, along with Alma Lavenson and Dorothea Lange, was sometimes invited to join in the group's shows. The exhibition was on view at Adams' gallery for only two weeks but reportedly was seen by five hundred people, an impressive number despite the show's short run during one of the bleakest periods of the Depression.[23]

Adams was deeply disappointed that his friends Stieglitz, Strand, and Sheeler turned down his requests to exhibit their work at the new gallery. From Stieglitz, it was the first of many such rejections, and Adams gradually became inured to them. He had written to his mentor soon after his return to San Francisco: "my meetings with you touched and clarified deep elements within me"; as a result, he claimed, he had decided to try his hand at exhibiting photography in a gallery setting and was hoping to show not just a cross-section of work by his contemporaries but nineteenth-century photography as well. Adams went on:

> My venture is not an attempt to imitate what you have done . . . that would be more than ridiculous to try. . . . It is an attempt to experiment with the public response to fine photography. The support of the project so far has been more than encouraging. I may go down in ignominious defeat, but I am willing to take the first step, and I have chosen to do so. Pray for me.[24]

Even though Stieglitz brusquely declined to send his own work or that of his wife Georgia O'Keeffe to Adams, he replied, "I know your 'Experiment' will be a good one. I know well it won't be an imitation of anything else."[25]

Adams also outlined his plans to Strand, whom he had first met in Taos, New Mexico, in 1930.

> Since my return I have attempted a new venture. . . . I have opened a small gallery. . . . I am trying to bring things to San Francisco that should have come many years ago. Despite a certain sneering attitude in the East about California I can truthfully say to you that I would rather live here and work here than in any other American city I have seen.[26]

In another note, written to Reed on the same day as his letter to Stieglitz, Adams repeated the phrase "center for photography" in describing his new undertaking and went on to say that he anticipated not only holding fine art exhibitions in the space but also hosting lectures and showing motion pictures there.[27] He believed that the Bay Area was starved for the type of gallery that he envisioned, and that San Francisco had the potential to become an important center for the arts, especially photography.[28] This concept of a place to promote, teach, and exhibit photography was a theme that Adams returned to over and over again during the next decade, and it ultimately led him to participate in projects such as the landmark "A Pageant of Photography" exhibition at the Golden Gate Exposition in 1940 and to the founding of the first-of-its-kind fine art photography program at the California School for the Arts in 1945.

Like Stieglitz at An American Place, Adams, for his gallery, planned to focus on what he deemed the best of modern art in all media, not just photography. And although Adams' gallery closed after only eight months, he managed to organize a number of notable exhibitions of painters and sculptors, such as Jean Charlot, Jane Berlandina, John Marin, Marguerite and William Zorach, Ralph Stackpole, and Benny Bufano, as well as solo shows of photographs by Anton Bruehl and Edward Weston. In a letter to Stieglitz in May 1934, Adams recounted the eventual demise of the gallery and his inability to "operate both my photography and an art gallery and do them both well."[29] Nevertheless, Adams' "Experiment" was a significant first step for a young photographer who was actively carving out a place for himself in the art world of San Francisco.

Concurrent with his own gallery venture, Adams was exploring an opportunity to exhibit contemporary photography on a much larger scale. Still energized by his meeting with Stieglitz, Adams wrote to him in the summer of 1933 that he was in the early stages of collaborating on a large international exhibition of photography with Lloyd Rollins, the sympathetic director of the M. H. de Young Museum:

5. MONOLITH—THE FACE OF HALF DOME, YOSEMITE NATIONAL PARK, *1927*

I am scared to death that unless I am certain of my sources I will get things of inferior worth. I am anxious to know just who to apply to in England, France, Germany, etc. in order to secure a few prints from each country of the best photography. I have seen so many dreadful things in "International Salons" that I am anxious for this show to convey only the most significant elements of present-day work.[30]

Rollins, an important early supporter of photography in the Bay Area, had given Weston and Adams their first one-man exhibitions at the de Young. He had also played a critical role in cementing the relationships of the seven original members of the f/64 circle when he offered them an exhibition in 1932, the earliest and most cohesive showing of an otherwise short-lived group. The international photography exhibition that Adams was organizing with Rollins was apparently never realized, but that it was being considered at all is remarkable. In 1933 there would have been very few models for Adams to follow in coordinating such an ambitious exhibition (and there was not a single museum in America as yet with its own department of photography). Having established himself as a photographer only recently, Adams was too young and lacked the necessary connections to have had his work included in the groundbreaking "Film und Foto" exhibition in Stuttgart in 1929, and Beaumont Newhall's pivotal "Photography: 1839–1937" survey exhibition at the Museum of Modern Art (MoMA) in New York, in which Adams' work would appear, was still four years off.[31]

MAKING A PHOTOGRAPH

During the 1930s, an increasing number of fine art and photography magazines wielded a growing influence on the field of photography, and this trend was not lost on Adams. Although he had a limited formal education, having received only an eighth-grade diploma, he was a surprisingly confident writer and critic, even very early in his career. As a result of having written a series of photography exhibition reviews for *Fortnightly* magazine in 1931 and 1932 and technical articles for *Camera Craft* magazine in 1934 and 1935, he became known for his well-reasoned critiques of exhibitions and his expertise on a wide range of subjects, such as landscape, architectural, portrait, commercial, and even winter photography.[32] Soon after the first of the *Camera Craft* articles were published, Adams sent some of his work to *Modern Photography*, a London-based magazine published by the Studio Limited and recommended to him by Imogen Cunningham. Although he was gratified to have one of his pictures chosen to appear in the magazine, he was dismayed to see

his black-and-white photograph and another by his friend Weston reproduced in colored inks—his in brown and Weston's in blue![33] Adams complained about the poor quality of the photomechanical reproductions to the editor Charles Geoffrey Holme, explaining that straight photography should never be altered or manipulated in such a way. Holme's response was to invite him to contribute an essay, "The New Photography," to their 1934–35 yearbook.

Adams' essay featured a brief history of photography, divided into four distinct periods of development. He identified the first phase, the *experimental period* of prephotography, as the era of the camera obscura and other chemical and optical experiments that led to the invention of the medium in 1839. The second, the *factual period* of nineteenth-century photography, Adams claimed, was characterized by photographers such as David Octavius Hill, Mathew Brady, and Eugène Atget, who were carefully selected by Adams to support his argument for a venerable lineage of straight photography leading up to his day. He praised the work of these men for what he referred to as "the microscopic revelation of the lens," or as "pure photography" that objectively revealed the world to the viewer. By contrast, Adams portrayed the third phase, the *pictorial period*, as one of superficial and sentimental excess, typified by turn-of-the-century photographers who had experimented with matte and textured papers and had manipulated their prints to suggest the look of other artistic media. Such decadence had slowed photography's progress, wrote Adams, and had required an emancipator like Stieglitz to liberate its followers from their shallow, imitative tendencies. Not surprisingly, Adams placed himself squarely in the final period, the *photographic renaissance* of straight photography, which he described as a return to the direct and honest representation found in even the earliest photographic images of the nineteenth century and as a trend clearly "anticipated by Stieglitz."[34] This fervent argument against pictorialism, which Adams perceived as still a threat to "the true identity of the art," reads, as one of his contemporaries described it, like a virtual manifesto of the f/64 movement.[35]

Not long after receiving "The New Photography," Holme proposed that Adams also write a beginner's guide to photography as the eighth volume in the Studio's series of How to Do It books (falling between *Pottery* and *Embroidery Design*). Adams' *Making a Photograph*, which came out in 1935, was the first how-to book to tackle both the mechanics and the aesthetics of photography.[36] Like his *Modern Photography* article and his writings in *Fortnightly* and

Camera Craft during this period, Adams used the opportunity to lay out his thoughts on the merits of straight versus pictorial photography. As photo-historian John Szarkowski explains it, Adams "seemed by the mid-thirties to understand more about the theoretical basis of practical photographic technique than any other working photographer, and he was willing—eager!—to share the fruits of that understanding with anyone who would listen."[37] Unlike Stieglitz, Adams relished the chance to convert the general reader to photography as a fine art, in particular photography that was tonally rich, sharply focused, printed on glossy paper, and did not try to replicate other art forms.[38]

To that end, *Making a Photograph* was meant to be not a detailed textbook but rather a straightforward outline of his methods for successfully making and printing photographs. Adams acknowledged that some readers would be disappointed because he had not included color and motion-picture photography in his text, and because he had discussed only large-format camera technique and not the use of miniature, handheld cameras (something he remedied in later manuals). The book was just under one hundred pages long and included practical drawings for a basic darkroom layout and Adams' first discussion of the characteristic curve in the sensitometry of photographic emulsions. Later, in the mid-1940s, Adams would codify these calculations for exposure and development (originally published in 1890 by Ferdinand Hurter and Vero C. Driffield) and present them as the Zone System. In fact, *Making a Photograph* was such a success that it remained in print for nearly twenty years, with subsequent editions published in 1939 and 1948. It also set the stage for the Basic Photo series of technical manuals that Adams produced in the 1940s and '50s and then revised in the 1980s as the Ansel Adams Photography series.[39]

The foreword of *Making a Photograph* was written by Adams' friend Edward Weston; in it he described the unique aspects of the medium and the relative strengths and limitations of camera "vision," as defined by the straight photographer. On the one hand, he celebrated the camera's capacity to render objective reality, especially elements such as texture and detail, and on the other, he cautioned against the camera's indiscriminate, mechanical recording of whatever appears before the lens. Weston argued that self-expression should not be the photographer's goal; he asserted that instead there must be a "directing intelligence" behind the final image, which should be "seen and felt on the camera's ground glass complete in every detail" before the exposure is made and the image fixed.

Weston's emphasis on the strict previsualization of a photograph was at odds with Adams' own preference for control and variation at every step of the process—from the initial visualization of the image, to the calculation of the exposure, all the way through the final printing—to achieve one's desired ends.[40] Unlike Weston, Adams' more flexible definition of straight photographic technique led him to think of the entire practice in musical terms and to conclude that the negative was like a composer's score and each print was a distinct performance of that piece.

In his introduction, Adams returned to a theme from his earlier essay "The New Photography," where he lamented that only a very few contemporary practitioners could compare with the accomplishments of photographers active in the 1840s, such as David Octavius Hill. The Scotsman Hill (whose partner Robert Adamson was not yet recognized) was singled out as a kind of naive genius by Adams, who called him the "pioneer" of the new art and admired the expressive power of his photographs, especially in light of the rudimentary paper negative process he employed. It is striking that Hill was also the only historic photographer whose pictures Stieglitz ever exhibited at his gallery; his work was featured in Alvin Langdon Coburn's landmark "Exhibition of Old Masters of Photography" at the Albright Gallery in 1915 and Beaumont Newhall's history of photography survey exhibition at MoMA in 1937; and Adams chose to reproduce one of his pictures on the cover of his 1940 catalogue *A Pageant of Photography* (fig. 3, p. 26).[41]

The only non-Adams image reproduced in *Making a Photograph* was Dorothea Lange's *White Angel Breadline* (1933), a testament to the long friendship between the two and to Adams' deep respect for Lange's approach to social documentary photography. In a letter to Stieglitz, Adams described her iconic image of a downtrodden man waiting in line for food as "a grand photo-document."[42] He greatly admired Lange's ability to combine fine print quality and composition with emotionally moving subject matter, and during the 1940s the pair collaborated on a number of photo-essays for magazines, including stories on the Richmond, California, shipyards and the agriculture of the San Joaquin Valley for *Fortune* and the Mormon communities in Utah for *Life*.

Never one to downplay the practical aspects of photography, Adams also illustrated examples of his own commercial assignments and personal work in the book, including two skiing images, a view of the Ahwahnee Hotel in Yosemite, a formal table setting, the "hands of a commercial lithographer," and an image of his baby

6. O'KEEFFE SUNFLOWER PAINTING IN STOREROOM, AN AMERICAN PLACE, NEW YORK CITY, *1939*

7. O'KEEFFE PAINTING AND REFLECTIONS, AN AMERICAN PLACE, NEW YORK CITY, *ABOUT 1938*

son, Michael, in the bath. These pictures cover the whole range of his non–fine art photography, from the myriad views he made for the Yosemite Park and Curry Company—his major employer during the 1930s—to the portrait and product photography that comprised much of the rest of his "bread and butter" work from this period.

Adams also took up a familiar refrain in *Making a Photograph* with his argument for another type of "center for photography," in this case, art schools that would focus on more than just the commercial aspects of the work and better prepare students for lives as both creative artists and professional photographers. He went on to express his belief that the field of photography in general, in the mid-1930s, was in a state of confusion. The serious student had virtually nowhere to turn for guidance and instruction, and looking for answers in books would only leave one feeling even more bewildered. Adams also prefigured the Museum of Modern Art's department of photography (the first in an American museum, which he helped found in 1940) when he wrote: "what is required above all else is a number of centralized institutions which combine competent instruction in theory and practice with library and museum features. Repositories of the most significant photography, past and contemporary, are sorely needed."[43] In fact, several years later, in a 1939 letter to David McAlpin, Adams thanked his friend for the one-thousand-dollar "seed money" recently given to Beaumont Newhall to begin collecting photography at MoMA: "You have done the most important thing that anyone could for Photography in the larger sense—you have made it possible for a large and very potent museum to incorporate photography in the presentation of the Fine Arts. . . . It is especially touching to me insofar as I wrote quite strongly about the need of just such a foundation in my book [*Making a Photograph*]."[44]

Adams' book also had an important influence on Newhall, the first curator of photography at MoMA. Newhall claimed that reading *Making a Photograph* changed his life and inspired him to study photography, which at the time had little written history. In fact, twenty-five years later, he wrote to Adams: "I never anticipated that what you wrote would mean so much. . . . your dream of a photographic museum, institute, library, collection, became my goal."[45] Reviewing the book for the *American Magazine of Art* in 1935, Newhall, who had not yet met Adams, singled out its clear and thoughtful text and commented in particular on the unusually high quality of its reproductions. Adams recalled that people seeing the varnished half-tone illustrations printed on heavy stock were often confused as to whether they were tipped-in photographs.[46] As such, *Making a Photograph* represented a level of excellence in photomechanical reproduction that became the standard for all of Adams' later books.

Stieglitz, too, wrote to Adams admiring the publication: "It's so straight and intelligent and heaven knows the world of photography isn't any too intelligent—nor straight either."[47] Adams, pleased by the approbation from the older man, replied: "It was wonderful to hear from you and to know that you approve of the Book. Frankly, I was doubtful that you would like [it]. Not that I did not have faith in what I was writing about or faith in you that your criticism would be just. I felt that you might react to it as just more *writing* and not enough *doing*."[48]

The year 1940 was exceptionally busy and productive for Adams: he taught his first photography workshop at Yosemite (sponsored by *U.S. Camera* magazine); he and Virginia collaborated on the *Illustrated Guide to Yosemite Valley*, as well as a children's book, *Michael and Anne in Yosemite Valley* (based on an imaginary day in the life of their son and daughter); and, along with Beaumont Newhall and David McAlpin, he helped found the Department of Photography at the Museum of Modern Art and curate the exhibition "Sixty Photographs," which opened in late December. The least-often discussed, but most remarkable, project of that year was Adams' organization of the "Pageant of Photography" exhibition at the Golden Gate International Exposition on Treasure Island in San Francisco.

Adams described the groundbreaking show as one of his proudest accomplishments.[49] According to a letter he wrote to Stieglitz in the spring of 1940, Adams had apparently complained to Timothy Pfleuger, the director of the fine arts section of the exposition, that the previous year's fair had featured only a very conservative, heavily pictorialist exhibition sponsored by the Photographic Society of America, meant to represent the entire field of photography.[50] Having called the earlier presentation a "camera club debacle" and argued that the medium warranted better treatment in the future,[51] Adams should not have been surprised when Pfleuger approached him a few months before the opening of the 1940 exposition to offer him the job of organizer of that year's presentation.

The planning and installation of the "Pageant of Photography" exhibition took Adams less than six weeks, from mid-April through late May—a seemingly impossible feat, for which he received no pay.[52] He was assigned a stenographer-assistant, had special stationery printed, and quickly went to work calling all his contacts on the East and West Coasts for potential loans. His coorganizers were Tom Maloney, editor of *U.S. Camera* magazine, who was responsible for helping him gather historical material, as well as contemporary color photography, and Grace McCann Morley, director of the San Francisco Museum of Art, who was in charge of the moving-picture segment of the show and of coordinating the films that were to be presented. The exhibition was designed to cover the entire history of the medium, ranging, as Adams described it, "from Timothy O'Sullivan landscapes to Man Ray 'Rayographs.'"[53] Like the pioneering 1929 "Film und Foto" exhibition in Stuttgart, which featured everything from advertising and news photography to industrial and fashion photography, Adams' "Pageant of Photography" included a wide variety of scientific, commercial, documentary, and fine art photographs. With more than two hundred prints on view at any given time, and several galleries changing their shows every two to three weeks, it was the largest and broadest showing of photography to be seen on the West Coast.[54]

Couching a letter to Stieglitz that April with "you may lift your eyebrows at my nerve," Adams explained that Pfleuger had offered him several good-size galleries, a large entrance hall, and a theater for screening "experimental, documentary and historical moving pictures," with the proviso that "if the Fair of 1940 is going to have any photography it's up to you." Knowing how Stieglitz disliked such big shows, Adams went on to assure him that he had been given carte blanche regarding the scope of the exhibition and, even though time was short, he would not compromise on quality.[55] Fully aware that he was introducing a large segment of the public to very different work from what was being shown at most photography clubs and salons of the day, Adams was particularly proud of the fact that the "Pageant" was to have three regularly changing spaces devoted solely to straight contemporary photography, one focusing on work by his fellow Californians and the second and third featuring other photographers (mostly Americans) working in color and black and white.[56] Although he acknowledged that by doing so he was setting himself up for criticism (from the "Camera Clubites" and "ambitious amateurs"), he also understood that he was establishing standards by which photography would be judged within the context of the other arts. In an article for *Camera Craft*, he

8. YOUNG BOY [MICHAEL ADAMS], YOSEMITE NATIONAL PARK, *1940*

9. WHITE HOUSE RUIN, CANYON DE CHELLY NATIONAL MONUMENT, ARIZONA, 1941

explained, "All in all, the Pageant of Photography is an exhibit of the greatest importance; next to the great show at the Museum of Modern Art in 1937, it is perhaps the most comprehensive exhibition of photography ever given in America. What is of even greater significance is the fact that, for the first time, photography is given a place in a Fine Arts Department of a great Exposition." Critics agreed. *New York Times* reviewer Tom White, for example, noted: "Photography as an art is this year fully recognized as such, in the Palace of Fine Arts," and an anonymous preview of the exhibition acknowledged that "Photographers in general owe Ansel Adams a debt of gratitude."[57]

After speaking with Stieglitz in New York, McAlpin wrote to Adams of the older man's apprehension regarding Adams' ambitious plans for "A Pageant of Photography": "Stieglitz is gravely concerned—he called me up to say he just couldn't understand it—trying to put on a show in three months. 'Why,' said he, 'even [MoMA] took over a year for their "History of Photography" show—and look how that was.'—'What can he be thinking of.'"[58] Of course, a period of three months was much longer than Adams had to organize the exhibition, but he replied to McAlpin with his newfound confidence: "I am still in full control of my standards, and fully aware of the complexities of the various things I have undertaken."[59] And to Stieglitz, he wrote: "Keep well and save yourself as much as you can. The Place means more than anything else in photography. Some of us have to be out on the front line, but it is always wonderful to know that the pattern of perfection exists somewhere."[60]

The scale and timing of the show would have been daunting to a less motivated person, but Adams approached the entire undertaking as just one more challenge to overcome. Although he described himself as "not a museum man at all,"[61] he saw the "Pageant" as an ideal opportunity to further the cause of photography in general and as especially exciting because it was being held in his hometown of San Francisco. In trying to sum up the century of progress since photography's invention in 1839, Adams' goal was to emphasize what he considered the simplest and most basic qualities of the medium and to treat "photography as an *independent* means of expression" with distinctive characteristics all its own.[62] To that end, he offered one-man shows, each only two or three weeks long, to photographers who shared his modernist vision and a straight, unmanipulated approach to printing. These included Charles Sheeler, Margaret Bourke-White, Paul Strand, Berenice Abbott, Clarence Kennedy, Edward and Brett Weston, as well as others, like László Moholy-

Fig. 2. Timothy O'Sullivan (American, born in Ireland, 1840–1882), *Ancient Ruins in the Canon de Chelle* [*sic*], 1873. Albumen print, 27.5 x 20.3 cm (10¹³⁄₁₆ x 8 in.). Courtesy of George Eastman House.

Fig. 3. Ansel Adams, "A Pageant of Photography" exhibition catalogue, published 1940.

ty American daguerreotypes by Albert Sands Southworth and Josiah Johnson Hawes and their contemporaries; ten David Octavius Hill calotypes (in the form of copy prints by Alvin Langdon Coburn); several plates from Eadweard Muybridge's Animal Locomotion series; a large group of Western views by William Henry Jackson, Carleton Watkins, Timothy O'Sullivan, and George Fiske; as well as Civil War, American Indian, and early railroad images by Mathew Brady, Alexander Gardner, A. J. Russell, and J. K. Hillers. As Adams scholar Anne Hammond pointed out, in this exhibition he placed a particular emphasis on the nineteenth-century photographers of the American West.[64] Adams had come to recognize their importance as precursors of his own landscape photography, admiring their incredibly sharp and detailed documentary images and seeing them as, "technically, the equal of any work of their time."[65] In fact, three years earlier, he lent one of these pieces, O'Sullivan's 1873 *Wheeler Survey* album (presented to him originally by his Sierra Club friend Francis Farquhar), to Newhall's "Photography: 1839–1937" exhibition at MoMA. Adams exhibited the album again in "A Pageant of Photography," and gave the Canyon de Chelly image from it a full-page reproduction in the accompanying catalogue. He described it there as "one of the most extraordinary photographs made in America."[66]

The large spiral-bound catalogue that accompanied the "Pageant of Photography" show featured an introduction by Adams and essays by photographers Edward Weston (on his own approach to straight photography), Dorothea Lange (on documentary photography), László Moholy-Nagy (on experimental photography), and Paul Outerbridge (on color photography). Beaumont Newhall also provided a brief overview of the history of photography; Grace Morley wrote an essay on the history of filmmaking; and N. U. Mayall of the Lick Observatory contributed a piece on astronomical and scientific photography. The richly illustrated volume also highlighted large-scale black-and-white, as well as color, reproductions of work by a wide range of nineteenth- and twentieth-century photographers, from Southworth and Hawes daguerreotypes to a film still from Charlie Chaplin's *City Lights*.

Once again, Stieglitz had declined Adams' request for the loan of his work to the show.[67] Nevertheless, determined to honor his mentor, Adams dedicated the exhibition catalogue to him and included a photographic portrait of the elderly Stieglitz by Imogen Cunningham in its opening pages.[68] As Adams wrote to McAlpin, he was not really surprised that Stieglitz had turned down the loan of his own photographs; he continued (with a hint of pique):

Nagy, whose work he recognized as significant to the field, though he did not care for it personally. In adjacent gallery spaces, Adams organized group exhibitions that highlighted an even wider range of contemporary work; for example, a show entitled "The American Small Town," produced by the government-sponsored Farm Security Administration; the Harlem Document series by the Photo-League of New York; selected photographs made for various newspapers and *Life* and *U.S. Camera* magazines; student work from the Art Center School in Los Angeles; and a small Group f/64 show.

Still seeking Stieglitz's approval for the exhibition, Adams wrote to him in late May: "I am certain that you would react happily to the show I have pulled together. You know I make no pretense to define or 'seal' photography. . . . I have tried in this show, to establish standards. Some of the early work of the 1860s and 70s sets an incredible standard."[63] The historical section of the "Pageant" set the standards he described to Stieglitz by including more than twen-

I frankly confess I did not anticipate his attitude towards the whole thing to be negative—especially as he knows practically nothing about what is being shown. . . . He has what almost amounts to a phobia regarding the preciousness of art. I am all for the finest possible work and presentation, but I never could accept the remoteness and imposed unavailability of his work and the work of his group. I think you can be a great artist and of the world at the same time. Most great artists were. Not only do I want to be, but I have to be.[69]

Stieglitz's refusal to lend his work to the "Pageant" meant that he was represented only by two issues of his early magazine, *Camera Work*, which were shown in the "historical section" of the show, and two photogravures, *The City, Fifth Avenue* (1896) and *The Steerage* (1907), which were lumped together with works by Edward Steichen, Alvin Langdon Coburn, Clarence White, Gertrude Käsebier, and others.

It is telling to see Adams' selection of his own photographs listed in the exhibition catalogue, too: *Monolith—Face of Half Dome* (1927), *Golden Gate before the Bridge* (1932), *Family Portrait* (about 1935), a portrait of a longshoreman (1940, courtesy of *Fortune* magazine), and a Japanese-style folding screen and overmantel, both made from photographic enlargements.[70] His choices seem carefully calculated not only to reflect the broad range of his work—landscape photography, portraiture, commercial subjects, and decorative photographic enlargements—but to attract future jobs and commissions as well.

His friends Beaumont and Nancy Newhall, whom he had met only the previous year, came out for a visit in the summer of 1940. This was their first trip to California, inspired at least in part by their desire to see Adams' show. Although Nancy and Beaumont were critical of the lack of color on the walls and the simple, rather conservative (at least by MoMA standards) installation of prints, Nancy wrote enthusiastically about the exhibition:

> [W]hat a survey of Western photographers, both early and contemporary; there were many we did not know and were rejoiced to see. . . . By far the finest art we saw in the West was in photography, not in painting, nor sculpture, not even architecture. Beyond question, photography was the art of the West—"A new art in a new land."[71]

The Newhalls were particularly impressed by the mural-size prints of the solar eclipse and starry nebulae, with the negatives supplied by the Astronomical Society of the Pacific and enlarged by Adams to a massive scale. These and the X-ray, photogram, aerial, and high-speed photographs and photomicrograph murals (of, for example, a bullet breaking glass by Harold Edgerton and a micro-

scopic detail of the head of a fly) had all been individually printed by Adams with a very simple enlarger and by rolling the large sheets of photographic paper through the trays by hand. Adding to the general spectacle, the exhibition also included a stereo photography section organized by Edwin Land and Clarence Kennedy featuring enlarged Kodachromes of famous artworks that could be viewed through a special stereo viewer by the thousands of visitors to the show.[72]

At the end of May, Adams wrote to Stieglitz, knowing that the older man did not approve of the exhibition but still enthusiastic about its outcome: "The show is up, and—except for a few changes and perfections—I am very much pleased with it. . . . It's been a big job—but I am pleased to say that a lot of people out here will see some good photography." Adams went on to describe how peculiar he felt celebrating the show in San Francisco when all the while the war in Europe was intensifying: "It was certainly strange to attend a brilliant exposition opening (very good and very gay) while so many terrible things were going on in other parts of the world."[73]

TEACHING PHOTOGRAPHY: THE ART CENTER AND
THE CALIFORNIA SCHOOL OF FINE ARTS

Although he had had little formal training, Adams was a great believer in the teaching of photography, something with which he was particularly involved during and just after World War II. In his *Autobiography*, he joked that his own disastrous childhood experiences with organized education very likely inspired his commitment to passing on knowledge when it came to his craft. Adams' early training as a classical pianist also influenced his concept of teaching, and throughout his career he regularly referred to the "music conservatory method" as having been his model for instruction.[74] For Adams, art education was a democratic ideal, which ran counter to Stieglitz's elitist leanings. In his popular Yosemite workshops, for example, he opened his classes to all levels of ability, keeping things "direct and simple," because, he claimed, "one never knows who will be touched by the message."[75] His years of teaching are rarely given more than a few pages in his biographies, but his role as mentor and educator was something about which he felt a keen responsibility. He once mused: "What if Alfred Stieglitz in 1933 had dismissed my work with a shrug?"[76]

Except for a few short courses and workshops, including the U.S. Camera Photographic Forums in Yosemite (initiated in the summer of 1940 and later transformed into the Yosemite workshops [1955 to 1981]),[77] Adams' first formal teaching experience came in 1942 when he was hired to work with Army Signal Corps recruits at the Art Center School in Los Angeles.[78] The school, founded in 1930 and located on West Seventh Street, was known for the strength of its programs in commercial art, illustration, and industrial design and was run by a young advertising man, Edward "Tink" Adams (no relation to Ansel). The center's slogan, "A Faculty of Professionals Rather Than a Professional Faculty," reflected its practical vocational bias and its highly qualified staff of commercial artists and designers.[79] Anxious to help the war effort, and to ensure a steady income to support his family, Adams received the Art Center job offer at an ideal moment. The only other war-related work that he had been able to cobble together during this period was teaching a few photography classes for soldiers at Fort Ord and the Presidio in San Francisco, taking naval patients at the Yosemite hospital out on photographic excursions, and documenting army convoys during their maneuvers in the park for the Department of the Interior.[80] Adams' training courses at the Art Center eventually grew to include basic photography education for airplane factory workers and civil defense personnel, as well as a class in photographic methods of corpse identification, taught at the city morgue![81]

One of his fellow instructors at the Center was Fred Archer, a specialist in portraiture with whom Adams collaborated on his now-famous Zone System, a method of controlling photographic exposure and development that Adams later claimed to have "roughly worked out in two weeks."[82] Few who practice the Zone System realize that its initial inspiration was the codification of what Adams described as an ideal teaching tool "[that] would be of immense service to the Military."[83] In the end, though, Adams' tenure at the Art Center was short-lived, and after only a few months (and many differences of opinion with the director) he wrote to Nancy Newhall that he was leaving Los Angeles, the "vale of bunk, sweat and beers," feeling that he had done all he could at the school and happy to head home to San Francisco.[84]

In 1944 Adams made another foray into teaching, which had an even more lasting impact on the field. He was invited by his friend, the architect Eldridge Theodore "Ted" Spencer, who was then president of the San Francisco Art Association, to give a series of lectures on photography at the California School of Fine Arts (CSFA, renamed the Art Institute of San Francisco in 1961). The success of these six lectures, which he had originally delivered at the Museum of Modern Art earlier that year, led the CSFA's administration to suggest that Adams be the person to found the school's first department of photography and develop a three-year program unlike any in the country.[85] Adams' name had also come up a decade earlier, when the idea of creating a photography course at CSFA had been suggested, but the plan had been shelved for lack of funds at the height of the Depression.[86] Adams was excited by the possibilities that such an undertaking presented, although he recognized that the time commitment required by a teaching job would take away from his creative work and more lucrative commercial projects. Despite the initial conflict, Adams eventually concluded that he was a natural teacher and that the work was gratifying; in 1947 he wrote to Nancy Newhall: "I think I should pay no attention to journals, schools, books, and lectures but just go out and make photographs, and then I realize that that is a form of rationalization, and that my field is really instruction."[87]

The California School of Fine Arts was a lively place after World War II. It served as a magnet for the many older and committed art students taking advantage of the GI Bill during the postwar years. Under the enlightened leadership of Douglas MacAgy (CSFA's new director as of June 1945), it became a center for West Coast abstract expressionist painting with the arrival of such well-known figures as Mark Rothko, Clyfford Still, and Elmer Bischoff. The school's administration had granted MacAgy the freedom to shake up the curriculum and add to the faculty, in light of its dire financial situation and the fact that during the war it had nearly closed on two occasions due to a lack of students. MacAgy's mission was to turn CSFA into a kind of "laboratory" of contemporary art, a place of experimentation rather than a standard art school program, and give it a national reputation by recruiting major artists from the world of painting, sculpture, and filmmaking and by founding a brand-new department of photography.[88]

To that end, Adams and Spencer set out in the fall of 1945 to raise fifteen thousand dollars to construct and outfit a basement darkroom and first-floor studio in the school's existing Chestnut Street building. By the first of November, ten thousand dollars had been promised by the Columbia Foundation, and classes began soon after.[89] The two friends collaborated on the design of the CSFA photography workspaces, and afterward Adams described the layout as perfect.[90] The curriculum he proposed was meant to be extremely flexible, based on the principle that although all the school's photography students would be required to attend certain group lectures,

10. FENCE NEAR TOMALES BAY, CALIFORNIA, *1936*

demonstrations, and presentations, these would be complemented by individualized instruction and assignments worked out in consultation with their teacher. This one-on-one instruction (which his successor Minor White dubbed the "apprentice-tutorial-conservatory" method) was virtually unheard of as a manner of teaching photography at the time, but Adams insisted that this approach was the only way to nurture individual talent and prepare students for the demands of future freelance work ("photography as a way of life"), rather than the more structured life of the commercial studio.[91]

Adams set out to create a department that would place photography on par with the other arts, and, as he wrote to his friend McAlpin: "It's GOT to be the best photo school in the USA!"[92] Although CSFA had important precedents in the photography training offered at the turn of the century at Columbia Teachers College in New York under Clarence H. White and Arthur Wesley Dow, and at the Institute of Design in Chicago in the late 1930s under László Moholy-Nagy, at the time most photography departments were not much more than trade schools, producing what Adams called "shutter parrots."[93] Adams argued for an emphasis on technical training for a period of at least three years (with the option of a fourth year for the qualified few), maintaining that only through mastery of technique could a photographer truly achieve the satisfaction of independent creative work. According to Nancy Newhall, he insisted that his students spend their first year of schooling learning the fundamentals of the 4 x 5 camera, the basic techniques of visualizing a photograph, calculating exposure, and the fundamentals of using sheet film and making contact prints. In the meantime, he also hoped to give them the same sound background in aesthetics and art history that the other CSFA students received.[94] He arranged to regularly bring in guest instructors (a practice that Minor White continued after Adams left full-time teaching in 1947), including Dorothea Lange, Imogen Cunningham, and Lisette Model, and the students were frequently treated to working trips down the coast to Carmel to study with Edward Weston.

Adams did not overlook the need for practical professional training either, and he planned to put his students through a rigorous period of apprenticeship in the second and third years of the program, teaching them how to achieve the status of journeymen photographers and to shoot many kinds of subjects under variable conditions. He also came up with actual commissions for them (for which they were paid), including a series of photographs of the Stanford University campus, another of the Feather River power plants for Pacific Gas and Electric, and yet another documenting the architecture of Bernard Maybeck in the San Francisco Bay Area.[95] Adams was the ideal choice of photographer to found such a department because he brought to the process a genuine understanding of the world of commercial photography and, unlike Stieglitz, knew the trials of such work and the difficulty of keeping one's personal creative photography alive at the same time. Ever pragmatic, Adams often used his assignments as a way to test out his own ideas on the students, some of which he then hoped to present in the Basic Photo Series books that he had been commissioned to write by his New York publishers, Lester and Morgan, in the late 1940s. In fact, in a letter to Nancy Newhall, he wrote (somewhat sheepishly): "I must confess I am learning a great deal at this time in clarifying factual matters about photography," in this case, during a brief three-week teaching stint back at the Art Center in 1945.[96]

Adams was newly energized at the end of World War II. Like many of his fellow San Franciscans, he was optimistic about the possibility of the city flowering into "a second Manhattan" and leading the way to what he described in his report to the school's board as "an intense cultural development on the West Coast."[97] As Stieglitz aged and gradually played a less public role, Adams consciously took on his mentor's mantle and increasingly came to see himself as Stieglitz's successor and principal promoter of the cause of photography. With the war over and photography just beginning to take hold at the San Francisco Museum of Art (later SFMoMA), he was full of plans for furthering the "cause" in the form of "a photographic journal, a creative photography center, and an art school to teach creative photography as part of a municipal cultural complex—a triad of school, museum and university."[98] Adams also hoped to link the CSFA photography department with the University of California as a way to diversify the private art school's program and give it higher standing (since it was not, strictly speaking, a college). Unfortunately, this ideal of a "cooperative degree program" was never realized, although the two schools did share a long-running affiliation. In a 1952 article entitled "The Profession of Photography," Adams suggested that the ideal connection to a college or university would allow, for example, academic study in journalism for students interested in news or magazine photography or courses in the social sciences for those wanting to pursue social documentary photography.[99]

In 1945 his good friends Beaumont and Nancy Newhall recommended Minor White to Adams as a potential assistant at CSFA, and although the two men had very different personalities, a mutual respect and deep friendship quickly developed between them.[100] While living in New York, White had taken night classes in art history with Meyer Shapiro at Columbia and worked as an assistant to the Newhalls at MoMA. The decision to move to California was a difficult one for the young photographer, but more than a decade later, he described the CSFA program that Adams had started as "that fabulous experiment" and the general atmosphere of the school as one of "creative excitement."[101] Soon after his arrival in San Francisco, he moved into the Adams' old family home next to Ansel's own house and ended up working at CSFA until 1953.

When Adams agreed to take on the job of founding the photography department at CSFA in 1945, it was always with the understanding that he would eventually move on, gradually teaching less and less, once the program was fully staffed and under way.[102] At about the same time that he began at CSFA, Adams applied for a Guggenheim Fellowship, and in April 1946 he learned that it had been granted to him; he was only the fifth photographer in the history of the program.[103] As a result of the Guggenheim, he was in a position to give up full-time teaching and focus instead on photographing the national parks of the United States, a project he had begun in 1941 under the auspices of the Department of the Interior but had been forced to abandon when funds dried up during the war.[104] Luckily for him, Minor White had proven himself a talented and popular instructor and was willing to take over Adams' job beginning the following fall semester, making the transition at CSFA relatively easy. However, Adams continued to be involved with the school for the next few years and reveled in his role as mentor. He wrote to his friend Ted Spencer in 1947:

> I think that the students do reflect my influence, and . . . maybe I should stop fussing around and just be an influence! Actually what has happened is this—by some trick of fate I developed my work at the time of a general renaissance of straight photography, and . . . it just happened to be me who walked into the arena at the right time.[105]

Stieglitz's failing health, combined with Adams' concerns about the state of the world after the close of the war, may also have spurred him to leave teaching and return to his personal work. In the summer of 1945, he wrote to McAlpin:

> The War is probably over; the war of guns anyway. It seems that there is another war to take up almost without a chance to celebrate the end of the shooting one; and that war may be the most important, after all. I am thinking more and more of Stieglitz and what he reflects . . . , and all the people, great and small, who have the Potential of creative action.[106]

Stieglitz and his American Place gallery had certainly been the inspiration behind many of the projects that Adams undertook over the dozen or so years of their friendship, but he had also long since moved out of the older photographer's orbit, extending his reach beyond the gallery walls and all they stood for.

By the time of Stieglitz's death in July 1946, Adams found himself in a position to effect change in the field simply by being a photographer and influencing others through his work and by his example. His search for the "center for photography" also clearly did not end with Stieglitz's passing—Adams continued to teach classes and workshops, write articles, produce books, and create opportunities for people to come together in the name of photography. In 1952, for example, he played a major role in the development of the pioneering photography journal *Aperture*; in 1967 he took part in the creation of the Friends of Photography, an institution committed to photographic publishing, education, and exhibitions in Carmel (and later San Francisco); and in 1975 he cofounded the Center for Creative Photography at the University of Arizona, Tucson, a program much like the one he had dreamed of in the 1940s: an archive, museum, and research institution for the study of the history and preservation of the medium, in a university setting.[107] His reputation as a folk hero remains intact and is well deserved, but to truly know Ansel Adams one must also recognize the many facets of his early career—the groundbreaking experiments as teacher, curator, writer, and arbiter for photography—that ultimately formed the figure we so admire today.

11. WIND, JUNIPER TREE, YOSEMITE NATIONAL PARK, *ABOUT 1919*

12. LYELL FORK MEADOWS, YOSEMITE NATIONAL PARK, *ABOUT 1921*

13. MARION LAKE, KINGS RIVER CANYON, CALIFORNIA, *ABOUT 1925*

14. ON THE HEIGHTS, YOSEMITE NATIONAL PARK, *1927*

15. SKIER, YOSEMITE NATIONAL PARK, *ABOUT 1929*

16. CLOUDS REST FROM MT. WATKINS, WINTER, YOSEMITE NATIONAL PARK, *ABOUT 1929*

17. SHIPWRECK SERIES #1, STEEL AND STONE, SAN FRANCISCO, *ABOUT 1932*

18. ROCKS, BAKER BEACH, SAN FRANCISCO, *ABOUT 1931*

19. ROSE AND DRIFTWOOD, SAN FRANCISCO, *ABOUT 1932*

21. THE GOLDEN GATE BEFORE THE BRIDGE, SAN FRANCISCO, *1932*

22. SUTRO GARDENS, SAN FRANCISCO, *1933*

23. WHITE CROSS, SAN RAFAEL, CALIFORNIA, *ABOUT 1936*

24. WRECKING OF THE LURLINE BATHS, SAN FRANCISCO, *1938*

25. DISCUSSION IN ART, SAN FRANCISCO, *1936*

26. MUSEUM STOREROOM, DE YOUNG MUSEUM, SAN FRANCISCO, *ABOUT 1935*

27. POLITICAL CIRCUS, SAN FRANCISCO, *1932*

28. AMERICANA, CIGAR STORE INDIAN, POWELL STREET, SAN FRANCISCO, *1933*

29. DATE OF MY BIRTH, MOVIE SET, LOS ANGELES, *1940*

30. WESTPORT, CALIFORNIA, *ABOUT 1936*

31. INTERIOR, PENITENTE MORADA, NORTHERN NEW MEXICO, *ABOUT 1930*

ANSEL ADAMS IN THE AMERICAN SOUTHWEST

Taos and Santa Fe were his Rome and his Paris. —Nancy Newhall, *Eloquent Light*

FROM THE TIME OF HIS INITIAL VISIT, at the age of twenty-five, Ansel Adams quickly came to cherish the American Southwest's dramatic landscape, glittering light, and diverse mix of Anglo, Indian, and Spanish cultures.[1] In fact, he so loved it there that he considered retiring to Santa Fe: when he and his wife, Virginia, decided to leave San Francisco, they were torn between New Mexico and Carmel, on the California coast.[2] They ultimately relocated to Carmel in 1962, to be close to Ansel's commercial work in San Francisco and Virginia's national park concession, Best's Studio, in Yosemite, but Adams' connection to the Southwest was enduring. Toward the end of his life, he wrote, "[W]henever I return to Santa Fe and other areas of the Southwest, it is, indeed, a homecoming."[3]

Adams recognized the region's photographic promise when he first visited in the late 1920s. Writing from Santa Fe in November 1928, he extolled the virtues of New Mexico to Virginia, who was back home in San Francisco.

> There is no use now trying to tell you of the possibilities that seem to stare me in the face—there is no one here, nor has there been anyone, who has had the least luck with pictorial photography on a large scale. I am amazed at the fresh prospect that no one has touched. If I were to work here, the country would give me the same opportunity that the Sierras gave the first artist that came to it. I do not understand this opening at this late day. Hardly anything is more "photographic" than these old towns and mesas and mountains, and yet nothing has been done.[4]

Whereas Adams met scores of writers and artists during those early trips to New Mexico, he came across surprisingly few photographers. Certainly, earlier photographers had spent time there, particularly those on government surveys, such as John K. Hillers and Timothy O'Sullivan in the 1870s and 1880s. Others who exclusively recorded the American Indian way of life in the area had also visited; Edward Curtis, by far the most renowned of this group, came at the turn of the century and again in the 1920s, hoping to document what he saw as a disappearing cul-

ture.[5] Laura Gilpin, Adams' senior by eleven years, also became known for her photography of New Mexico and the American Southwest, but she was not part of Adams' New Mexico circle in the late 1920s and did not reside in Santa Fe until 1946.[6]

Adams himself would go on to spend extensive time in the Southwest, photographing the landscape and its inhabitants for various personal, collaborative, and commissioned projects. His experiences in the region offer an important counterpoint to his long and varied career and demonstrate his ongoing concern with making a living through his photography. Although he is well known today for his landscape views and the impressive prices his prints often bring, in fact Adams spent much of his life trying to come up with creative ways to make ends meet. His fame and success have eclipsed this mundane reality, but his southwestern projects demonstrate his determination to make photography as financially rewarding as it was personally fulfilling. In these endeavors, Adams was open to collaboration; he enjoyed working with authors, including Mary Austin and Frank Applegate in the 1920s and Nancy Newhall in the 1950s, as well as with editors, such as Raymond Carlson of *Arizona Highways* magazine. He benefited greatly from social interaction and often found artistic inspiration in the company of friends, as on his excursion with Georgia O'Keeffe and David McAlpin in the 1930s or on his travels with his son, Michael, and his friend Cedric Wright, photographing national parks in the early 1940s.

The wealth of southwestern works in The Lane Collection provides a unique opportunity to learn from Adams' pivotal experiences there: little-known pictures are brought to light, and well-known views are given new context. By examining four different periods of Adams' time in the region—the late 1920s, 1937, 1941, and the early 1950s—and the images he made during these trips, it is possible to observe developments in Adams' photographic style and approach. Close-up pictorialist-inspired studies of Indian dancers from the 1920s (little known to Adams' public) give way to the awe-inspiring panoramic views he made

32. ALBERT BENDER, *ABOUT 1928*

In the spring of 1927, Albert Bender, a San Francisco insurance man and patron of the arts, invited the young Ansel Adams to accompany him from San Francisco to Santa Fe (plate 32). The only stipulation was that Adams drive Bender's Buick the twelve hundred miles each way. In his *Autobiography*, posthumously published in 1985, Adams remembered the journey as being mostly over rutted washboard roads.[7] He also recounted a humorous anecdote regarding the return drive from New Mexico with their companion, the author Bertha Pope:[8]

> We finally made our way home, stopping at Zuni and Laguna Pueblos and the South Rim of the Grand Canyon. At each of these places Bertha added to her purchases, while insisting on sitting in the front seat. I shall never forget Albert, squeezed in the back, draped with rugs and adorned with pots, literally covered with Bertha's collection. There was no air conditioning, of course, and if the backseat windows were opened, the blast of air would damage the feathers of the Hopi Kachina dolls. Red as a beet and dripping with perspiration, Albert manfully endured the three-day ordeal of the hot return trip.[9]

Aside from painting a colorful picture, this story speaks volumes about Adams' early experiences in New Mexico. Bertha Pope's accumulation of American Indian objects made a powerful impression on him, as did the many visits they made to the pueblos in the area. The American Indians Adams was familiar with in Yosemite had suffered profound attacks on their way of life and were greatly diminished in population and territory.[10] In contrast, New Mexico's Pueblo Indians continued to practice their arts and religion and resided in villages that they and their ancestors had inhabited for centuries. On his return visits to the Southwest, Adams often photographed American Indians, their dwellings, and their ancient ruins, and over time he came to appreciate the intimate connection between the people and their physical surroundings.

In addition to exposure to New Mexico's American Indian culture, the trip afforded Adams two other important introductions: his first taste of the magical southwestern light and a warm welcome into the lively and intellectual New Mexican social scene. The distinctive quality of the light and the region's dramatic and changeable weather especially appealed to Adams. He described how discouraged he felt about his chances of making successful photographs when a dust storm swirled to life upon their arrival; however, things changed quickly: "the next morning all was diamond bright and clear, and I fell quickly under the spell of the astonishing New

as part of the national parks project in the 1940s. He gained self-assurance with experience; early in his career, he gratefully accepted work with accomplished authors, but by the 1950s he confidently approached Raymond Carlson with a long list of his own proposals for *Arizona Highways* projects.

Unlike many of his contemporaries, Adams did not travel to Europe during his formative years as an artist; rather, as Nancy Newhall described it, "Taos and Santa Fe were his Rome and his Paris." Although the Southwest was geographically nearby, its ancient and "exotic" cultures, distinctive architecture and landscape, and social scene replete with wealthy patrons and talented artists all contributed greatly to Adams' artistic development into the successful photographer we know today.

Fig. 4. Frank Applegate and Ansel Adams, "Southwestern American Colonial Interiors and Fabrics," from the December 1930 issue of *Ladies' Home Journal* ® magazine. Used with permission of the publisher.

few photographs.[12] During his various stays, he worked with an array of cameras, producing negatives that ranged in size from 3¼ x 4¼ inches to 8 x 10 inches, from which he made both fine prints and reproductions for books and magazines. Unlike many of the artists he met in New Mexico, Adams was not drawn to the region initially by the American Indian culture or the influence of the Spanish on the customs, architecture, and religions of the people. However, it was exactly these "exotic" cultures, along with the stunning landscape, that he ultimately parlayed into marketable photographs.[13] From his collaboration with Mary Austin and Frank Applegate, an artist, anthropologist, collector, and restorer of Spanish Colonial objects, on two major projects—one taking pictures for a book on Spanish Colonial arts and the other photographing the Taos Pueblo—Adams learned to value these non-Anglo peoples and to see that their ways needed protection in the face of change. These two undertakings inspired several return visits, and other smaller jobs and portrait commissions filled the gaps. Although only the Taos Indian project ultimately came to fruition—in the luxurious book *Taos Pueblo*, of 1930—Adams spent much of his time during this period working on photographs for the Spanish Colonial arts book.

Initially, he had great aspirations for his Spanish Colonial arts pictures. The book in which they were to appear was the brainchild of Austin and Applegate. In 1925 the two had founded the Spanish Colonial Arts Society to protect this work and to encourage interest in the folk arts of the Spanish peoples of New Mexico and southern Colorado. Austin planned to write on the Spanish Colonial history and folklore, Applegate was to handle the chapters on art, and Adams was hired to supply the photographic illustrations.[14] In a letter to Applegate, simply datelined "On Train, Monday," Adams referred to the proposed project, emphasizing the pressing need for such a publication: "The Missions, the dances, the types, and the architecture and arts should be carefully and completely secured by the camera before they have altered too greatly or vanished."[15] Writing again to Applegate, this time before his extended stay in New Mexico during the spring of 1929, Adams included a postscript that underscored his desire to also make the trip financially worthwhile: "P.S. Perhaps it might help if word is started that I am coming; portraits are always most acceptable. I will take pictures, buy pots and even sweep up the Camino in order to stay a while in Santa Fe."[16] Such concerns about income are a common theme in his correspondence during these years.

Mexican light."[11] It was on this trip to Santa Fe that Adams met the nature writer and Indian activist Mary Austin and the poet Witter Bynner, who accepted Adams into their group of writers, artists, and activists. These new acquaintances also provided photographic opportunities that brought him back to New Mexico many times over the next several years.

The surviving records are vague, but it is apparent that Adams visited New Mexico at least six times between 1927 and 1930, including the first trip with Bender, during which he made relatively

The Spanish Colonial arts book was tremendously important to both Applegate and Austin, for nothing of the sort had yet been written. As the project took shape, Applegate's enthusiasm for the subject led him to expand the scope of the proposed book. By late August 1929, when he wrote to Adams about a group of photographs Adams had sent for his review, the original publication seems to have become at least two different books in his mind: Applegate described dividing the pictures into those for the Spanish arts book, those for the architecture book, and "those that would hardly fit in either."[17] After his initially expansive ideas, however, he realized it was too ambitious to try to do both book projects at the same time. Writing to Adams on April 9, 1930, Austin laid out their revised plan: "Frank discovered, when he got down to it, that he was not at all prepared to write the book on Architecture . . . so we are now at work on a book on Spanish Arts, which is going very well."[18]

Although Adams enjoyed his participation in the book, the photographs did not require the kind of creative vision that he employed when working on the Taos Pueblo project. Intended as straightforward illustrations to accompany Applegate and Austin's text, Adams' photographs document a wide range of artworks: carved wooden chests and furniture, woven blankets and embroidery, *santos* (images of saints, both flat painted figures called *retablos* and painted sculptures called *bultos*), tinwork, and architectural details. Some objects were set against spare backgrounds; others were photographed in situ or shot outdoors on a patio, where more light was available. Adams mentioned to Austin that he expected the engraver to completely eliminate the background from the images of the *santos*, isolating the figures, which suggests that the range of different image styles had more to do with circumstance than aesthetic intent.[19] As the main function of these images was to document and describe the little-known artworks, clarity was of the utmost importance.[20]

Despite the enthusiasm of the three collaborators and the work they had already completed, the project was ultimately abandoned. Applegate's sudden death in early February 1931 left both Adams and Austin shocked and grieving.[21] Austin insisted she would finish the manuscript, but the impact of the Depression led Yale University Press to cancel the original contract, and she struggled to keep the project moving forward while juggling her other commitments.[22] Just three days before her death on August 13, 1934, Austin sent the completed text to another publisher, Houghton Mifflin, but attempts by others to revise the manuscript and applications to various publishers over the next seven years failed to produce a book.[23] Adams never

tried to complete the project on his own, writing in 1967 that the Spanish Colonial arts book "[had] apparently died a natural death."[24]

Adams undertook a wide range of other assignments during those early years in New Mexico. Applegate, who was actively publishing articles from the Spanish Colonial arts material, twice paid him for reproducing his photographs: sixteen dollars for use in an unnamed "art magazine" and twenty-five dollars for illustrations in a story in *Ladies' Home Journal* (fig. 4).[25] Adams also made photographs for the celebrated Santa Fe architect John Gaw Meem, documenting his remodeling of the La Fonda Hotel, as well as other commercial and domestic commissions in the area.[26] (Meem was known for his blend of Spanish, Indian, and Anglo architectural styles and had designed Austin's home.)[27] In addition, Adams took a number of portraits while in New Mexico, including several of the poet Arthur Davison Ficke in the spring of 1928.[28] During the same trip, Adams wrote to Virginia saying he thought he had five additional orders for portraits and was still getting commissions for another trip later that year, recounting that he had received six more requests for sittings.[29]

An idea for another southwestern project was inspired by Adams' satisfaction with a group of photographs he had taken in the spring of 1929 of Indian dances. Adams thought of these as personal, creative work, in contrast to his more commercial assignments of making portraits, photographing Spanish Colonial objects, and documenting Meem's architecture. Writing to Austin during the summer of 1929, he enthusiastically reported that he had made some "stunning" Indian dance negatives.[30] After discussing his upcoming Sierra Club trip and the Spanish Colonial art photographs he was sending to her, Adams concluded by asking, "By the way, if I do a portfolio of Indian Dance pictures, as I hope, may I dedicate it to you?"[31] This letter is the only mention of his plan to produce such a portfolio, which was apparently never realized; however, Adams did make several prints of these images, sending a group of them to Austin in late 1929.[32]

Although Adams is best known for his glossy, high-contrast, and sharp-focus black-and-white photographs, much of his work of the 1920s, including the Indian dance photographs, looked markedly different. Under the influence of the pictorialist movement, which favored photographs that imitated other art forms, including subjects more typically seen in painting and surfaces reminiscent of charcoal drawings or richly inked etchings, Adams frequently printed his work on uncoated, textured papers during the 1920s. He experimented with different types of printing papers and mounting methods—a

34. EAGLE DANCE, TESUQUE PUEBLO, NEW MEXICO, *1929*

typical pictorialist practice—and even tried a variety of croppings on a particular negative, something he rarely did later in his career. The surviving Indian dance photographs reflect this process of cropping, as well as the use of uncoated, matte-surface papers, which were characterized by warm, rich tones and soft lines. In fact, Adams commented later in his life that some of these early negatives were almost impossible to print successfully on contemporary glossy papers, because he had originally intended that they be printed on matte papers.[33]

To understand the process he used to produce the Indian dance photographs, it is possible to consult Adams' proof prints, which were made for reference purposes and replicate the original negatives before cropping. Comparing some of these proof prints with the fine art prints Adams ultimately made informs us not only about his working method during this period but also about the settings in which he saw these Indian dances. Adams photographed at two New Mexican pueblos—Tesuque and San Ildefonso—in each case taking pictures from several different viewpoints, moving around the courtyard in which the dancers performed, and at Tesuque even photographing from atop the two-story Pueblo church (plates 35 and 42). In some instances, superfluous details were captured along with the dancers who were his focus, and so Adams cropped his images, sometimes radically, to eliminate background elements such as architecture, spectators, and, in one case, cars parked at the edge of the plaza (plate 34 and fig. 5). The resulting prints emphasize the dancers' costumes, postures, and expressions and eliminate the extraneous information Adams found distracting. The movement of the dancers and Adams' use of an uncoated, matte printing paper produced soft, warm-toned prints imbued with a hazy, dreamlike quality that is, indeed, stunning.

Indian dances had been a popular American tourist attraction since the mid-1890s, when railroads brought increasing numbers of visitors to the region.[34] After automobiles began to cut into the railroads' tourist trade, the Atchison, Topeka, and Santa Fe (ATSF) Railroad even devised the so-called Indian Detour in 1926. Touring cars met railroad passengers at the train station to take them on multiday tours, which included pueblos where visitors could observe dances and buy pottery, and then returned them to the train.[35] John Sloan's 1927 etching (fig. 6) spoofs these Indian detours and the resulting conditions at the dances, showing large touring cars and fashionably dressed non-Indian tourists crowding around the dancers. However, the elements that Adams cropped out when he printed his negatives indicate that both the Eagle Dance he attended

Fig. 5. Ansel Adams, proof print of *Eagle Dance*, 1929. Gelatin silver print, 7.6 x 10 cm (3 x 3¹⁵⁄₁₆ in.). Courtesy of the Center for Creative Photography, University of Arizona.

at Tesuque Pueblo, just north of Santa Fe, and another unidentified dance at San Ildefonso had only relatively small audiences, who were evenly divided between Indians and Anglos. The dances Adams photographed were not yet major tourist attractions and thus probably felt like the religious ceremonies they were, rather than performances for the entertainment of an audience.

From 1895 until the Depression, the ATSF Railroad advertising office maintained an active program of buying artworks featuring the New Mexican scene to decorate its passenger stations, restaurants, and offices and to use in calendars, brochures, and menus.[36] Taos Society painters such as E. Irving Couse, Joseph Henry Sharp, and Ernest Blumenschein found the railroad and the Harvey Company of hotels and restaurants a rewarding source of income for this type of work.[37] Aware of this practice, Adams likewise saw a potential for earnings and recognition, and he apparently considered proposing his photographs for railroad advertising during the late 1920s. He contacted Albert Bender during his trip in the fall of 1928, saying that Mary Austin would use her influence with the railroad to get him "special work."[38] With his typical blend of enthusiasm and irreverent humor, he also wrote to Austin the following year: "I am quite amazed at some of my Indian pictures. With the grace of Gawd and a proper approach to the managing powers, I should be able to do something big with the Santa Fe

Fig. 6. John Sloan (American, 1871–1951), *Indian Detour*, 1927. Etching, 15.2 x 18.4 cm (6 x 7¼ in.). Courtesy of Kraushaar Galleries, New York.

Railroad."[39] There is no evidence, though, that he was successful in selling pictures to the ATSF Railroad.

Adams also suggested that his Indian dance photographs appear in his solo exhibition at the Smithsonian Institution in 1931. In the fall of 1930, before his book *Taos Pueblo* was published, Adams received an unsolicited offer for a one-man exhibition from A. J. Olmstead, curator of the Section of Photography at the Smithsonian Institution, in Washington, D.C.[40] Though small exhibitions of his work had been held at the Sierra Club offices, and he had published his first portfolio, *Parmelian Prints of the High Sierras*, several years earlier, this was Adams' first recognition by a museum. He was just beginning to establish his photographic reputation, and an offer of this nature must have both excited and encouraged him. Olmstead had heard about some of Adams' mountain pictures from H. S. Bryant, also of the Smithsonian, who described them by writing, "The photographs to me presented a very unusual appearance, most of them very closely resembling etchings" (the reference to etchings probably relates to the matte printing papers Adams was using).[41] On November 20, 1930, Olmstead wrote to Adams asking how many photographs he might want to send for a monthlong show.[42] Adams quickly responded with a range of options: "I have a comprehensive collection of photographs of the Sierra Nevada, and many photographs of Indian Dances, Indian and Mexican Types,

and Southwest Architecture. I also have quite a few Canadian Mountain photographs (of the Jasper Park and Mt. Robson regions)."[43] He clearly considered his southwestern pictures a major part of his work. In addition, in the postscript he wrote that he had "some stunning ski photographs taken in the Yosemite High Sierra," referring to the upper elevations of the Sierra Nevada, in which Yosemite Valley is nestled. He and Olmstead finally settled on sixty High Sierra and Canadian Rockies pictures, including twelve skiing subjects, and in the end the Indian dance pictures were not exhibited. By the following year, Adams had left pictorial photography behind and wholeheartedly embraced straight photography and glossy photographic papers, and, perhaps not surprisingly, these images of Indian dancers were dropped from his exhibition repertoire.[44]

By far the most successful of Adams' various New Mexican endeavors was *Taos Pueblo* (fig. 7), released in late December 1930. The book combined fourteen pages of text by Mary Austin with twelve photographs by Adams—eleven of the Taos Pueblo and one of the Ranchos de Taos Church, a few miles south of the pueblo. Adams engaged the Grabhorn Press, renowned San Francisco printers, to produce just 108 letterpress copies of the publication, set in Goudy Newstyle type and printed in rich black and orange ink. The folio was large—more than seventeen inches tall—and bound in orange linen and calfskin, with the title blind-stamped into the fine leather. Valenti Angelo designed the book, using a stylized thunderbird image as a decorative element throughout the text, and Hazel Dreis, who worked with Adams on a couple of Sierra Club portfolios, did the binding.[45] Unlike most photographically illustrated books of the time, which featured tipped-in photographs or photomechanical reproductions (such as gravures, halftones, or lithographs), part of the paper stock from Crane and Company was specially coated with photographic emulsion by Adams' friend the San Francisco photographer and papermaker William Dassonville. Thus, Adams printed the photographic illustrations, one image per page, on the same high-quality paper as the letterpress text, and they were then bound directly into the book. The time, labor, and expense of this method were prohibitive for most book projects, which meant that Adams' *Taos* remained a rare example of this process in twentieth-century bookmaking.[46]

The idea for a Pueblo book—originally discussed as a portfolio—seems to have come first from Adams, who mentioned it to Bender, who in turn suggested that Austin might be willing to contribute a text. Austin was indeed agreeable, and discussions began in the spring of 1928, initially focusing on the Acoma Pueblo in western New Mexico. However, Acoma fell through because the ethnographic filmmaker Robert Flaherty was already working there, and soon thereafter, Charlie Chaplin arrived to shoot an Indian film for Hollywood.[47] Once the subject of the Taos Pueblo was chosen, Tony Lujan, the Taos Indian husband of Mabel Dodge Luhan, a socialite and patron of the arts, negotiated photographic rights for Adams, charging twenty-five dollars plus a copy of the book for the pueblo.[48] Adams proceeded to make his pictures, and Austin wrote her description of the pueblo and its history. Although they did not actively collaborate, Adams decided which photographs to include only after having read Austin's typewritten manuscript in October 1929.[49]

The images Adams chose for the book reflected his interest in the architecture and activities of the pueblo. Of his twelve photographs, five include Taos Indians, in both close-up and more distant views, and five feature sacred structures—a pueblo kiva, the old pueblo church, the new pueblo church, the new church gate, and the neighboring Ranchos de Taos Church. A pair of these photographs, one of a Taos woman winnowing grain and another of fields of harvested wheat, also point to Adams' growing awareness of the close relationship between Indian life and the agricultural cycles of the land. The remaining two photographs depict the monumental North House of the pueblo—one showing its distinctive stacked structure as seen from the plaza, the other taken from the west end.

The sparkling light and variable weather that had so impressed Adams on his first trip to New Mexico also pervade these views of Taos. In the opening picture of the North House (fig. 8), for example, sunlight is a major subject of the photograph, sculpting the architecture and casting deep shadows that become tangible forms. In other images, such as *South House, Harvest*, the clouds, rather than the light, are important elements in the composition, creating a third layer of depth beyond the buildings and fields of the pueblo. Adams also set the pueblo architecture off against the mountains in *North House*, so that it became the visual equivalent of the surrounding topography. He aligned the top of the North House with the crest of the Taos Mountains, equating the man-made and natural forms. Both adobe houses and their mountain setting represented home to the Taos Indians, and Adams' photographs make it clear that he understood this concept.

Whereas he certainly strove to create a group of beautiful photographs of the pueblo, an even more pressing issue for Adams was

TAOS ·· BY MARY AUSTIN

PUEBLO MOUNTAIN

stands up over Taos pueblo and Taos water comes down between the two house-heaps, North house and South house, with a braided motion, swift and clear flowing. As you look at it from the south entrance to the valley, Pueblo Mountain, bare topped above, and below shaggy with pines, has the crouched look of a sleeping animal, the great bull buffalo, turning his head away and hunching his shoulders. Beyond him the lower hills lie in curved ranks of the ruminating herd. It is not so much the animal contours that give the suggestion as the curious quiescent aliveness of the whole Taos landscape, as if it might at any moment wake and leap. You look and look away, and though nothing has altered you are quite certain that in the interval the hills have stirred, the lomas have exchanged confidences. Far out, to the north, where Taos Valley ceases to be valley without having lifted again to hill proportions, there is a feeling of the all but invisible tremor of a sleeping sea.

From the air, looking down, there is the same sense of wild animality, but of a different creature; Mokiatch, my lord puma, taking his ease across all Colorado, but with his tail hanging down into New Mexico, a long flexile tail that crooks out to the east and then curls at the tip, far down at Santa Fe, into a cat coil, the final knot of the Culebra ranges. Culebra, snakey; that is how they curve about the eastern rim of Taos Valley, of which the upper cañon of the

Fig. 7. Mary Austin and Ansel Adams, first text page of *Taos Pueblo*, published 1930. Courtesy of the Center for Creative Photography, University of Arizona.

making an exquisite and marketable product from which he eventually could realize a profit. Adams' lengthy correspondence with Austin surprisingly contains almost no discussion of issues of Indian culture. Instead, his letters repeatedly refer to two aspects of the book project: his financial concerns and the importance of a high-quality production. On February 23, 1930, Adams wrote to Austin: "The Taos Portfolio is gradually taking shape, and I will know just what's what in a month. The Grabhorn Press will do the typogra-

35. DANCE GROUP, SAN ILDEFONSO PUEBLO, NEW MEXICO, *1929*

phy, and I am sure it will be a grand piece of work. . . . The book will be sold entirely on subscription both to individuals and dealers. Would you be willing to autograph some of them?"[50] On April 4 of the same year, he wrote another long letter regarding the pricing of the book:

> I have been carefully weighing in my mind the number of copies to be made, and the price to charge. The practical phase of the venture is too serious to be secondary: were I to be "stuck" and take in less than the book cost it would be rather disastrous to our affairs. Here is [sic] the comparative specifications on the two propositions regarding the book: 1. 250 copies @ $50 will require the sale of 90 copies to meet the material cost of the edition. 2. 100 copies @ $75 will require the sale of 45 copies to meet the material cost of the edition.[51]

To these suggestions regarding price, Austin replied, "Two hundred and fifty copies of a book at fifty dollars a copy seems to me to be beyond belief, and a hundred copies at seventy-five dollars a copy leaves me gasping."[52] Adams recommended that the latter might be the safer course of action, and they ultimately did decide to make just one hundred copies at the incredible price of $75 each (roughly equivalent to $825 today). However, even at this high price, Adams felt confident about their likely sales. In his letter of April 4, he continued, "I believe the subject itself, your name and the printer's name will certainly more than assure the success of the book, to say nothing of the clientel [sic] I have built up here."[53]

Austin had hoped that a less expensive version of the book might also be printed, with a broader distribution, to ensure that her recounting of the history and values of the Taos Pueblo would reach a larger audience. In several letters between them, Adams and Austin discussed this idea, but no such volume was ever produced. In fact, when a reprint of the deluxe edition was finally done in 1977, it was still a luxury presentation sold by subscription for $375. Other correspondence between the author and photographer refers to the possibility of doing a series of books on the pueblos and marketing them as a set. To this end, Austin wrote on March 31, 1931, "I was advised by [my publishers] not to sell out Taos completely, but to wait until the series is further along, and then raise the price on Taos for the remaining copies. Collectors who come into the series later will want to complete their sets."[54] Unfortunately, no further collaborations between the two were undertaken.

The *Taos* book, when it came out at the end of 1930, was well received. Adams had captured a view of the place that fulfilled the idealized vision of Pueblo Indian culture Austin celebrated in her text, and he had expressed his own interest in the perceived harmo-

Fig. 8. Mary Austin and Ansel Adams, *North House, Taos Pueblo (Hlauuma) and Taos Mountain*, first plate of *Taos Pueblo*, published 1930. Gelatin silver print, 15.2 x 21.3 cm (6 x 8⅜ in.). Courtesy of the Center for Creative Photography, University of Arizona.

ny between Indian culture and the natural world. Perhaps more important for Adams at this early moment in his career, the book sold well, was admired by his mentor Alfred Stieglitz, and was a beautifully designed publication of which he could be intensely proud.[55]

In the summer of 1930, while photographing for the Taos book, Adams met the photographer Paul Strand at Mabel Dodge Luhan's home. Strand, not having brought any photographic prints with him, allowed the younger photographer to examine the negatives he had been making while he was there. The experience made a lasting impression on Adams, and over the years he often recounted the transformative process of looking at Strand's exquisite 4 x 5 negatives with afternoon sunlight pouring through a south-facing window.[56] In later recollections, Adams even credited this encounter with his decision to become a professional photographer.[57] Although he had made his career choice well before 1930, the clarity, composition, and tone of Strand's work—qualities visible to Adams even in the negatives—certainly influenced his decision to switch to straight photography. The glossy papers that Adams used more and more often after 1930 revealed the sharp focus, crisp detail, and great depth of field that characterized his negatives for the rest of his career. By the time Adams next visited New Mexico, the look of his photographs had changed permanently.

As with the many artists and patrons he met during the 1920s, Adams greatly valued his relationship with the painter Georgia O'Keeffe, who was fourteen years his senior. Her quiet study of nature inspired Adams. He wrote to her husband, Alfred Stieglitz, during a 1938 High Sierra backpacking trip: "To see O'Keeffe in Yosemite is a revelation . . . she actually stirred me to photograph Yosemite all over again . . . [to] see things for myself once more."[58]

Adams first met O'Keeffe at Los Gallos, Mabel Dodge Luhan's fabled home in Taos, New Mexico. It was the summer of 1929, and Adams was at the height of his early New Mexico experience, photographing for several different projects, taking part in the lively social scene, and familiarizing himself with the unique qualities of the landscape. O'Keeffe, in contrast, had just returned to the desert Southwest, a place she had visited only once before, in 1917, with her sister.[59] Though Adams and O'Keeffe did not immediately become close friends, they quickly came to share a fascination with the southwestern landscape and an abiding interest in local Indian and Spanish cultures. O'Keeffe painted Spanish Catholic crosses and sketched at Taos Pueblo after Tony Lujan introduced her to his ancestral village. Meanwhile, Adams was engaged in making photographs for the Spanish Colonial arts project and the *Taos* book. Both Adams and O'Keeffe were particularly captivated by the New Mexican sky: Adams was drawn to the quality of the light and the unpredictable weather, and O'Keeffe was entranced by its seemingly endless expanse. For these two artists, northern New Mexico was a dramatic change of scene—it was a stark contrast to the foggy California coast and mountainous High Sierra that Adams knew so well, and for O'Keeffe it was a welcome change from the New York cityscapes and Lake George environs where she had spent much of the previous ten years.

New Mexico fulfilled different needs for Adams and O'Keeffe. The camaraderie and exposure to other artists appealed to Adams. He regularly attended festivities with the Santa Fe poet Witter Bynner, frequently starring as the life of the party. He trekked to Indian dances with the Irish writer Ella Young and visited homes in small Spanish Colonial towns with Frank Applegate.[60] In 1930 Adams met the artist John Marin and was impressed by the older man's character and his modernist paintings. Adams was deeply moved by Marin's passion for art and was particularly touched by the painter's willingness to share ideas with him and to encourage his photography. Toward the end of his life, Adams wrote of Marin,

Fig. 9. Ansel Adams, *Georgia O'Keeffe Painting in Her Car, Ghost Ranch, New Mexico,* 1927. Gelatin silver print, 21.1 x 30.8 cm (8¹⁵⁄₁₆ x 12⅛ in.). Courtesy of the Center for Creative Photography, University of Arizona.

[He] was someone who took the time to pass on his thoughts to me. He had been generous with comments on art and on my photography since our meeting at Mabel Dodge Luhan's many years before. . . . Marin would spend days wandering around the Taos country, sometimes painting but mostly looking about, watching cloud formations and "Just sitting on a rock waiting for something to happen." . . . [He] would make statements such as, "I am always exploring something—a rock, a tree, a face or a cloud—the more I look, the more I see," and, "Keep the camera-eye going; it can't hurt you!"[61]

This careful observation of the natural world was something that Adams shared with the painter and admired in the older artist.

Whereas Adams appreciated and enjoyed his southwestern social contacts, O'Keeffe came to the Southwest in search of solitude. In her first years there, she stayed at Luhan's home, which was a lively social center in the small town of Taos. She often avoided the communal atmosphere, however, and was known to ride on horseback after dinner until dusk, taking in the quiet landscape on her own.[62] During her first summer in Taos, she also bought a black Model A Ford, as her goal was to explore the country independently.[63]

In 1937 O'Keeffe invited Adams and her friend David McAlpin, an investment banker and client of Stieglitz's gallery, to come to Ghost Ranch, where she had been spending her summers since 1934, about sixty miles northwest of Santa Fe, in the Chama River Valley of New Mexico.[64] Adams anticipated the excursion with excitement, writing to McAlpin in August, "It will be wonderful to see you and

36. WHITE CROSS AND CHURCH, COYOTE, NEW MEXICO, *1937*

O'Keeffe. As I think I said before—I feel like a six-year-old on Christmas Eve!"[65] Adams, McAlpin, and Godfrey and Helen Rockefeller, McAlpin's cousin and his wife, arrived in mid-September. They spent two weeks at Ghost Ranch before starting their road trip to several nearby attractions. Adams took advantage of his time in the valley to make a number of photographs. The thunderstorm activity over the flat-topped mesas fascinated him, and in just one day he made forty exposures of the dark storm clouds (plate 44).[66] Adams also took a portrait of O'Keeffe painting a desert landscape from inside her car, a setup that protected her from the intense sun; using his Zeiss Contax, his first 35mm camera, he photographed O'Keeffe as she worked, producing an unusually intimate and casual portrait (fig. 9).[67] Even before embarking on their road trip, Adams found himself once again entranced by New Mexico, and he wrote to Stieglitz:

> It is all very beautiful and magical here—a quality which cannot be described. You have to live and breathe it, let the sun bake it into you. The skies and land are so enormous, and the detail so precise and exquisite that wherever you are you are isolated in a glowing world between the macro and the micro, where everything is sidewise under you and over you, and clocks stopped long ago.[68]

On September 27 the group finally set out in two roadsters and a station wagon with Orville Cox, the head wrangler at the ranch, as their guide.[69] The exact order of the itinerary remains unclear, but their tour took them to Laguna, Zuni Pueblos, and Inscription Rock in New Mexico; through Hopi and Navajo lands; and to Monument Valley and Canyon de Chelly in northeastern Arizona. The group crossed northern Arizona to visit the Grand Canyon, and the final leg of the trip was through southwestern Colorado, with stops in the former mining towns Silverton and Ouray, the Indian ruins at Mesa Verde, and the scenic Dolores River country.[70] Adams brought three cameras with him—the 35mm, a 5 x 7 Juwell, and a 4 x 5 Korona.[71] Working with all three cameras, he was optimistic about the photographs he made on the trip; only a few, however, are well-known images today, among them a candid portrait of O'Keeffe and their guide, Orville Cox, at the rim of Canyon de Chelly (plate 45).[72] Shooting with his 35mm camera, unencumbered by a tripod or large-format camera, Adams captured O'Keeffe and Cox in conversation. He dropped down on one knee to isolate their figures against the cloud-filled sky, producing a spontaneous and evocative portrait. Adams described Canyon de Chelly as a high point of the trip; the group watched the dramatic progress of a lightning storm, and even many years later the sensations of that day remained fresh in his mind. In the early 1980s, he wrote of the double portrait:

This photograph recalls for me the brilliant afternoon light and the gentle wind rising from the canyon below. I remember that we watched a group of Navajos riding their horses westward along the wash edge, and we could occasionally hear their singing and the echoes from the opposite cliffs. The cedar and pinyon forests along the plateau rim were gnarled and stunted and fragrant in the sun.[73]

Another photograph made on this trip was *Aspens, Dawn, Dolores River Canyon*, taken in southwestern Colorado (plate 48). In this striking image, a grove of bare aspen trees forms a screen of delicate repeating lines against a darker wooded backdrop. The fragile pattern of this forest vignette contrasts starkly with the grander and more iconic views Adams made on later trips to the Southwest.

Adams returned from his travels renewed and confident about the future. He wrote to McAlpin, finding himself at an unusual loss for words, "As it is quite impossible for me to tell you how much the trip meant to me, I will not try to write it out here. It was a very wonderful experience."[74] In November he wrote again, buoyed with ideas for a fruitful 1938 and full of plans for making the next several years productive ones. He concluded the accounting of his future plans by saying, "After that, I expect to retire to a fine-grained photographic heaven where the temperatures are always constant. I imagine Heaven must look a bit like the Ghost Ranch country."[75]

THE NATIONAL PARKS PROJECT

In the fall of 1941, Adams embarked on a new commission that brought him back to the Southwest once again. He was hired by the secretary of the interior, Harold Ickes, as a photomuralist to document the national parks of America. It was Adams' first governmental commission, and it resulted in two of the best-known photographs of his career.

Adams' relationship with Ickes dated from early 1936, when Adams first went to Washington, D.C., to lobby Congress on the Sierra Club's behalf. Adams had joined the Sierra Club in 1919, actively participating in the club's trips and writing and photographing for the *Sierra Club Bulletin* beginning in the 1920s; he became a member of the board of directors in 1934, a post he held for nearly forty years. The Sierra Club had long wanted the Kings River Canyon, south of Yosemite Valley, to be added to the National Park System and maintained as wilderness land. Adams, wielding the many photographs he had made in the region, appeared before a congressional hearing and made a case for the transfer of Kings River Canyon from the Forest Service to the National Park Service, emphasizing the club's desire to preserve the area in its undeveloped state.[76] Apparently, during this visit he met the secretary of the interior, who that year purchased one of Adams' Japanese-style folding screens (*Leaves, Mills College*, 1936) for his Washington, D.C., office.[77] Two years later, in 1938, Adams produced a stunning first book of landscape photography entitled *Sierra Nevada: The John Muir Trail*. As it featured a number of images of the Kings River Canyon region, which had not yet been granted national park status, he sent a copy to Arthur Demaray, the National Park Service director. Demaray wrote to Adams saying he had forwarded the book to Secretary Ickes, who had then shown it to President Roosevelt, who was so impressed that he had kept the volume for himself. Demaray was writing to request a second book for Ickes, who hoped to have a copy as well.[78] The astute decision on the photographer's part to send *Sierra Nevada* to Washington gave Ickes another opportunity to admire his work and surely contributed to Ickes's choice of Adams as a national parks muralist.

Thus, in 1941 Ickes hired him to make images of America's national parks, which Adams would then enlarge to wall-size photographic murals to adorn the new Interior Building in Washington.[79] A number of artists had already been engaged to paint murals for the new building, but Adams was the first photographer to be included in the project.[80] He relished the opportunity to work on such a high-level commission, and having spent so much time in Yosemite, he had a sympathy for the subject and a deep appreciation of the national parks. Apparently, the initial arrangement was for just a few photographs, but Adams convinced Ickes that a more thorough documentation was in order.[81]

Adams set out in October of that year to make some of his first photographs for the commission, driving south through Death Valley in Southern California with his young son, Michael, and his friend Cedric Wright (plate 52). In addition to national parks and monuments, Adams was assigned to photograph other Department of Interior jurisdictions, such as Boulder Dam in Arizona and the Indian nations in New Mexico. He first traveled to the American Southwest photographing the Grand Canyon, Canyon de Chelly, Zion National Park, Saguaro National Monument, Mesa Verde, Walpi Pueblo, and Carlsbad Caverns. He was on the road for a total of forty-six days and billed the Department of the Interior for just five and a half days. During the remaining time, he made photographs for his own creative projects, as well as working on commission for the U.S. Potash Company (plate 39).[82] Adams knew U.S. Potash's vice president and general manager, Horace Albright, from his previous role as director of the National Park Service. He spent several days in the potash mine near Carlsbad, New Mexico, photographing miners at work, and the income from this commercial assignment helped to offset the expenses of the long road trip.

In the early weeks of the 1941 trip, he made two photographs that would become icons of his career: *White House Ruins, Canyon de Chelly*, made for the parks project, and *Moonrise, Hernandez, New Mexico*, a scene Adams immortalized while driving through northern New Mexico. Adams had visited Canyon de Chelly four years earlier on his tour with O'Keeffe and McAlpin. In April 1931 the canyon, with its ancient Indian cliff ruins and petroglyphs, had been set aside as a national monument. A goal for Adams during this trip was to re-create one of his favorite photographs by another U.S. government photographer: Timothy O'Sullivan's 1873 photograph of the White House Ruins (fig. 2, p. 25). Adams had long been aware of O'Sullivan's photographs of the American West, made on assignment with George M. Wheeler's government survey expeditions. In the 1930s, a Sierra Club friend, Francis Farquhar, had given Adams a copy of Wheeler's *Geological Surveys West of the 100th Meridian* (1871–73), which was illustrated in part with thirty-five of O'Sullivan's albumen photographs.[83] Impressed by what he saw, Adams familiarized himself with O'Sullivan's experience as an expedition photographer; he admired the intrepid adventures and studied the technical details of O'Sullivan's wet-plate collodion photography. Adams was so taken by O'Sullivan's southwestern views that when the Museum of Modern Arts's Beaumont Newhall contacted him about contributing his own work to the museum's groundbreaking exhibition "Photography, 1839–1937," Adams wrote:

> Following the mailing of my first letter to you today, I thought of something I have on hand here which might interest you as an item for exhibit. It is a collection of original prints, chiefly by a man named O'Sullivan, taken in the Southwest about 1870. A few of the photographs are extraordinary—as fine as anything I have ever seen.[84]

Newhall was familiar with O'Sullivan's work only from Alexander Gardner's *Sketch Book of the Civil War* (1865); he did not know the southwestern work and was delighted to exhibit the album Adams owned.[85]

In October 1941 Adams paid homage to his nineteenth-century predecessor (plate 9, p. 24). Standing on the floor of Canyon de Chelly and looking up at the Anasazi Indian structures tucked into a niche in the cliff face, he must have considered the fact that O'Sullivan's collodion negative was sensitive only to blue light, whereas his own modern panchromatic film was sensitive to nearly the full spectrum of colors.[86] He knew that if his image was to re-

37. MOONRISE, HERNANDEZ, NEW MEXICO, *1941*

create O'Sullivan's, he would have to make adjustments. Writing many years later in his book *Examples: The Making of 40 Photographs*, Adams recounted that the ideal filter to approximate O'Sullivan's glass-plate negative was yellow, but his yellow filter was missing, so he chose green instead.[87] He was aware that this would result in slightly less luminous shadows, a quality he particularly admired in nineteenth-century photographs, but that it would still enhance the vertical striations on the expanse of the cliff face, as in the O'Sullivan print. Later that month, Adams wrote to his friends Beaumont and Nancy Newhall from Mesa Verde National Park in Colorado with characteristic excitement, saying he had spent "two spectacular stormy days at Canyon de Chelly. I photographed the White House Ruins from almost the identical spot and time of the O'Sullivan picture!! Can't wait until I see what I got."[88] Adams was pleased with the results, and the photograph remained one of his favorites, appearing in many of his subsequent publications.[89]

The other significant picture made in the Southwest that October was his striking *Moonrise, Hernandez, New Mexico* (plate 37). A friend once noted that Adams could vividly recall the emotions he felt when making a meaningful photograph, even when the circumstances of the moment were lost to him.[90] Certainly, the making of *Moonrise* offers a telling example of just such an experience. Adams remembered it as a day when he had been photographing in the Chama River Valley, near Ghost Ranch, where he had stayed with O'Keeffe in 1937. He had had little success in making any promising negatives that day. It was late afternoon, and he was driving south along Highway 84 toward Santa Fe with his son, Michael, and Cedric Wright. As the Pontiac station wagon sped through the darkening landscape, the small town of Hernandez under the rising moon caught his attention; set by the side of the road with the distant mountains beyond, the town's adobe church, which he had photographed in the past (plate 38), absorbed the sun's rays, and the rows of white crosses in its small graveyard sparkled in the dwindling light.

Acting quickly, Adams pulled his car off the road and frantically began to set up his 8 x 10 camera and tripod. As he stood behind his view camera, composing the scene on the ground glass, his light meter was nowhere to be found. In his telling of the story, Adams had a moment of epiphany—his experience came to him, and he remembered the luminance of the moon. With this knowledge, Adams was able to approximate an exposure time that would give him a negative that was neither too dark nor too light. He must have rechecked the composition and then released the shutter, expos-

38. ADOBE CHURCH, HERNANDEZ, NEW MEXICO, *1937*

ing the film to what has become one of the best-known scenes of the southwestern landscape. To be sure he had the picture, Adams prepared to make another exposure, but as he turned over his film holder and pulled the slide, the sun slipped away, and the small town fell into shadow before he could make a second image.

This account suggests the drama and excitement Adams experienced when making a great photograph. The most surprising element of the story, however, is that for decades Adams could not remember exactly when this famous photograph had been made. For years he had dated it anywhere from 1940 to 1944, but in the summer of 1980 a solar physicist, David Elmore, visited the site. He identified the location of Adams' camera, plotted the lunar movements on a computer, and determined that the position of the moon depicted in *Moonrise* could have occurred only on October 31, 1941, at approximately 4:03 P.M.[91] This date was disputed by another scientist, the astronomer Dennis di Cicco, who also attempted dating the photograph based on celestial coordinates; di Cicco was ultimately more accurate with his November 1, 1941, 4:49 P.M. attribution, because he correctly determined Adams' tripod placement on the *old* road (rather than the newer highway) that runs from the Chama River Valley to Santa Fe.[92] The precise date for *Moonrise* allowed Adams to reconstruct the story, including his son and friend as participants, as he then knew it had taken place on his first national parks trip through the Southwest.

39. U.S. POTASH COMPANY, CARLSBAD, NEW MEXICO, *1941*

financial assistance on his own. He applied for the Guggenheim Fellowship in 1945 and was awarded the grant in 1946 and 1948, which allowed him to travel to more distant national parks, including Glacier Bay and Mount McKinley in Alaska (plates 53 and 54), Hawaii National Park, the Great Smoky Mountains in Tennessee (plate 56), and Acadia National Park in Maine. From this large group of national park negatives, Adams made individual fine prints for sale and exhibition; a limited-edition portfolio, *The National Parks and Monuments*; and a more broadly distributed book, *My Camera in the National Parks*, the latter two in 1950.[94] In these ways, he shared his message about the positive and transformative power of the parks with the widest possible audience. As Adams wrote in *My Camera in the National Parks*,

> The grandeurs and intimacies of Nature as presented here will, I hope, encourage the spectator to seek for himself the inexhaustible sources of beauty in the natural world about him. Fortunate he is, indeed, to see Mount McKinley against the summer midnight sky, the lush fern forests of Kilauea, the white jubilance of Yosemite's waters, and the somber Atlantic rock and surf of Acadia. But perhaps in his own garden—even in a flower pot on a window sill—a single leaf turned to the sun will hint of the revelations of Nature so grandly expressed in the domains of the National Parks.[95]

ARIZONA HIGHWAYS

Adams had been working on the national parks project for only a few months when the world picture suddenly changed: on December 7, 1941, Japan attacked Pearl Harbor, and the United States was drawn into World War II. Adams lobbied for the continuation of his project, but with America's entry into the war, the necessary funds were withdrawn. Even his attempt to couch his appeal in terms of supporting the war effort, arguing that the photographs represented "an emotional presentation of 'what we are fighting for,'" failed to maintain the financial support.[93] He continued to work through June 1942—the end of the fiscal year—traveling through Colorado to photograph in Rocky Mountain National Park and then north to make another group of images, including a view of the Snake River in Grand Teton National Park and a series of pictures of Old Faithful Geyser in Yellowstone (plates 50 and 51). After the photography was complete, Adams made prints of his negatives and sent them to Washington, retaining the negatives in order to make the mural-size prints once funding could be renewed. Unfortunately, the money was never forthcoming and the photographic murals were not made, but Adams was left with some of his most lasting and powerful photographs of the southwestern landscape he so loved.

Even though the government never renewed the commission, Adams felt so strongly about the value of the project that he sought

Writing to Raymond Carlson, the editor of the travel magazine *Arizona Highways*, in November 1951, Adams proposed an idea that would allow him to make several more trips to the desert Southwest.[96] He described a series of regional books he hoped to do with his close friend Nancy Newhall, explaining, "So many southwest books are so dull and factual, so lacking in imaginative imagery, that we feel the opportunity exists for us to apply what pictures we have, new pictures, and a high order of editing and writing to the structure of a new kind of book."[97] Adams went on to describe how *Arizona Highways* might figure into the project, suggesting that he and Newhall submit short articles and photographs (both black-and-white and color) to the magazine relating to the books they were already developing.[98] The money *Arizona Highways* paid them would provide much-needed financial support for travel and expenses, as well as contribute toward "the persistent obligations of hearth and larder."[99]

Adams must have been encouraged when he received Carlson's letter, written just eight days later: "As editor of the magazine, I have never been as proud as when I have had the opportunity, on

rare occasions, to present your work. . . . Frankly, we would be interested in anything that you would care to send along. . . . The name of Ansel Adams in our magazine adds worth, character and value to our publication."[100]

Adams' letter to Carlson had listed numerous possibilities for article topics, ranging from thematic concepts, like the development of a thunderstorm or sunrise on the desert, to more concrete studies of small Arizona towns, such as Jerome and Tombstone. The list also included natural wonders: Sunset Crater in northern Arizona; Monument Valley on the Utah-Arizona border; the Enchanted Mesa, a sandstone butte near the Acoma Pueblo in central New Mexico; and the Grand Canyon, suggesting close-ups of "intimate trail details, fossils and plant forms."[101] Adams also proposed a few man-made and historical structures—Fort Logan in Denver, Colorado, built in the late nineteenth century to protect pioneers from the resident Indians; Inscription Rock, which Timothy O'Sullivan had also photographed; and, north of Santa Fe, the Santuario at Chimayo, which had interested Adams ever since Mary Austin's efforts to preserve it in the late 1920s. Adams had already made a number of pictures of some of these subjects; the rest he hoped to photograph in more detail for the regional books he and Newhall were planning.

Of the myriad proposals, Carlson showed particular interest in the Arizona topics—quite naturally, since his magazine was devoted to promoting Arizona tourism. Ultimately, *Arizona Highways* featured seven of Adams and Newhall's articles, the first in June 1952 on Canyon de Chelly, in northeastern Arizona.[102] Others soon followed on Sunset Crater and the Ruins of San José de Tumacácori Mission—the oldest mission site in Arizona, founded in 1691.[103] Later subjects included the Death Valley National Monument in southeastern California; the Organ Pipe National Monument, a preserve of the Sonoran Desert landscape in southern Arizona; and Mission San Xavier del Bac, which was built south of Tucson, Arizona, only one year after Tumacácori Mission.[104] A final collaborative piece entitled "Mary Austin's Country," with seven photographs of the desert Southwest and a short biography of Austin, appeared in the April 1968 *Highways* edition, long after it was submitted to the editors.[105] Although only two of these subjects finally resulted in book-length treatments—*Death Valley* and *Mission San Xavier del Bac*, both issued by Virginia Adams' publishing company, 5 Associates, in 1954—the self-selected *Arizona Highways* assignments allowed Adams to undertake extensive photography projects in the Southwest that otherwise would have been impossible.[106]

On the opening page of the June 1952 issue, Carlson introduced the photographer to the magazine's readers: "Ansel Adams, one of America's truly distinguished photographers, will be with us quite regularly from now on to interpret and help us wrap up our country with his camera."[107] Compared to Adams and Newhall's later *Arizona Highways* features, the Canyon de Chelly text was quite brief: just a page and a half focusing on the site and another page describing Adams' photography. The piece began with an image of the White House Ruins—the photograph that Adams had made as part of his national parks project for the Department of the Interior—filling the left-hand page. In her short text, Newhall described three of Adams' photographic trips to the canyon: the first in 1941 under the aegis of the national parks project, during which Adams replicated O'Sullivan's famous view; the second in 1947 as part of his Guggenheim project of photographing the national parks; and a third in the fall of 1951, when Adams photographed weather-eroded rock formations and Indian pictographs.[108] The article included examples of Adams' photographs from each of those three excursions, as well as a two-page spread of a view down into the winding canyon made from the rim. Adams particularly admired Newhall's Canyon de Chelly text, which is ironic because she wrote it without having visited the site, an unusual situation for her. She composed her lyrical description of the place based solely on books and other publications, and many years later Adams boasted, "She was widely complimented on the perception and precision of her essay."[109]

Adams' Death Valley feature in *Arizona Highways* reflected his deep-seated interest in the Southern California desert, and he again culled the images for the article from a number of trips he made over several years.[110] Adams once commented that just as he had been the one to introduce the photographer Edward Weston to the Sierra Nevada, Weston had been responsible for introducing him to Death Valley. Weston first photographed the area in 1937 as part of his Guggenheim Fellowship, which he spent traveling through California and surrounding states, making the series of stunning landscape views that he and his wife, Charis, published as *California and the West* in 1940.[111] When Adams began photographing Death Valley in 1941 as part of his national parks project, he described his view of the place as having been greatly inspired by these photographs by Weston.[112] The Death Valley landscape was perfectly suited to Weston's photographic vision; it allowed him to create nonreferential, abstract pictures and to emphasize the sculptural qualities of the stark setting. Adams, whose images tended to focus on the effects of weather and light on the land, found the dry expanse of Death Valley enormously challenging. He acknowledged the difficulty of finding his own vision of the distinctive desert landscape, writing to fellow photographer Minor White in 1947: "Death Valley is

DEATH VALLEY

PHOTOGRAPHS by ANSEL ADAMS

TEXT by NANCY NEWHALL

Unearthly and immense, Death Valley so seizes the imagination that its history during the century white men have known it, is a history of illusions.

At first sight, it seems more an apparition than a reality.

Spectacular mountains and deserts surround it, yet somehow you are never quite prepared for what lies before you. Suddenly you notice that the distances are no longer serene and lonely. The mountains darken, sharp and turbulent as waves under an approaching storm. Pale mudhills, torn by gullies, crowd the narrow road. Pale shrubs grow in the steepening washes. Towering peaks loom ahead. Then, beyond shimmering fins and pinnacles, the ghostly gleam of the salt flats opens below.

Thousands of people, on first looking into Death Valley, have seen the landscape from a nightmare, there is no life, no water visible. Thousands have seen in the naked chaos of rocks and sediments untold wealth waiting to be mined. Geologists and naturalists have seen mysteries worth a lifetime's work to solve. And nearly all, shocked by the strangely intense beauty before them, have felt they were looking into another world.

From the bare crest of the Black Mountains, you look down dark, plunging spurs more than a mile to where the salt flats, sloping down to two hundred and eighty feet below sea level, glimmer for forty miles through the deepest sink in the western hemisphere. North and south Death Valley reaches into the distances, one hundred and thirty miles long, widening and narrowing between vast alluvial fans poured from the mouths of mountain canyons. Beside you, the eastern ranges, the Black, the Funeral, and the Grapevine, rear up in a sombre wave six thousand to eight thousand feet high. Ahead, to the west, the Panamints rise thousands of feet higher, to summits bright half the year with snow, and the eleven-thousand foot peak of Telescope. Overhead, in the intense and blazing blue, nearly always there float a few remote and delicate wings of cirrus cloud.

The Indians called it Tomesha — the Ground Afire.

When summer began to burn and shimmer, the Shoshones climbed out of their wickiups in the mesquite clumps and followed the ripening of fruits and seeds higher and higher up into the Panamints. On the lower slopes there were also lobes of prickly pear to dry, seeds of devil' pincushion to save, and crickets, grasshoppers and grubs to eat. Then rabbits and quail. Thousands of feet up, piñon nuts to gather. Perhaps a mule deer to roast, or, with luck, a bighorn sheep. Then, with cold returning, and snow frosting the heights, back down to the balmy warmth of the valley floor, to pick the beans of the honey mesquite, now hanging ripe, to ambush and dry the ducks alighting from their migrations in Salt Creek. All winter there were the mice, packrats and other small inhabitants of the dunes to catch, and now and then a chuckwalla, a big harmless lizard, to corner in a crevice of the rocks, deflate with a sudden jab, and eat raw. Uncertainties hung over this wandering, hand-to-mouth existence. If winter brought no rain, there would be few seeds to ripen, no succulent buds to attract rabbits and sheep, no nuts to shuck from the dry cones of the piñon. Delay might spell hunger or even

famine for the whole tribe. Those troubled by evil spirits, too old to keep up, chose the only honorable alternative: to drop behind alone and starve to death.

In the winter of 1848, the Shoshones saw their valley invaded by frightening beings: white men with long beards, great horned beasts, creaking wagons.

A lying map had brought a wagon train of forty-niners to the unsuspected brink of Death Valley. Fear of dying from thirst and starvation in this vast and unknown desert had already split the train into several groups, the young men pushing ahead, the men with families struggling behind. A young Vermonter named William Lewis Manly, who stayed behind to help the families as scout and hunter, wrote years later of his first look at Death Valley country after a night's vigil on a high butte:

> I was glad enough to see the day break over the eastern mountains, and light up the vast barren country . . . it seemed as if pretty near all creation was in sight . . . and from anything I could see it would not afford a traveller a single drink in the whole distance or give a poor ox many mouthfuls of grass. In a due west course from me . . . the high peak we had been looking at for a month . . . glistened in the morning sun.

A day or so later he climbed a peak probably in the Funerals:

> . . . and had the grandest view I ever saw. I could see north and south almost without limit. The surrounding region seemed lower, but much of it was black, mountainous and barren. On the west the snowpeak shut out the view . . . To the south the mountains seemed to descend for twenty miles . . . it was the most wonderful picture of grand desolation one could ever see.

> . . . I remained on this summit an hour or so bringing my glass to bear on . . . anything that might help us or prove an obstacle to our progress. The more I looked the more I satisfied myself we were yet a long way from California, and the serious question of our ever living to get there presented itself to me . . . I might be forced to see our party choke up and die, powerless to help them. It was a darker, gloomier day than I had ever known could be, and alone I wept aloud, . . . I believed I could escape at any time myself, but all must be brought through or perish.

Scouting ahead, Manly camped one night on the salt flats with the young men who called themselves the Jayhawkers. They had slaughtered some of their starving oxen, and were burning the now useless wagons to smoke the meat.

> One fellow said he knew this was the Creator's dumping ground where he had left all the worthless dregs after making a world, and the devil had scraped these together a little. Another said this must be the very place where Lot's wife was turned into a pillar of salt, and the pillar must have been broken up and spread around the country . . . It seemed as if there were not bad words enough in the language to express their contempt and bad opinion of such a country as this.

On that first invasion, only one man, a Captain Culverwell, is known to have died in Death Valley itself. But of the journey

PAGE SIXTEEN • ARIZONA HIGHWAYS • OCTOBER, 1953   MANLY BEACON ⬇

Fig. 10. Ansel Adams and Nancy Newhall, "Death Valley," spread from the October 1953 issue of *Arizona Highways* magazine.

41. THE NAVE FROM THE SANCTUARY, MISSION SAN XAVIER DEL BAC,
TUCSON, ARIZONA, *ABOUT 1952*

Having personally experienced the disorienting characteristics of the valley, Adams cautioned in his section of photographic advice: "never go blithely off photographing over the hills without first getting your bearings by the sun and the huge salient landmarks; a car can become a surprisingly small object to find in Death Valley."[115]

Both Adams and Newhall appreciated the otherworldly qualities of the place, but in conceiving their *Arizona Highways* feature, they also wanted to promote this land of extremes to potential tourists. Newhall began her lengthy ten-page history by emphasizing the strangeness of Death Valley.

> Thousands of people, on first looking into Death Valley, have seen the landscape from a nightmare, there is no life, no water visible. Thousands have seen in the naked chaos of rocks and sediments untold wealth waiting to be mined. Geologists and naturalists have seen mysteries worth a lifetime's work to solve. And nearly all, shocked by the strangely intense beauty before them, have felt they were looking into another world.[116]

In contrast, Adams' opening color image offered a much more appealing vision: rolling golden-brown hills under a marine blue sky, with the peak of Manly Beacon visible in the background (fig. 10). The photograph also includes four tourists, visible on close inspection. These tiny figures, in two pairs, do not carry large packs or wear hats, suggesting they are strolling for pleasure, just an easy walk from their cars. Their presence gives the viewer a welcome sense of scale and shows the landscape to be both dramatic and reassuringly manageable. This photograph, combined with the article's fifteen others, creates a dynamic vision of Death Valley as vast and awe-inspiring, yet worth a visit on a family vacation.

Following the Death Valley feature, Carlson wrote to Adams explaining that the text he and Nancy had sent to him for that article was enough for three magazines, and that in fact he would prefer "pictorial features to be so complete in themselves that only a few long captions would be necessary to tie up the feature."[117] In a return letter, Adams agreed that the essay had been too long, but the Mission San Xavier piece for April 1954 was even more extensive, stretching to fourteen pages.[118] Carlson was obviously willing to acquiesce, however; he described the Adams-Newhall collaboration in the San Xavier issue:

> Ansel Adams, with his sensitive camera, and Nancy Newhall, with her deft prose, have joined their talents to portray in all of its romance and all of its beauty the White Dove of the Desert. As far as we know this is the most complete coverage of this engrossing subject that has ever been done. At least this humble publication has never told the story of San Xavier so well before.[119]

SOMETHING!!! . . . it's just a tremendous nest of photographic opportunity. Interesting to recognize many of Edward's pets, and also interesting to figure how I would do them my way."[113]

Among Adams' early Death Valley photographs used for *Arizona Highways*, a view west from Zabriskie Point illustrates the deceptive sense of scale presented by the desert landscape. Referring to the visually confounding aspects of his picture in the accompanying essay, Newhall described the white streaks of the salt flats seen in the distance: "[They] look smooth at first, mere dried deposits on the desert floor. Actually they are beds of jagged rock crystals three or four feet high, interspersed with pools and creeks of crystalling [*sic*] brine."[114] Adams' image depicts the seemingly limitless field of white flame-shaped formations as if they were a forest of pine trees.

As a collaborative project, the San Xavier article seems to have benefited from Carlson's suggestion that it focus on the life and activity of the church. Adams wrote to Father Celestine Chinn, the superior of the Franciscans at San Xavier, in late November 1952: "I have been to San Xavier several times in the past, and have some good photographs of the exterior of the building. But my collection is very incomplete, and I have nothing of the life related to the Mission."[120] He then went on to ask when it might be best to come and assured Father Chinn that

> [i]t is our desire to work as unobtrusively as possible and with a mini-
> mum of photographic equipment so as not to distract the natives in
> any way, or cause you any effort to accommodate us. [The piece] will
> treat . . . the building itself, its history and environment, beautiful
> interior decoration, and the people to whom it serves as the center of
> their spiritual existence.[121]

He was granted access to the church and made a variety of photographs at San Xavier, nine miles south of Tucson, including a subtle color image of the church bathed in early evening light that was featured on the cover of the magazine. He photographed distant and close-up exterior views, a large number of interior details—mostly of the colorful frescoes and sculptures—and several overview shots that were meant to give the reader a sense of standing in the main aisle of the church (plate 41). To bring the place to life, Adams also made a series of eight individual portraits of one of the friars and seven of the Papago (now referred to as Tohono O'odham) Indian members of the congregation, as well as a full-page color image of Papago Indian acolytes carrying the Saint Francis of Assisi sculpture during the Fiesta of San Xavier. Adams shot an unusually large number of photographs in preparation for this article and the book that followed, requiring him to make several trips to the church.

Father Chinn was very pleased with the final product. He wrote to Adams and Newhall:

> Hearty congratulations for your symphonic opus on [San Xavier]!
> What sheer delight for the eye, what melody for the ear—now soft
> and sweet with romance, now mighty and resounding with epic
> grandeur! I confess dire poverty of speech to convey my sentiments.
> . . . The Santos look more benign, the acrobatic cherubs are breaking
> past records, the lions lift their heads a bit higher in pride, the great
> shell of San Xavier now sheds that "self-contained" light in even
> greater effulgence.[122]

The last phrase refers to Newhall's compelling description of the Mission church: "no matter when you come, even in twilight or in storm, somehow San Xavier is luminous, as though it had its own light within it."[123]

In 1976, after making photographs for sixty years, Adams selected 109 images he had taken in the Southwest and compiled them into a book simply titled *Photographs of the Southwest*. In the short, three-page statement that accompanies this collection of photographs, Adams recounted some of the important events of his life that took place there: the first trip to Santa Fe with Albert Bender and Bertha Pope, his collaborations with Mary Austin, the experience of seeing Paul Strand's negatives, and his later work with Nancy Newhall for *Arizona Highways*. He also commented on the selection of images, the majority of which had never before been published. He hoped that the few that had been published previously would benefit from their new context and arrangement, which was neither chronological nor strictly geographic. According to Adams, the group of photographs was meant to evoke a "flow of meaning," rather than to document his many travels through the region.[124]

Clearly, the Southwest had tremendous significance for Adams, and he chose to commemorate his time there with this book.[125] His southwestern photographs also held great appeal for Boston-area collectors William H. Lane and his wife, Saundra. In putting together their collection of Adams' work, between 1967 and 1973, the Lanes chose prints of seventy southwestern subjects, almost one-sixth of their total collection of his photographs.[126] In fact, when *Photographs of the Southwest* came out in 1976, the Lanes could find twenty-four of their seventy southwestern images illustrated within it.

At the end of *Photographs of the Southwest*, Adams wrote: "wherever one goes in the Southwest one encounters magic, strength, and beauty. Myriad miracles in time and place occur; there is no end to the grandeurs and intimacies, no end to the revival of the spirit which they offer to all."[127] Certainly, the southwestern photographs that Bill and Saundra Lane chose abound in exactly these qualities: magic, strength, beauty, grandeur, and intimacy. Perhaps what the Lanes understood best of all is that it is not just the southwestern land but Adams' photographs of these places that hold the power to revive the spirit of all who fall under their spell.

42. INDIAN DANCE, SAN ILDEFONSO PUEBLO, NEW MEXICO, *1929*

43. PUEBLO INDIAN PASSING OVEN AT TESUQUE, NEW MEXICO, *1929*

44. THUNDERSTORM, GHOST RANCH, CHAMA RIVER VALLEY, NORTHERN NEW MEXICO, *1937*

45. GEORGIA O'KEEFFE AND ORVILLE COX, CANYON DE CHELLY NATIONAL MONUMENT, ARIZONA, *1937*

46. ROCKS, JOSHUA TREE NATIONAL MONUMENT, CALIFORNIA, *ABOUT 1942*

47. SAGUARO CACTUS, SUNRISE, ARIZONA, 1942

48. ASPENS, DAWN, DOLORES RIVER CANYON, COLORADO, *1937*

49. ASPENS, NORTHERN NEW MEXICO, *1958*

50. OLD FAITHFUL GEYSER, YELLOWSTONE NATIONAL PARK, WYOMING, *1942*

51. OLD FAITHFUL GEYSER, YELLOWSTONE NATIONAL PARK, WYOMING, *1942*

52. FROM ZABRISKIE POINT, DEATH VALLEY NATIONAL MONUMENT, CALIFORNIA, *1941*

53. INTERGLACIAL FOREST #3, GLACIER BAY NATIONAL MONUMENT, ALASKA, *ABOUT 1948*
54. INTERGLACIAL FOREST #1, GLACIER BAY NATIONAL MONUMENT, ALASKA, *ABOUT 1948*

55. FROM HURRICANE HILL, OLYMPIC NATIONAL PARK, WASHINGTON, *1948*

56. DAWN, AUTUMN, GREAT SMOKY MOUNTAINS NATIONAL PARK, TENNESSEE, *1948*

57. CLEARING WINTER STORM, YOSEMITE NATIONAL PARK, *ABOUT 1937*

"A GREAT DAY FOR PHOTOGRAPHY"

ANSEL ADAMS AND WILLIAM H. LANE first met in San Francisco in the autumn of 1954, when they were introduced by their mutual friend, the artist Charles Sheeler. Lane and Sheeler flew to the West Coast together in October of that year on the occasion of Sheeler's major retrospective exhibition at the University of California, Los Angeles. Their plan was to attend the opening on the 11th and then to travel north to visit Sheeler's photographer friends, Adams in San Francisco and Edward Weston in Carmel. Not long after their arrival at Ansel and Virginia Adams', however, Lane was called home by a threatened strike at the plastics manufacturing company he owned in central Massachusetts. He would miss the expedition to visit Weston, a photographer he was always sorry not to have met.

On October 25, Sheeler wrote to Lane from San Francisco, having just returned from a jaunt to Yosemite with Adams:

> This is it—the place where those who prefer our way of life may come—my America! I need a dictionary of adjectives to convey a glimpse of what I am seeing and feeling here—it is something I have not experienced before. The Yosemite is wonderful as you have known, but I don't see anything I can do about it beyond putting my forehead to the earth in reverence. . . . I am sorry that you could not stay to share in this. As for this fellow Adams there isn't enough I can say in his favor. I wouldn't knowingly have missed these days of association with him. He recharges my batteries—and how they needed that![1]

Adams, too, seems to have greatly enjoyed his friend Sheeler's company; he described him warmly in his own letter to Lane as "that benign prophet you left in my care."[2]

For Lane—businessman, music lover, and collector of American modernist paintings—this initial contact with the charismatic Adams, although brief, made an enduring impression, and the two began a friendship that lasted for the next thirty years. In early November 1954, Lane wrote to Adams: "The pleasure of hearing from you so soon has been recently exceeded only by the greater pleasure of meeting you after having looked forward to it for at least a few years. And under what circumstances! I had not expect-

Fig. 11. Saundra Lane, *Ansel Adams and Bill Lane*, October 1967.

ed to seek out a photographer and discover such a superb musician. I am indebted to Charles for many things, not the least of which is that he brought this about."[3]

Lane and Adams kept in touch during the late 1950s, and Adams, who was working as a consultant for Edwin Land at Polaroid and traveling regularly to the corporation's headquarters in Cambridge (across the Charles River from Boston), sometimes visited Lane at his home, about an hour west of the city. Through him Adams also met and became friends with the renowned tenor Roland Hayes, for whom Lane acted as business manager. Not long after Lane's second marriage in 1963, he and his young wife, Saundra, made the first of many trips to California, this time to accompany Hayes on one of his concert tours. During their travels, the Lanes visited Ansel and Virginia Adams at their beautiful new oceanfront home in Carmel Highlands, a place where they soon became regulars, always made to feel welcome by the warmth of the Adamses and the myriad photographers, assistants, and friends who filled the house.

While in San Francisco, the Lanes took the opportunity to see Adams' critically acclaimed "Eloquent Light" exhibition, which recently opened at the M. H. de Young Museum. The sprawling exhibition of more than four hundred of Adams' photographs was organized by his great friend and collaborator Nancy Newhall and was described by the artist as "probably the best show I've ever had or will have."[4] Nearly four years later, a smaller version of "Eloquent Light," this time more than halved in size, went on view at the Museum of Fine Arts, Boston. It became the catalyst for Lane to begin thinking about collecting Adams' work in a concerted way. On July 5, 1967, he wrote to Adams: "Saundy and I have been twice to see your exh[ibition] at the Boston Museum. It is truly magnificent. Would you give me a call the next time you come to Boston? There are some things I would like to discuss with you."

Lane's beginnings as an art collector dated from 1952, with his early patronage of Edith Halpert's Downtown Gallery in New York's Greenwich Village. His impressive holdings of twentieth-century American paintings, drawings, and watercolors, acquired over the course of about fifteen years, included major works by Arthur Dove, Georgia O'Keeffe, Stuart Davis, Marsden Hartley, and Charles Sheeler, among many others. His first acquisition of photographs, however, did not occur until his friend Sheeler's death in 1965, when the Lanes purchased the entire estate of more than two thousand photographs directly from the artist's widow. Virtually overnight, the couple, who had never before bought a single photograph, came to possess the beginnings of what would soon be a world-class collection.

A letter from Adams to Lane in August 1967 makes clear that the two men did, in fact, meet in Massachusetts in late July to discuss the idea of the Lanes purchasing a substantial group of his photographs.[5] This notion of acquiring large numbers of a single artist's work was a model they had initiated with the Sheelers and one they continued in their future collecting as well. Unlike many of their contemporaries, the Lanes never chose to own just one or two pieces by artists they admired if there was an opportunity to purchase the work in greater depth. During the late 1960s and well into the 1970s, there was only a very small market for fine art photography and very few dealers specializing in it, so even for a successful photographer like Adams, the offer of a large purchase by interested collectors such as the Lanes held great appeal.

Later that August, the Lanes were already back in California with the Adamses, this time to look at prints and to formalize their arrangement to buy several hundred of Adams' photographs over the course of the next few years. Adams' first letter to Bill and

58. GRASS AND BURNED STUMP, SIERRA NEVADA, CALIFORNIA, *1935*

Saundra after this visit begins in his quintessential style: "I can't get used to the old shack without you in it!! It was a wonderful experience having you with us! Please repeat—soon!!!!" and ends (with more of his characteristic capital letters and exclamation points): "It was a GREAT DAY for photography when you came this way!!!"[6]

The whole process of acquiring the approximately five hundred photographs in The Lane Collection would take nearly ten years of

59–63. SURF SEQUENCE, *1940*

visits on both the East and West Coasts, numerous letters and trunks full of pictures sent back and forth, lists and revised lists of images, and many plaintive messages from the eager Bill Lane, including: "PLEASE SCHEDULE SOME DARK ROOM TIME FOR ME! . . . On all the rest GO-GO-GO."[7] The lengthy inventories of photographs sent to the Lanes on approval are heavily annotated by Adams with abbreviations such as CDB for "can do better" and by Lane, with "R" for returned or "O" for ordered and reflect the wide range of work they were discussing for acquisition.

Coming to the relatively new field of photography collecting from the world of paintings and drawings, Lane was something of an anomaly because of his desire, whenever possible, to purchase "vintage prints," those made closest to the date of the negative, and for his interest in Adams' less-known early work, including the Parmelian prints of the 1920s. Lane was also a stickler for the dating and documentation of the photographs he acquired, much to the dismay of Adams, who often claimed to remember nearly every detail that went into taking a specific photograph but could only rarely recall a date, even for some of his most famous images. As a result of Lane's prodding, Adams' photographs in the collection have more lengthy inscriptions on the verso of their mats than the majority of his extant prints; they frequently include valuable information on the type of camera, lens, and film he used.

During these years, the Lanes' photography collection also grew to include work by a number of other California-based photographers, especially Edward Weston, who had died of Parkinson's disease in 1958. Once again, it was Ansel and Virginia Adams who were behind it all, making introductions between the Lanes and Weston's sons, Cole, Brett, Neil, and Chandler, as well as Imogen Cunningham, Wynn Bullock, Morley Baer, and several younger photographer-assistants in Adams' circle, including Ted Orland, Gerry Sharpe, and Liliane De Cock. Ultimately the Lanes acquired work by these and many other West Coast photographers, and the number of their holdings of Weston's photographs eventually rivaled even those by Sheeler.

Over the next decade, the regular visits and crisscrossing shipments of photographs between Adams and the Lanes continued, as Ansel's often humorous letters indicate: "It was great seeing you in the east. We miss you here!!!! Of course, we miss Saundy even more than we miss you, because she is not only intelligent (as you are), but she is BEAUTIFUL which neither you nor I (or either you or I) (or is it ME?) would claim for ourselves! You will hear from me very soon. And, very soon, some vintage prints will come your way."[8] Typically Bill Lane would then reply with news of their lives in Massachusetts, interspersed with his aspirations for the collection: "When all is done I hope to have the SOUL of ANSEL ADAMS—the definitive cross section of your work,"[9] or, on another occasion: "I feel my 'eye' has

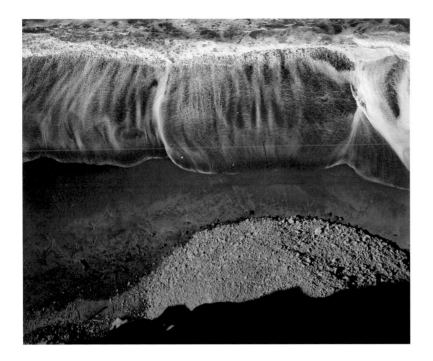

improved since I began seriously to study your work a year ago, and I have some hope that I shall be able to pull together a DEFINITIVE collection. I would value your advice."[10] Frequently, correspondence such as this would then be followed (sometimes within a matter of days) by a letter from the Lanes expressing their desire to return for a visit, ending with, for example, "Saundra and I are becoming a little restive with New England weather. Could we count on a good Point Lobos storm if we decide to travel to the Coast soon?"[11] or signed "Warmth from the land of freezing rain,"[12] a joking reference to Ansel's 1950 book project, *The Land of Little Rain.*

Finally, on May 10, 1973, Bill Lane wrote to Adams: "All shipments received in good order and now complete." The friendship between the Lanes and the Adamses, however, did not end there. Bill Lane continued to attend board meetings of the Sierra Club and the Friends of Photography, both of which Ansel had invited him to join. And, although the Lanes made fewer and fewer trips to California, the two men maintained their correspondence until 1983, the year before Adams' death at the age of eighty-two. Adams never forgot Lane's role as one of his first major supporters, and in 1974 he wrote that he was taking stock of things generally: "I am unloading junk, clearing files, re-organizing negatives, etc. Little did I realize that I would approach being an 'institution'! It seems all to the good— and you had a tremendous part in it all!"[13] Lane also appreciated

the significance of what they had accomplished in creating the collection with Adams, and in 1976 he wrote: "In reflecting on our deal and the events leading up to it and . . . surrounding it I am astonished at what has happened in the market for prints. . . . It is altogether appropriate and becoming for you to be riding the crest of UNIVERSAL RECOGNITION. Hurrah! Hurrah! HURRAH!"[14]

The last decade of Adams' life continued to be very productive, much of the time spent filling the final photography orders that had resulted from his decision in 1975 to stop taking individual orders to print from his own negatives, as well as with plans for the founding of the Center for Creative Photography in Tucson, to which he eventually donated his archives, prints, and negatives. During this period, Adams also enjoyed the public acclaim that accompanied two major New York retrospective exhibitions of his work: one at the Metropolitan Museum in 1974 and another, five years later, at the Museum of Modern Art. The latter he described in a letter to the Lanes as "boffo-terrif" and then went on to say:

> I am only now beginning to recover from a full portion of adulation and the joy of seeing so many old friends convened for the celebration. But we did miss you, especially as some of your prints are in the show and look very beautiful, if I do say so myself! . . . You do have a fine eye, Bill, and you made an outstanding selection of my work when you were forming your collection some years back. It was good to see those old friends on the walls at the Museum, and I'm just sorry that you weren't with us.[15]

As the years went by, the correspondence and visits between the Adamses and the Lanes gradually grew less frequent, but in 1981 Bill wrote to Ansel, who was by this time suffering from heart troubles and in declining health: "I miss being in contact with you, think of you more than you might suppose—with love, gratitude, admiration, respect and—what the hell—AWE. We are delighted to note the honors with which you are being pelted-belted-gowned-crowned-knighted."[16] Quite fittingly, Adams' last letter to Lane, written on July 15, 1983, on receipt of a gift copy of a Museum of Fine Arts, Boston, catalogue featuring the Lanes' painting collection, has a similarly reflective tone. In it he again writes of old friends: "The selection of paintings reminds me of a conclave of old friends. You have certainly built a remarkable collection of works of art! I hope someday the world can see your photography collection!"

The Lanes' collection today remains the largest holdings of Adams' work in private hands. It falls roughly into four broad categories: the rare, early prints of the High Sierra, the Canadian Rockies, and the Southwest, made before 1931; the Eloquent Light subjects, some of them the actual prints from the exhibition; the so-

65. GERRY SHARPE, OURAY, COLORADO, *1958*

called Classic Photographs (Adams' term), which he came to think of as his "greatest hits," such as *Moonrise, Hernandez, New Mexico* (1941) and *Aspens, New Mexico* (1958); and a smaller group of images that appealed to the Lanes, in part because they were conceived of as sets or series of pictures, for example, the Shipwreck Series (about 1932) and the Surf Sequence (1940). The great depth and range of the Lanes' collection make it an invaluable resource for scholars and curators, as well as the general public, for whom Adams is such a beloved figure. With this catalogue and exhibition, our hope is that this significant group of Adams' photographs will be better known and appreciated, as the artist himself would have wished.

66. PINE FOREST IN SNOW, YOSEMITE NATIONAL PARK, *ABOUT 1932*

67. LONE PINE PEAK, SIERRA NEVADA, CALIFORNIA, *1948*

68. LEAVES ON POOL, SIERRA NEVADA, CALIFORNIA, *ABOUT 1935*

69. POOL, TUOLUMNE MEADOWS, YOSEMITE NATIONAL PARK, *ABOUT 1937*

70. EDWARD WESTON, LAKE TENAYA, YOSEMITE NATIONAL PARK, *1937*

71. CHARIS WESTON, SIERRA NEVADA, CALIFORNIA, *1937*

72. DEAD TREE, DOG LAKE, SIERRA NEVADA, CALIFORNIA, *ABOUT 1936*

73. TREES, ILLILOUETTE RIDGE, YOSEMITE NATIONAL PARK, *ABOUT 1945*

74. GRASS AND REFLECTIONS, LYELL FORK OF THE MERCED RIVER, YOSEMITE NATIONAL PARK, *ABOUT 1943*

75. RAIN, YOSEMITE VALLEY, CALIFORNIA, *ABOUT 1940*

76. WALL WRITING, HORNITOS, CALIFORNIA, *ABOUT 1960*

77. SODIUM SULPHITE CRYSTALS, *1962*

78. HOUSING DEVELOPMENT, SAN BRUNO MOUNTAINS, SAN FRANCISCO, *ABOUT 1966*

79. FREEWAY INTERCHANGE, LOS ANGELES, *1967*

80. CROSSES, MONO LAKE CEMETERY, CALIFORNIA, *ABOUT 1960*

81. SPIRITUAL AMERICA, HORNS AND BELFRY, FOOTHILLS, SIERRA NEVADA, CALIFORNIA, *ABOUT 1966*

82. BANNER PEAK—THOUSAND ISLAND LAKE, SIERRA NEVADA, CALIFORNIA, *1923*

THE SIERRA CLUB OUTING ALBUMS, 1920–1945

ANSEL ADAMS' RELATIONSHIP with the Sierra Club began not long after his introduction to Yosemite Valley in 1916. After his first few trips to the park, Adams began to seek out ways to extend his time in Yosemite, and in 1919, at age seventeen, he joined the Sierra Club and applied to be summer custodian of the LeConte Lodge, the Sierra Club's headquarters in the valley.[1] During the next several summers, the young Adams relished the job of watching over the small stone lodge, nestled at the foot of the valley's south wall. Over the course of his duties, he met many of the club's members, who came in to use the various botanical, geological, and historical resources of the lodge, and every spring he installed the heavy cable system that enabled hikers to climb one of Yosemite's most distinctive features, the sheer-faced granite Half Dome, which rises nearly five thousand feet from the valley floor.

Adams' early connection to the club is recorded in a series of photographic albums now in the Bancroft Library at the University of California, Berkeley. Fifteen albums, spanning the years from 1920 to 1945, demonstrate his development as a photographer during this crucial period of his career and illustrate the impact that the Sierra Club experiences had on him.[2] Adams compiled nearly all of these albums from photographs made on the annual Sierra Club outings, called "high trips," he took part in each summer. He was named official photographer of the high trip in 1928, when the club traveled to the Canadian Rockies for its yearly four-week trek. However, even before this appointment (for which he was not paid), Adams was making photographic albums to commemorate the Sierra Club trips and, in the process, taking part in a long tradition of amateur photography during the summer outings.

The Sierra Club was founded in June 1892, bringing together two groups: those who wanted a mountain outing organization, like some of the newly formed alpine hiking clubs, and those who hoped for a watchdog group to protect Yosemite Park.[3] Adams' initial interest was in hiking and photographing the mountains, but over time he became a vocal advocate for their preservation. The club's incorporation papers described its goals: to explore, enjoy, and render the mountains accessible; to publish authentic information about them; and to enlist the support and cooperation of the public and the government in preserving the forests and other natural features of the Sierra Nevada.[4] The original members, mainly Berkeley and Stanford professors, U.S. Geological Survey scientists, and legislators, unanimously elected writer and naturalist John Muir as their first president; the group quickly expanded to include scholars, doctors, lawyers, and bankers.

The first Sierra Club outing was held in the summer of 1901 and was attended by ninety-six members, who hiked to Tuolumne Meadows, just north of Yosemite Valley. From their base camp, the participants took short side trips and climbed the surrounding mountains, with a commissary providing all their meals. Although the earliest outings used the base-camp format, by the time Adams took part in the trips during the 1920s, the group, which by then numbered about two hundred participants, usually established a new campsite every few days.

Adams' first outing with the club was in 1923, when he joined the annual monthlong trip for just one week. Following this brief trek in Yosemite Park's Pate Valley and Muir Gorge, he created an album of forty-three photographs, which included a price list stating that members could buy contact prints or enlargements; prints could be made "plain or soft-focus" and ranged in price from 50¢ for a small print to $1.25 for an "attractively mounted" enlargement.[5] Although this outing album, complete with prices, suggests that Adams' entrepreneurial spirit was well developed at a young age (he was only twenty-one at the time), in fact, the sale of prints from outing albums was an established Sierra Club practice.

By the 1920s, a tradition had developed of placing amateur photograph albums from the High Country trips on view in the Mills Tower offices of the club's San Francisco headquarters. The August 1928 *Sierra Club Bulletin* referred to the photographic exhibition, which included "the photographs taken on the recent outing to Jasper and Mount Robson Parks in the Canadian Rockies by Mr. Ansel E. Adams, who was with the party for the special purpose of taking photographs." The announcement also suggested that other Sierra Club members send their own albums in for exhibition, noting that "each photograph should be numbered to facilitate ordering of copies," thus allowing members to exchange prints.[6]

The leadership abilities Adams demonstrated on the 1928 trip led to his appointment as assistant manager of the outings beginning in 1930, in addition to his role as official photographer.[7] Adams selected each day's route and campsite, identified possible climbs along the way, arranged for evening entertainment, and supervised the lost and found (perhaps, he commented, because he was already responsible for so much camera equipment). He also laid out camp, requiring that he arrive before the pack train to identify the men's, women's, and marrieds' camps and locations for the commissary and latrines. Adams played this role for a number of years, allowing him to choose routes most conducive to his photographic pursuits.

Because Adams was a landscape photographer and outdoorsman, the bulk of each album's pictures recorded the terrain from a hiker's point of view. Many of the images made on these outings became part of his regular repertoire, and he continued to print some of them—such as *The Black Giant, Muir Pass* (1930), *Frozen Lake and Cliffs* (1932, plate 87), and *Lake Near Muir Pass* (1933, plate 90)—throughout his career. Others, however, were related to specific trips and were meant to commemorate a particular group's experience. They included whimsical details of Sierra Club camping gear, especially the tin cups and plates; close-ups of plants, trees, and rocks for botanical and geological study; pictures of group activities, such as climbers atop a recently scaled mountain peak or seated around a campfire listening to the violin; as well as individual portraits of outing members. In four years—1928, 1929, 1930, and 1932—Adams offered for sale not only individual prints but also special portfolios of his Sierra Club prints. Each portfolio combined what Adams felt were the best twenty-five pictures from that year's album, presented together with a specially printed title page and portfolio case.

Ten prints in The Lane Collection derived from negatives originally taken on Sierra Club outings. Two of the images were initially featured in one year's album and then reused in a later album.[8] An additional seven prints of subjects from Adams' 1927 portfolio *Parmelian Prints of the High Sierras* appear in both The Lane Collection and the Sierra Club albums (one, *Banner Peak*, appears in both the 1929 and 1931 albums). This portfolio, Adams' first, featured eighteen of his views of the Sierra Nevada, made between 1921 and early 1927. Each image was printed on Kodak Vitava Athena Grade T parchment, a semi-translucent paper, and presented within a folder imprinted with the title; the eighteen folders were then held together in a black and gold silk portfolio case. The title *Parmelian Prints* was given by the publisher, who felt that potential buyers would not be enticed to pay so much simply for a group of photographs. The exact derivation of the word is unclear, but Adams recounted that the "melian" portion related to the Greek term for "black."[9] Adams "reused" some of this portfolio's negatives in the Sierra Club albums when their subjects coincided with a particular year's trek.

What follows is an accounting of each of the Sierra Club albums for which there are related prints in The Lane Collection. For each album, the date, the title, and the Bancroft Library's

album number are listed. All of the images in the album that have corresponding prints in The Lane Collection are identified, even those that are not illustrated in this catalogue. The Sierra Club origin of the Lane photographs not only aids in dating the negatives (a notoriously common concern with Adams' works) but also brings new context to the images. The subsequent text focuses on one or two images in each album, discussing their placement and arrangement, their relationship to the Sierra Club outing, or the circumstances of their making.

1927 SIERRA CLUB OUTING: SEQUOIA NATIONAL PARK (1971.031.1927:01-ffALB)

• *Granite Ridge, Milestone Mountain, Sequoia National Park, California*; labeled in album, "59. *Milestone Mountain*" (plate 83)

• *Glacial Cirque, Milestone Ridge, Sequoia National Park, California*; labeled "60. *Peak on Milestone Ridge*" (plate 88)

These two views, both taken with a telephoto lens, appear together on one page of the 1927 album. Adams wrote of them to his friend and patron Albert Bender from the Junction Meadow Sierra Club camp in the Kern River Canyon on July 25, 1927:

> I wish I could set out to tell you of this marvelous summer—but I shall have to let my pictures do that. If nothing unfavorable happens to the plates—and I hope nothing does—I will have to show you the best set of mountain pictures I have ever had. But the pressure of my work has allowed me little time for rest and writing. Up at four or five in the morning—rushed breakfast—then off on the trail with 30 pounds on my back and a tripod in my hand—and by the time I return I feel like doing just nothing until the next morning. Yesterday I climbed Milestone Mountain—13,600 feet and hauled my camera to the craggy top. The peak is about the most majestic I have ever seen—and the view incomprehensible.[10]

Although the rule governing the sale of prints from Sierra Club albums was that they be made available to other members at cost, Adams realized that people might be willing to pay extra

for special prints. In the 1927 price list, single six-by-eight prints were offered at $1 apiece or $10 for twelve, on either white or buff matte-surface paper. Adams also listed individual prints on "parchment" for $2.50 apiece and asked that patrons wishing this treatment request "Parmelian Prints." (Once he had used this term to describe the photographs in his *Parmelian* portfolio, he commonly referred to all of his prints by this fanciful, made-up name.) To this end, he provided an example of a parchment print at the back of the album, for interested customers. Adams' special treatment of these prints—using delicate, slightly translucent paper packaged in individual paper folders—suggested that they were fine works of art meant to be carefully handled and intimately studied. Rather than on parchment paper, however, the large early photographs *Granite Ridge* and *Glacial Cirque* in The Lane Collection are printed on heavy, textured, matte-surfaced paper whose broad areas of warm tones dominate the earth and sky, creating mountain landscapes that seem more at home on the moon than in the Sierra Nevada.

1928 SIERRA CLUB OUTING: JASPER AND MOUNT ROBSON PARKS, CANADIAN ROCKIES (1971.031.1928:04a-ffALB AND 1971.031.1928:04b-ffALB)

• *Blackhorn Peak, Tonquin Valley, Canadian Rockies*; labeled "30. *Black Horn Peak—Telephotograph*" (plate 84)

• *From Moose Pass, Canadian Rockies*; labeled "129. *Peak East of Moose Pass—Telephotograph*" (plate 85)

• *Mount Robson from Mount Resplendent, Canadian Rockies*; labeled "156. *Mount Robson from Resplendent*" (plate 89)

A photogravure of Adams' *Mount Robson from Mount Resplendent* appeared as the frontispiece in the 1929 *Sierra Club Bulletin*, which described the previous summer's outing to the Canadian Rockies. The author, Walter L. Huber, referred several times to Adams' antics, including this humorous anecdote: "When at last we halted for lunch we looked back to see our photographer friend far up on the mountain, entranced by the view and handicapped by his pack. The [Swiss]

83. GRANITE RIDGE, MILESTONE MOUNTAIN, SEQUOIA NATIONAL PARK, CALIFORNIA, *1927*

guides fully understood his position, and in a tone of affection one remarked to the other: 'I go back and get dat Hansel.'"[11] The stunning view and Adams' handsome gravure of it are also mentioned in Huber's article, as part of his lengthy account of the ascent of Mount Resplendent:

> Before us lay one of the world's finest mountain scenes—the summit of Mount Robson from the east and the great ice-fall below it. Mere words cannot adequately describe such views. Our photographer spent little of his precious time eating lunch, but the results of his work during that brief period will give the reader, who is here referred to the frontispiece, an idea of the scene which those of us who viewed it will never forget.[12]

Adams featured Mount Robson in several photographs in this album, confirming its importance as a landmark for the outing members. He included two similar pictures of Mount Robson from Mount Resplendent: the vertical view illustrated in the *Bulletin* (and in The Lane Collection) records the glacial ice below the summit, and a close horizontal variant emphasizes the dramatic shape of the mountain against the sky. Other photographs are taken from surrounding viewpoints, such as the Sierra Club camp, with tents in the foreground or hikers ascending the snow-covered peak.

1929 SIERRA CLUB OUTING: BLANEY MEADOWS TO YOSEMITE VALLEY (1971.031.1929:03-ffALB)

• *Banner Peak—Thousand Island Lake, Sierra Nevada, California*, from *Parmelian Prints of the High Sierras* (plate 82)

• *On the Heights, Yosemite National Park*, from *Parmelian Prints of the High Sierras* (plate 14, p. 35)

• *The Sentinel, Yosemite National Park*, from *Parmelian Prints of the High Sierras*

• *Monolith—The Face of Half Dome, Yosemite National Park*, from *Parmelian Prints of the High Sierras*

The 1929 Sierra Club outing traversed territory Adams had photographed in the past, and as a result, he incorporated several prints from previously made negatives into this album. Four of his

84. BLACKHORN PEAK, TONQUIN VALLEY, CANADIAN ROCKIES, *1928*

85. FROM MOOSE PASS, CANADIAN ROCKIES, *1928*

images from *Parmelian Prints of the High Sierras* were included, allowing his fellow club members to purchase these prints individually rather than having to buy the whole set. One of them, *Banner Peak—Thousand Island Lake*, was first made in 1923, and Adams later remarked that it was among his earliest successful photographs. Featuring a dramatic, cloud-filled sky, it stands out in his work of this period; most of his other *Parmelian* portfolio subjects have blank white skies reminiscent of nineteenth-century landscape photographs and typical of the orthochromatic glass plates he still used. These negatives, sensitive only to blue and green light, frequently overexposed the sky, producing an empty void. However, for the *Banner Peak* image, Adams employed a newly purchased panchromatic glass plate, which rendered a wider spectrum of colors accurately in terms of their relative brightness and allowed him to depict a more natural sky. Despite this achievement, he continued to use the less-expensive orthochromatic negatives until 1932.[13]

1930 SIERRA CLUB OUTING: SOUTH FORK OF THE SAN JOAQUIN RIVER AND MIDDLE FORK OF THE KINGS RIVER (1971.031.1930:02-ffALB)

• *Black Giant, Muir Pass, Sierra Nevada, California*; labeled "78. *Muir Pass/The Black Giant*"

• *Mount Winchell Sunset, Sierra Nevada, California*; labeled "138. *Mount Winchell*" (plate 86)

Adams' 1930 album price list advertised "Twenty-five Prints made on Dassonville Charcoal Black," complete with a title page and fabric-covered portfolio case.[14] The portfolio was priced at thirty dollars (about ten dollars more than ordering twenty-five prints individually) and contained, Adams noted, "the best and most representative selection of my Photographs of the 1930 Outing." The Lane Collection includes prints of two of the 1930 album images, which were also featured in the portfolio. Adams made only eight copies of the 1930 portfolio, presumably based on the number of orders he received. His profit margin on such a small edition was probably not high, but offering prints packaged in various ways was intended to broaden the market for his photographs.

86. MOUNT WINCHELL SUNSET, SIERRA NEVADA, *1930*

• *Banner Peak—Thousand Island Lake, Sierra Nevada, California*, from *Parmelian Prints of the High Sierras*; labeled "108. *Banner Peak and Thousand Island Lake*" (plate 82)

• *Sierra Junipers, Upper Merced Basin, Yosemite Valley*, from *Parmelian Prints of the High Sierras*; labeled "80. *Mount Clark from Fletcher Creek Trail*"

As with the 1929 album, in which Adams employed earlier negatives to augment his new photographs, the 1931 album contains two *Parmelian* portfolio subjects. In this case, Adams called attention to their inclusion in the typewritten price list adhered to the front cover: "A few of the photographs herein—chiefly relating to the second part of the outing—were secured in past summers, but [are] included for their representative value. The atmospheric conditions during our 1931 outing were generally poor—due to almost continual forest and brush fires in the lower ranges. The lack of snow contributes most distressfully to the aspect of barrenness in pictures of the high mountains."

87. FROZEN LAKE AND CLIFFS (PRECIPICE LAKE), KAWEAH GAP, SIERRA NEVADA, CALIFORNIA, *1932*

• *Mount Brewer*, from *Parmelian Prints of the High Sierras*; labeled "45. *Mount Brewer from Bullfrog Lake*"

• *East Vidette*, from *Parmelian Prints of the High Sierras*; labeled "51. *East Vidette*"

• *Granite Ridge, Milestone Mountain, Sequoia National Park, California*; reused from 1927 outing album, labeled "98. *Milestone Mountain*" (plate 83)

• *Frozen Lake and Cliffs (Precipice Lake), Kaweah Gap, Sierra Nevada, California*; labeled "159. *Lake Below Kaweah Gap*" (plate 87)

Of the four Lane Collection prints whose images appear in the 1932 album, three are reused from earlier years: two from the *Parmelian* portfolio and one from the 1927 Sierra Club outing album.

The remaining photograph, now known as *Frozen Lake and Cliffs*, is conspicuous for its powerful, abstract qualities. In the album, it is alone on a page, singled out for special attention. Four other images of the same location—the area near Kaweah Gap, in Sequoia National Park—accompany it on surrounding pages (fig. 12). The related photographs provide a larger context for this famous image by Adams, showing the pass in the distance, the cliffs and lake in the middle ground, and the shore in the foreground. Thus, Adams made both "conventional" landscapes of the area and the strikingly stark *Frozen Lake and Cliffs*. He referred to this more abstract image as the equivalent of his personal experience of the place, writing of the picture, "I believe I was able to express in this photograph the monumental qualities of the subject that I responded to so intensely at first sight."[15]

• *Lake near Muir Pass, Kings River Canyon, California*; labeled "51. *Wanda Lake*" (plate 90)

• *Thunderstorm over North Palisade, Sierra Nevada, California*; labeled "75. *North Palisade*" (plate 91)

• *Mount Winchell Sunset, Sierra Nevada, California*; reused from 1930 outing album, labeled "90. *Mt. Winchell*" (plate 86)

Thunderstorm over North Palisade, with its threatening thunderclouds piling up above the mountain, was one of Adams' particular favorites. He made a number of prints from this negative and chose to illustrate it in the account of that year's trip in the *Sierra Club Bulletin*. In addition, he included it in his earliest book of landscape photographs, *Sierra Nevada: The John Muir Trail* (1938), a large folio dedicated to the memory of Walter Starr Jr., who died while mountain climbing in the Sierra. Nancy Newhall also featured it in Adams' first biography, *Ansel Adams: Eloquent Light*, in 1963, and it reappeared more than twenty years later in Adams' posthumously published *Autobiography* (1985).

Adams' interest in the constantly changing mountain skies can be seen in many of his photographs, but to the outing participants, this photograph recorded specific clouds and a specific thunderstorm. For those who were camping outdoors for four weeks, thunderclouds signified the potential for treacherous lightning storms, which greatly affected their high country experience. The 1934 *Sierra Club Bulletin*'s trip report for the previous summer included Ethel Boulware's description of their few afternoons of rainfall:

> About ten o'clock soft patches of white would attract attention; by noon they had gathered ominously, becoming bigger and blacker; and promptly at 2:30, a roll of thunder would be heard, followed by a steady downpour. In spite of the protection of a sloping rock or of a poncho generously draped over the low branches of an albicaulis [*Pinus albicaulis* is a whitebark pine], most of us returned like draggled-tailed chickens.[16]

Adams photographed this great mass of clouds not just as a photographer trying to depict a visually stunning scene but as a Sierra Club backpacker, who saw it for its very real potential for rain. He knew that the members who perused the album would see the photograph that way, too, and that for them it would conjure the feeling of the coming storm, just as the clouds themselves had on the day the photograph was made.

—*Rebecca A. Senf*

Fig. 12. Ansel Adams, *Eagle Scout Peak from Kaweah Gap*, from Sierra Club Album, 1932. Gelatin silver print, 19.8 x 15.1 cm (7 ¹³⁄₁₆ x 5 ¹⁵⁄₁₆ in.). Photograph courtesy of Bancroft Library, University of California, Berkeley.

88. GLACIAL CIRQUE, MILESTONE RIDGE, SEQUOIA NATIONAL PARK, CALIFORNIA, *1927*

89. MOUNT ROBSON FROM MOUNT RESPLENDENT, CANADIAN ROCKIES, *1928*

90. LAKE NEAR MUIR PASS, KINGS RIVER CANYON, CALIFORNIA, *1933*

91. THUNDERSTORM OVER NORTH PALISADE, SIERRA NEVADA, CALIFORNIA, *1933*

92. OLD CHURCH, HORNITOS, CALIFORNIA, *1943*

HORNITOS THROUGH ADAMS' LENS

HORNITOS, CALIFORNIA, a twentieth-century ghost of a nineteenth-century gold-mining town, was a favorite subject for Ansel Adams. The seven Hornitos photographs in The Lane Collection range from informal street scenes to carefully composed architectural studies. They span the years from 1934 to 1960 and display a concern for human subject matter, unlike Adams' more typical photographs of untouched wilderness.

Hornitos is now home to fewer than one hundred residents, but it continues to appeal to tourists because of its relatively large number of surviving nineteenth-century buildings.[1] Following the discovery of gold at Sutter's Mill in 1848 and the beginning of the California gold rush, the surrounding region was flooded with prospectors. Many of these forty-niners, as they came to be known, were foreign immigrants, a significant fact in the history of Hornitos, which was settled largely by Mexican miners driven out of neighboring Quartzburg by their Anglo counterparts. Hornitos, Spanish for "little ovens," was named for its dome-shaped tombs, built aboveground because the hardness of the local soil discouraged traditional interment; the burial mounds were reminiscent of adobe bread ovens called *hornos*. Although mid-nineteenth-century population estimates of fifteen thousand are now considered quite high, in its heyday the town did boast a number of hotels, six fraternal organizations, a post office, a Wells Fargo Express office offering banking and delivery services, many saloons and entertainment halls, and six general stores, including one owned by Domingo Ghirardelli, founder of the San Francisco chocolate company.[2]

Located in the western foothills of the Sierra Nevada, Hornitos was not far out of Adams' way as he traveled back and forth between his San Francisco home and Yosemite Valley. The appeal of abandoned mining towns for modernist photographers like Adams and his friends Edward Weston and Alma Lavenson seems largely to have been due to their abundance of weathered man-made materials succumbing to nature: rusted metal, crumbling adobe, and splintering wood, often overgrown with weeds. In some cases, Adams and his fellow photographers even shared subjects. For example, Lavenson, in her extensive documentation of the Mother Lode mining region, photographed the same church in the town of Chinese Camp as Adams did; she recorded the entire building, but he isolated a detail of the door (plate 99).[3] Adams described the attraction of deserted mines in an article on photographing commonplace objects.

> Parts of iron machinery were scattered over a large area, some half-buried in the earth, some partially hidden by grass and shrubs. The metal possessed the patina of years of sun and storm; forms and textures were beautiful in the truest sense—their dispersal, being accidental, gave them as "natural" a quality as the scattered rocks and trees and clouds of a wild landscape . . . they were beautiful in their inter-relationships and in their balance of form, texture and mass.[4]

Whereas Adams called attention to the compositional potential of decaying mining equipment, Lavenson cited two particularly attractive qualities when she chronicled her work on ghost towns: the wealth of worn surfaces and their evocation of the past.[5] About the former, Lavenson explained: "Where half the story is told by the weathered texture of the boards and the aged appearance of the buildings, where a few little weeds straggling through the board sidewalk tell a tale of struggle and ultimate survival, [it is] necessary to record every detail and every bit of texture."[6] Her focus on the historical qualities of these towns meant that unlike Adams, she avoided signs of contemporary life: "Often I waited seemingly endless time for automobiles or present-day residents in modern dress to move out of the scene. I hoped that the spirits of the old-timers of bygone days would fill the streets instead."[7] Adams would have agreed with Lavenson's interest in the patina of time, but he was also interested in recording the town and its people.

The lure of ghost towns extended beyond modernist photographers, and even *Life* magazine, with its massive circulation, commissioned an article from Adams on Hornitos in the late 1930s.[8] Like many picture stories initiated by the magazine, the spread was never run, apparently bumped at the last minute by a pressing news item.[9] Nevertheless, Adams was eventually able to publish his Hornitos images thanks to his longstanding friendship with Tom Maloney, the editor of *U.S. Camera* magazine. In 1934 Maloney had begun publishing the *U.S. Camera Annual*, modeled on European publications featuring images of what the editors deemed the year's best photographs.[10] In the autumn of 1938, Maloney founded *U.S. Camera* magazine, and by 1940 he had published a number of photography essays by Adams. Mostly technical articles, Adams' titles included "Photography of Architecture," "Photo-Murals," "New York: On the 'Just Right' Conditions for a Picture"—detailing his process for making a particular city view—and "Practical Hints on Lenses."[11] In 1944 Adams wrote another series of stories, beginning with "Exploring the Commonplace" in May; a piece on Hornitos entitled simply "People" in June; a short discussion of his documentation of Japanese American internees at the Manzanar War Relocation Camp in eastern California's Owens Valley, entitled "Manzanar," in November; and a two-page spread of snow-covered trees in Yosemite, under the title "Christmas Trees," in the December issue.[12]

Fig. 13. Ansel Adams, "People," spread from the June 1944 issue of *U.S. Camera*.

The photographs of Hornitos townspeople in the *U.S. Camera* spread at first appear to be documentary in nature. However, Adams himself argued that their lack of an intended cohesive story belied this initial impression. Their true function is made clearer by contrasting the Hornitos essay with the one on Manzanar, which introduced Adams' one major exploration of documentary photography. Whereas the American social documentary style of photography tends to be associated with photographers like Dorothea Lange, Walker Evans, and Margaret Bourke-White, whose work during the Depression brought the plight of the rural unemployed to the attention of the nation, Adams had his documentary experience a decade later. He found the Second World War a frustrating time and desperately wanted to do something toward the war effort, but few opportunities seemed to come his way. When his Sierra Club friend Ralph Merritt offered him the chance to photograph the

Manzanar War Relocation Camp, to which Merritt had recently been appointed director, he eagerly took the job. According to Adams, Merritt was sympathetic to the plight of the American-born Japanese people who were incarcerated there under his care.[13] Adams was not inclined to depict the bleak conditions at Manzanar or the injustice of relocating American citizens of Japanese descent; instead, he focused on the resilience and strength he found among the camp's detainees. Tom Maloney suggested that the Manzanar pictures warranted being brought together as a book, and he published them in *Born Free and Equal* in late 1944.[14] Nancy Newhall curated a selection of the photographs for the Museum of Modern Art, but the brief exhibition was relegated to a basement space, and Adams felt that many people misunderstood the work as being pro-Japanese rather than pro–Japanese American.[15] The essay in *U.S. Camera* was excerpted from Adams' forthcoming book; a short text illustrated by four large images,

and one smaller one, described his approach to photographing the relocation camp and its residents.

In contrast to the Manzanar article, the magazine piece on Hornitos can be understood as an extension of Adams' teaching at the time, rather than a documentary project[16] (fig. 13). The text included only a minimal introduction to Hornitos and its annual "homecoming," a "colossal barbecue get-together" that was the focus of many of the images in the story. Instead, it provided practical advice and was clearly rooted in Adams' experience in leading workshops in Yosemite, under the sponsorship of Maloney and *U.S. Camera*, as well as his work at the Art Center School in Los Angeles. Adams discussed his strategies for working with a handheld 35mm camera in the low light and rainy conditions of the town gathering.[17] He went on to outline technical guidelines for his reader:

> I have been asked why flash was not used. My answer is that for merely factual purposes, flash would have been simpler and the pictures sharper. However, I feel that the mood is as important as the thing itself. . . . Even with the most elaborate lighting set-up imaginable, it would be practically impossible to re-create the feeling of rain, heavy skies, the wet earth and quiet light. A "snappy" print would not be in key and the ordinary flash-in-the-pan flashlight quality would be as false as inserting professional models into the pictures. . . . We can justify imperfect negatives only if we have done everything possible to make them perfect. Yet, the expressive purpose is of greater importance than mere technical perfection. . . . In other words, what is expressed is of greater importance than the arbitrary standards of expressing it.[18]

The text also addressed the image captioned "Moment in a Crowd" (plate 94), distinguishing it from the "documentary" mode, which is meant to tell a larger story, and describing it instead as "an *observation* of a moment from nature." Adams contrasted his approach to that of sports photography, in which the photographer's knowledge of the action helps him anticipate the crucial scene, or to news photography, in which significant events determine when a picture is made.

93. RESIDENTS, HORNITOS, CALIFORNIA, *ABOUT 1935*

He noted that there "is no time to *think out* a picture such as this" and that he was lucky to click the shutter at the instant that several people in the crowd were directing their attention to the little boy, giving the composition coherence.[19] Adams mentioned Henri Cartier-Bresson, Lisette Model, and Helen Levitt as photographers who successfully captured similarly complex moments.[20]

The opening page of "People" includes two small portraits, one in each lower corner. The two elderly men depicted appear together in an early enlargement now in The Lane Collection entitled *Residents, Hornitos* (plate 93). In the large print, Adams set off the figures of the two men against the texture of worn wooden clapboards and the lines and angles created by the porch beams, chairs, and windowpanes.[21] The gentlemen look as weathered as the building behind them and seem to be permanent fixtures on the porch. The individual portraits of the men, in contrast, omitted much of the lively background and were reproduced in the magazine as a pair of close-ups rather than a double portrait.

Adams clearly found Hornitos a valuable source of photographic material. He brought his Yosemite workshop students on day trips and took many of his own pictures there over the years. Although not reflected in the *U.S. Camera* piece, the wide range of subjects available in Hornitos is well represented in the seven prints in The Lane Collection. Adams' 1943 portrait of Saint Catherine's, the town's Catholic church, with its symmetrical white wooden facade and stone buttresses, is stunning in its simplicity (plate 92); another image of the same church, seen in the distance beyond a fence, was featured in his *Portfolio I* in 1948 (plate 96). Two pictures, one from early in his career and the other made much later, depict gravesites and graffiti, subjects that Edward Weston photographed as well. Adams' print from the 1930s isolates two headstones in the town's cemetery seen against the rolling hills beyond (plate 97), whereas a late print, made in 1960, forgoes context and focuses instead on a graffiti-covered wall (plate 76). Weston's photographs of these subjects, made on a day trip to

94. MOMENT IN A CROWD, HORNITOS HOMECOMING, CALIFORNIA, *1938*

Hornitos with Adams in 1940, during Weston's time in Yosemite teaching with the U.S. Camera workshop, are very different.[22] His graveyard picture makes the fenced gravesites seem incidental, nestled in the lower-left corner of a pale landscape, and his photographs of "wall scrawls" combine graffiti and recognizable elements—bricks and flaking plaster—to create complicated images of varied textures that evoke the process of decay. Another Adams "street scene" of three men talking in front of the mid-nineteenth-century Pacific Saloon exhibits a spontaneity similar to that of *Moment in a Crowd* and was probably made in 1938, along with the other Hornitos "homecoming" pictures (plate 95). By bringing

together this diverse group of images, made over a span of more than thirty years, The Lane Collection demonstrates the rich source of inspiration that the little town of Hornitos provided Adams, all just a stone's throw from Yosemite.

—*Rebecca A. Senf*

95. MEN AND DOG, HORNITOS HOMECOMING, CALIFORNIA, *1938*

96. CHURCH AND FENCE, HORNITOS, CALIFORNIA, *1946*

97. AT HORNITOS, CALIFORNIA, ABOUT 1934

98. MR. SHEPARD AT HIS HOME, INDEPENDENCE, CALIFORNIA, *ABOUT 1936*

99. DETAIL, CHURCH, CHINESE CAMP, CALIFORNIA, *ABOUT 1944*

100. WINDMILL, OWENS VALLEY, CALIFORNIA, *ABOUT 1935*

101. POPLAR TREES, OWENS VALLEY, CALIFORNIA, *ABOUT 1936*

102. OLD WALL PAPER IN HOUSE AT LUNDY, CALIFORNIA, *1939*

103. REMAINS OF OLD SQUARE PIANO, LUNDY, CALIFORNIA, *1939*

104. GRASS AND POOL SCREEN, *ABOUT 1948*

JAPANESE-STYLE FOLDING SCREENS

ANSEL ADAMS CREATED his first Japanese-style folding screen in 1936 from an enlargement of his photograph *Leaves, Mills College* (about 1931) and exhibited it in his one-man exhibition at the Katherine Kuh Gallery in Chicago the same year. The photographer wrote to his wife, Virginia: "The show looks very fine and the screen is a knockout."[1] The original inspiration for this first screen is not known, but its manufacture coincided with his growing interest in printing mural-size photographs. According to Adams, *Leaves, Mills College* was photographed on the Mills campus in Oakland, from the vantage of a bridge overlooking a waterway.[2] The image captures a dense bower of ferns and leaves along the water's banks, as seen from above, like a modern-day *millefleur* tapestry. In fact, Adams claimed that when he showed this picture to the dean of fine arts at Yale in 1933, the dean was convinced that it was a reproduction of a tapestry or a painting, rather than a photograph from nature.[3] Years later, perhaps with this in mind, Adams wrote that photographic screens should feature "patterns of leaves, natural or mechanical forms . . . patterns not dissimilar to tapestry effects, or to semi-abstract compositions."[4]

Adams is thought to have produced only twelve to fifteen decorative screens over the course of his career, beginning with the three-paneled *Leaves* from the mid-1930s and continuing into the early 1970s, when he seems to have stopped making them altogether.[5] The majority of his screens were created either for exhibitions, like Katherine Kuh's and his 1940 "Pageant of Photography" show, or as commissions or gifts for close friends.[6] Today most of them are in the collections of museums and other institutions or still owned by the artist's family. Adams' folding screens are surprisingly difficult to account for; several seem to have been damaged or destroyed over the years. To some extent, this was the result of the less-than-ideal materials from which they were constructed. The screens consist of enlarged photographic prints glued to plywood or Masonite panels and glazed with a thin coat of varnish, which, in a number of cases, rather than protecting the prints, seems to have caused severe yellowing and discoloration.[7] The single-sided screens, which are by far the most common, are often painted a flat gray or other neutral dark color on the verso; the photographs are held in place by a narrow aluminum channel along the edges, and several of the screens are supported by small spherical feet along the bottom. In most screens, the individual panels are joined by piano hinges (an interesting choice in light of Adams' beginnings as a concert pianist), which allows them to bend in either direction.

Adams' *Leaves, Mills College* screen was sold, not long after the close of the Kuh show, to Harold Ickes, head of the Department of the Interior.[8] Perhaps because it was his first screen and it had found such a prestigious home, Adams was diligent about keeping track of it over the years and apparently wrote to nearly every new secretary of the interior to check on it. A letter to Stewart Udall in January 1961 brought this reply from Washington: "Although I have admired your camera work at a distance, it excited me to know that you produced the screen which is at my elbow"; but a visit to Udall's office six years later led Adams to offer to replace the screen at his own expense, because he felt it was no longer in good condition.[9] Rather than replicate the earlier *Leaves, Mills College* image, he replaced it with a new enlargement of his 1947 photograph *Fresh Snow*.[10] In February 1968, he wrote to the secretary to explain the gift: "The Department of Interior has been a very potent influence in my life and career, from the days of Harold Ickes to the present. It has been a great experience to know you and to have participated in some of the activities and goals of your office." On receiving the new replacement, Udall replied: "The screen is superb!"[11]

In 1940 Adams wrote an article for *U.S. Camera* magazine describing various strategies for making photomurals, from the choice of subject matter and issues of composition to various methods of darkroom processing and the final mounting of the print. Written not long after Adams had produced a number of large-scale photographs for his "Pageant of Photography" exhibition at the Golden Gate Exposition in San Francisco, the *U.S. Camera* article went on to propose the idea of fabricating freestanding screens from photo enlargements.[12] The opening illustration is a close-up view of a group of old wooden wagon wheels lying on the ground in a complex pattern, which Adams recommended as an ideal screen subject.[13] The reproduction is marked with two small dots below it to demonstrate where he suggested one might divide the composition to create a tripartite screen; in fact, this image was the source for the now-lost screen that he exhibited at "A Pageant of Photography."[14] The picture on the following page is that of an actual screen, based on his earlier photograph *Branches in Snow* (about 1940); it is shown in situ at the bottom of a staircase at what was then Best's Studio in Yosemite (renamed the Ansel Adams Gallery in 1972). Emphasizing the decorative potential of mural and screen subjects like these, Adams advised using photographs that are as graphic, abstract, and tonally strong as possible. The challenge, he explained, is that with folding screens "the photograph is seen not as a flat surface, but as a combination of surfaces, each set at a different angle to the others," creating "effects not only of altered perspective and scale, but, on account of reflective properties of the panels, of light intensity as well."[15]

Fig. 14. Ansel Adams, *Clearing Storm, Sonoma County Hills* (recto) and *Oak Tree, Rain, Sonoma County* (verso) screen, 1969. Each panel 186.6 x 75 x 3.2 cm (73 7⁄16 x 29½ x 1¼ in.). Courtesy of the Center for Creative Photography, University of Arizona, Gift of Seeley W. Mudd II.

Fig. 15. Hashimoto Gaho (Japanese, 1835–1908), *Snowy Landscape* screen, mid-1880s. Ink and light color on paper, 169.2 x 361.4 cm (66⅛ x 142⅗ in.). Museum of Fine Arts, Boston, William Sturgis Bigelow Collection, 11.8724.

In an early unpublished biography of Adams, Nancy Newhall described the very rudimentary darkroom that he used to print the mural-size photographs that were employed in his screens; the surprisingly cramped space was in the basement of his parents' home (and had to be entered via a ladder from the garden!). Of his protracted method of designing the screens, she wrote:

> [He] undertakes a commission for a mural, screen or other decoration with the same care painters and sculptors devote to such projects. . . . Then he submits sketches—photographs of several possible subjects. . . . These he prints in several contrasts, with a scale model or two for the sake of visualization. . . . Idea and effect agreed on, he proceeds to make the final negative and the final print.

Newhall then went on to describe his printing process.

[His] large camera, converted to an enlarger by the bank of mercury argon tubes at its back, recoils on its tracks and throws an image on the wall, where roll by roll the mural paper will be pinned. . . . Then section by section, he examines the image and by intricate play with light withholds here, intensifies there. The huge exposure is rolled up, placed in the vats of developer and slowly, constantly, unrolled and rerolled, transferred to shortstop [stop bath], two baths of hypo, and finally two hours of washing, still being rolled and unrolled like a scroll. The matching of tones between the sections, imposed by the width of the mural paper, must be exact, and an inch or more leeway allowed for the perfect matching of the image when mounted.[16]

Living in San Francisco, with its wealth of Asian art, Adams would have been familiar with folding screens from an early age. His friendship with Asian art collectors, such as Albert Bender, would also have ensured his exposure to authentic examples of fine, non-Western screens. The folding screen as an art form was a relatively recent phenomenon in the West, dating only from the seventeenth century, but in China, where they were invented, and Japan, where they were adapted and popularized, screens had been a common domestic and ceremonial decoration for more than a thousand years.[17] During the Victorian era in America, a resurgence of interest in all things Japanese began, and women's magazines of the period featured screen designs as do-it-yourself projects, including some that were covered with embroidery, prints, stamps, wallpaper, and even photographs. The Arts and Crafts and Art Deco movements also capitalized on the practical and aesthetic appeal of the form, and by the time that

Adams was producing his streamlined, metal-framed screens, they were increasingly being created by artists, from Thomas Hart Benton to Yves Tanguy, and Man Ray to Jim Dine. Late in life Adams claimed not to have been directly inspired by Chinese or Japanese screens, but the affinities of his subject matter and compositional devices with those in Asian screens and paintings are unmistakable (see, for example, fig. 15).[18]

A three-panel screen of his lyrical and abstract image *Grass and Pool* was purchased at auction for The Lane Collection in October 2001 (plate 104).[19] At the time of the sale, the screen had been in the McAlpin family for more than fifty years, having originally been made for his good friend David McAlpin in late 1947 or early 1948.[20] According to McAlpin, the photograph from which it was created was taken in September 1938, during a seventeen-day pack trip that he, Georgia O'Keeffe, and four other friends made with Adams to the Yosemite High Country.[21] McAlpin recounted the route the group took out of Yosemite Valley over the Snow Creek Trail, past Tenaya Lake, up to Tuolumne Meadows, and through the Cathedral Range to reach their destination—the Lyell Fork of the Merced River. He also described Adams shooting this particular image with his 4 x 5 camera pointed down at the dark surface of the water near their camp in the river valley. The Lyell Fork of the Merced, with its dramatic views of Rodgers and Electra Peaks in the distance, was one of Adams' favorite settings in the High Sierra and a location that he photographed many times. As early as 1921, for example, he made a pictorialist-inspired, soft-focus image of lodgepole pines not far from there (plate 12, p. 33), and later in his career he took another picture of the mirrorlike water reflecting the far-off mountains, including the peak that was officially named Mount Ansel Adams following his death in 1984 (plate 74, p. 106).

The two folding screens by Adams currently in the collection of the George Eastman House in Rochester are derived from an image of sumac leaves made from a single 5 x 7 negative originally taken around 1937 in Owens Valley, California.[22] One of this pair was created in 1947 or 1948 (at roughly the same time as the *Grass and Pool* screen) for Adams' good friends New York lawyer George Marshall and his wife, Betty (fig. 16). In a letter to Beaumont Newhall, Adams claimed that, in their case, he had purposely printed the negative softer than he otherwise might have, "to match [Betty's] room"—another example of his taking into consideration a screen's eventual setting when designing it.[23] The second, more sharply printed but otherwise nearly identical screen was initially fabricated for an exhibition in Pasadena in 1950; however, after the show the intended purchaser changed his mind, deciding the work was too large for his space, and as a result Adams offered it as a loan to Newhall, who by this time had gone to work at the Eastman House as curator.[24] The sumac, with its luminous all-over pattern of delicate leaves, is closely related to the subjects of his other decorative screens made during the late 1940s. In both Eastman House sumac screens, as well as McAlpin's *Grass and Pool*, Adams' cropping and camera angle cause the ground to appear to tilt sharply upward, flattening and abstracting the calligraphic forms of the grasses and leaves that spread across the surface of each panel. The graphic qualities of these folding-screen images is further enhanced by their large scale, which inspires one to read them as decorative arrangements of dark and light tones, rather than depictions of specific natural forms.

During the 1950s and '60s, Adams again made a pair of screens, each several years apart but of the same subject, for two separate clients. These screens are unusual in his oeuvre in that they are double-sided, the rectos featuring his *Clearing Storm, Sonoma County Hills* (from a negative dated 1951) and the versos, *Oak Tree, Rain, Sonoma County* (about 1951).[25] The example that Adams produced in 1951 for Mr. and Mrs. Jack Skirball was his most ambitious screen thus far: it was five-paneled, rather than three, and stood on thin metal legs that raised it about a foot off the floor. Designed for Skirball Ranch, the couple's Santa Rosa home in Sonoma County, the screen was intended to be seen from both sides and to act as a room divider between their spacious dining and living rooms.[26] Eighteen years later, in 1969, Adams was commissioned to make a similar screen for Dr. and Mrs. Seeley W. Mudd of Carmel, which today is in the collection of the Center for Creative Photography in Tucson (fig. 14).[27] Although the subject is the same, for the Mudds' screen Adams returned to his more typical low, ball-footed design, and by altering the cropping and composition (in the case of the *Oak Tree, Rain* verso, for example, he flopped the negative and reversed the image), he produced an equally stunning four-panel variation on the earlier, Skirball screen.

Adams' third Guggenheim grant, in 1959, gave him a new impetus to focus on making mural-size prints and screens. The Guggenheim funding also allowed him to update his darkroom in his new home in Carmel and purchase the necessary equipment to produce even larger and more imposing photographs than he had previously. Adams' massive "Eloquent Light" exhibition, organized by his friend Nancy Newhall at the de Young Museum in 1963, featured a number of monumental photo murals and folding screens and succeeded in bringing these works to the attention of a much broader public.[28] Always open to novel ways of presenting large-scale imagery—from his Coloramas in Grand Central Station during the 1950s to the Polaroid murals of the 1960s and 1970s—Adams' folding screens are fascinating examples of the artist's innovative ideas regarding scale and utility in photography.

—*Karen E. Haas*

Fig. 16. Ansel Adams, *Leaves, Owens Valley, California* screen, 1950. Approximately 182.9 x 228.6 cm (72 x 90 in.).
Courtesy of George Eastman House, Gift of Mrs. George Marshall.

PARMELIAN PRINT

ANSEL EASTON ADAMS

P 13

Number

Label 1

PHOTOGRAPH
BY
Ansel Adams

NO_____ NEG NO_____
Mr. Shepard at his home
Independence, California
CA 1936

Label 5

ANSEL ADAMS
BOX 455
YOSEMITE NATIONAL PARK
CALIFORNIA

Stamp 3

PHOTOGRAPH
BY
ANSEL ADAMS
ROUTE 1, BOX 181
CARMEL, CALIFORNIA
93921

Stamp 7

ANSEL EASTON ADAMS

PARMELIAN PRINT
NO._____

Label 2

ANSEL ADAMS
131 24th AVENUE · SAN FRANCISCO · CALIFORNIA

To _____
YOSEMITE NATIONAL PARK
DETAIL: FOREST IN WINTER

SECOND CLASS MATTER. Postmaster: This package may be opened for postal inspection if necessary.

Label 6

PHOTOGRAPH
BY
ANSEL ADAMS
131 - 24TH AVENUE
SAN FRANCISCO

NEG. NO. 4-NPS- 164
Lower Glacial Forest
Glacier Bay, Alaska   #1

Stamp 4

TITLE Charles Erskine Scott Wood
CREDIT_____
DATE 1928 FILM
Dassonville Paper

Stamp 8

PHOTOGRAPH
BY
ANSEL EASTON ADAMS
SAN FRANCISCO

Label 3

PHOTOGRAPH
BY
ANSEL ADAMS

Stamp 1

PHOTOGRAPH
BY
ANSEL ADAMS
ROUTE 1, BOX 181
CARMEL, CALIFORNIA

Stamp 5

ANSEL ADAMS
ROUTE 1, BOX 181
CARMEL
CALIFORNIA
93921

Stamp 9

A
PHOTOGRAPH
BY
ANSEL ADAMS
SAN FRANCISCO

SUTRO GARDENS
1933

Label 4

PHOTOGRAPH
BY
ANSEL ADAMS

New York City

Stamp 2

ANSEL ADAMS
131 24th AVENUE · SAN FRANCISCO · CALIFORNIA

To _____
YOSEMITE NATIONAL PARK
DETAIL: FOREST IN WINTER

SECOND CLASS MATTER. Postmaster: This package may be opened for postal inspection if necessary.

Stamp 6

ENLARGED FROM A POLAROID LAND
TYPE 55 P/N NEGATIVE

Stamp 10

Photograph by Ansel Adams
MAYNARD DIXON ARTIST
ca. 1945   TUCSON ARIZONA
Route 1   Box 181   Carmel, California 93921

Stamp 11

CHECKLIST OF THE EXHIBITION

NOTE TO THE READER

The Ansel Adams photographs in The Lane Collection represent every aspect of the artist's career. Many of them have notations, labels, and stamps on the backs of original mounts. This wealth of documentation is, at least in part, the result of William Lane's approach to collecting: he specifically sought out vintage prints (those made close to the date of the negative) and frequently asked Adams to annotate prints with the dates of both the negative and the print, as well as the type of film, camera, photographic paper, and toner used. Dating Adams' work is notoriously difficult, so these inscriptions (often made at the time of purchase) are informative but cannot always be counted on as definitive. The artist often claimed to remember nearly every detail that went into taking a specific photograph but rarely to be able to recall a date, even for some of his most famous images.

GENERAL INFORMATION

All of the Adams photographs listed here are gelatin silver prints and are in The Lane Collection, unless noted otherwise. They are identified in the following manner:

Exhibition number. (Plate number in this catalogue)
Title of work, date of negative; print date if significant
Height x width cm (height x width in.)
Signature; inscriptions

Objects exhibited only in Boston (and not in the traveling exhibition) are indicated with an asterisk (*) after the exhibition number.

Print dates, when known, are provided if they are more than five years after the negative was made, or if they reflect early negatives printed in a later portfolio or a change in Adams' printing practice.

Dimensions indicated are the image size. When an original mat hides the print edges, the dimensions provided are those of the mat window.

SIGNATURES AND INSCRIPTIONS

Signatures are in graphite and located on the mount recto, below and to the lower right of the print, unless indicated otherwise.

Inscriptions on the mount verso begin with those in the upper left and proceed clockwise. All inscriptions are in black ink unless noted otherwise.

A few photographs in the exhibition have letterpress titles printed on the sheet below the image. All examples are from Adams' 1927 *Parmelian Prints* portfolio, and these titles are indicated as "printed," to differentiate them from titles inscribed by hand.

When checklist information contradicts the inscriptions, it is because new research suggests that the original inscription is inaccurate.

LABELS AND STAMPS

A number of the prints have small, white, adhesive labels inscribed with numbers. Each label designates the print's display in "The Eloquent Light" exhibition at San Francisco's M. H. de Young Museum in 1963. These labels are indicated by "EL" here.

Adams used a range of personal labels and inked rubber stamps to mark the mounts of his photographic prints throughout his life. Listed below, roughly in chronological order, are the labels and stamps found on prints in The Lane Collection. The number assigned to each one here corresponds to the label and stamp information provided in the checklist.

Stamps are in black ink unless stated otherwise. Please note that although Adams usually used each of these stamps for the date range indicated below, they were sometimes added to earlier prints and therefore cannot always be used to determine image or print date.[1]

Label one (used 1927 to 1928)

Label two (used 1928 to 1929)

Label three (used 1930 to 1935)

Label four (used 1936 to 1944)

Label five (used about 1940 to about 1953)

Label six (used about 1940 to about 1960)

Stamp one (used 1930 to 1960)

Stamp two (used about 1930 to 1960)

Stamp three (used from 1937 on)

Stamp four (used about 1950 to 1962)

Stamp five (used about 1962 to 1963)

Stamp six (frequently used with stamp five, about 1962 to 1963)

Stamp seven (used about 1963 to 1973)

Stamp eight (frequently used with stamp seven, about 1963 to 1970)

Stamp nine (used about 1963 to 1973)

Stamp ten (used about 1960 to about 1980)

Stamp eleven (used 1973 to 1977)

1. The authors are indebted to Andrea Gray Stillman, Adams' former assistant and editor, for her informative notes on his labels and stamps. Additionally, Adams' assistants Alan Ross and Don Worth provided helpful insights into the time periods during which some of the stamps were in use.

1. (PLATE 11)
Wind, Juniper Tree, Yosemite National Park, about
1919
15.2 x 20.2 cm (6 x 7 ¹⁵/₁₆ in.)
Recto: signed on sheet, lower right: Ansel E Adams;
inscribed on sheet, lower left, graphite: "Wind"
Verso: mount, upper left: label two [cut off],
graphite: P 79
top center, graphite: D.
center: stamp five; stamp six: Juniper Tree, snow
[crossed out] Yosemite Nat Park Calif / (very early
1919?); "Wind"; Dassonville Paper / "speed kodak" ?
upper right: 7-2

2. (PLATE 12)
Lyell Fork Meadows, Yosemite National Park (from
Parmelian Prints of the High Sierras), about 1921;
print date: 1927
14.6 x 19.7 cm (5 ¾ x 7 ¾ in.)
Recto: signed on sheet, lower right: A E Adams;
printed on sheet, bottom center: LYELL FORK
MEADOWS

3.
The Sentinel, Yosemite National Park (from
Parmelian Prints of the High Sierras), about 1923;
print date: 1927
14.6 x 19.8 cm (5 ¾ x 7 ¹³/₁₆ in.)
Recto: signed on sheet, lower right: A E Adams;
printed on sheet, bottom center: THE SENTINEL

4.
Roaring River Falls, Kings River Canyon, California
(from *Parmelian Prints of the High Sierras*), about
1925; print date: 1927
20.4 x 15.4 cm (8 ¹/₁₆ x 6 ¹/₁₆ in.)
Recto: signed on sheet, lower right: A E Adams;
printed on sheet, bottom center: ROARING RIVER
FALLS

5.
East Vidette, Kings River Canyon, California (from
Parmelian Prints of the High Sierras), about 1925;
print date: 1927
14.7 x 19.8 cm (5 ¹³/₁₆ x 7 ¹³/₁₆ in.)
Recto: signed on sheet, lower right: A E Adams;
printed on sheet, bottom center: EAST VIDETTE

6. (PLATE 13)
Marion Lake, Kings River Canyon, California
(from *Parmelian Prints of the High Sierras*), about
1925; print date: 1927
14.6 x 19.8 cm (5 ¾ x 7 ¹³/₁₆ in.)
Recto: signed on sheet, lower right: A E Adams;
printed on sheet, bottom center: MARION LAKE

7. (PLATE 82)
*Banner Peak—Thousand Island Lake, Sierra
Nevada, California* (from *Parmelian Prints of the
High Sierras*), 1923; print date: 1927
15.3 x 20.4 cm (6 x 8 ¹/₁₆ in.)
Recto: signed on sheet, lower right: A E Adams
Verso: inscribed on mount, lower left, graphite:
Banner Peak and Thousand Island Lake August,
1923

8.*
Glacier Point, Yosemite National Park (from
Parmelian Prints of the High Sierras), about 1923;
print date: 1927
15.1 x 20.4 cm (5 ¹⁵/₁₆ x 8 ¹/₁₆ in.)
Recto: signed on sheet, lower right: A E Adams;
printed on sheet, bottom center: GLACIER POINT

9.*
Abode of Snow, Yosemite National Park (from
Parmelian Prints of the High Sierras), about 1925;
print date: 1927
15.1 x 19.7 cm (5 ¹⁵/₁₆ x 7 ¾ in.)
Recto: signed on sheet, lower right: A E Adams;
printed on sheet, bottom center: ABODE OF SNOW

10.*
Mount Brewer, Kings River Canyon, California,
about 1925
28.1 x 38.3 cm (11 ¹/₁₆ x 15 ¹/₁₆ in.)
Recto: inscribed on sheet, in image, lower left:
MT. BREWER

11.*
Charles Erskine Scott Wood, 1928
20.2 x 15.2 cm (7 ¹⁵/₁₆ x 6 in.)
Recto: signed on sheet, lower right: Ansel E Adams;
inscribed on sheet, lower left, graphite: Charles
Erskine Scott Wood
Verso: mount, upper left: label one [cut off],
graphite: P 13
top center: stamp seven; stamp eight: Charles
Erskine Scott Wood / 1928
center: Dassonville Paper

12.
Mount Galen Clark, Yosemite National Park (from
Parmelian Prints of the High Sierras), 1927
20.4 x 15.3 cm (8 ¹/₁₆ x 6 in.)
Recto: signed on sheet, lower right: A E Adams;
printed on sheet, bottom center: MT. CLARK

13. (PLATE 14)
On the Heights, Yosemite National Park (from
Parmelian Prints of the High Sierras), 1927
14.7 x 19.8 cm (5 ¹³/₁₆ x 7 ¹³/₁₆ in.)
Recto: signed on sheet, lower right: A E Adams;
printed on sheet, bottom center: ON THE HEIGHTS

14. (PLATE 5)
*Monolith—The Face of Half Dome, Yosemite
National Park* (from *Parmelian Prints of the High
Sierras*), 1927
20.3 x 15.3 cm (8 x 6 in.)
Recto: signed on sheet, lower right: Adams; printed
on sheet, bottom center: MONOLITH—THE FACE OF
HALF DOME

15.
*Monolith—The Face of Half Dome, Yosemite
National Park*, 1927; print date: 1950–60
47.7 x 36.9 cm (18 ¾ x 14 ½ in.)
Recto: signed on mount, lower right: Ansel Adams;
inscribed on mount, lower right, graphite: Cat #8
Verso: mount, center: stamp seven; stamp eight:
Monolith, The Face of Half Dome / Yosemite Valley
/ CA 1923; 6² x 8² / Glass Plate; From the "Diving
Board" / West Shoulder of Half Dome. / wide-angle
lens.

16. (PLATE 84)
Blackhorn Peak, Tonquin Valley, Canadian Rockies,
1928
14.5 x 19.8 cm (5 ¹¹/₁₆ x 7 ¹³/₁₆ in.)
Recto: signed on sheet, lower right: Ansel E Adams
Verso: inscribed on mount, upper left, graphite:
Black Horn Peak, Tonquin Valley
top center: stamp seven; stamp eight: Black Horn
Peak, Tonqutn [*sic*] Valley / 1928
upper right, blue ink: 16-1

17. (PLATE 89)
*Mount Robson from Mount Resplendent, Canadian
Rockies*, 1928
20.4 x 15.2 cm (8 ¹/₁₆ x 6 in.)
Recto: signed on sheet, lower right: Ansel E Adams
Verso: inscribed on mount, upper left, graphite:
[3?]2 Mount Robson from Mount Resplendent

top center: Valuable only extant print
center: stamp five; stamp six: MOUNT ROBSON FROM MOUNT RESPLENDENT. Canada 1928 / 4 x 5 View Camera / Protar? / Dassonville Paper; EL label: 48
upper right: W. L.
lower right, graphite: 1

18. (PLATE 85)
From Moose Pass, Canadian Rockies, 1928
14.5 x 19.8 cm (5 11/16 x 7 13/16 in.)
Recto: signed on sheet, lower right: Ansel E Adams
Verso: inscribed on mount, upper right, graphite: View from Moose Pass
center: stamp five; stamp six: From Moose Pass (Telephotograph) Canada 1928
upper right, blue ink: 4-1
lower right, graphite: 1

19. (PLATE 83)
Granite Ridge, Milestone Mountain, Sequoia National Park, California, 1927
38.4 x 28 cm (15 1/8 x 11 in.)
Recto: inscribed on sheet, in image, lower left: Milestone Mountain

20. (PLATE 88)
Glacial Cirque, Milestone Ridge, Sequoia National Park, California, 1927
28.1 x 38.4 cm (11 1/16 x 15 1/8 in.)
Verso: inscribed on mount, lower left, graphite: [H]

21.
At Tuolumne Pass, Yosemite National Park, 1926
15 x 20.4 cm (5 7/8 x 8 1/16 in.)
Recto: signed on sheet, lower right: Ansel E. Adams
Verso: inscribed on mount, upper left, graphite: At Tuolumme [*sic*] Pass, Yosemite National Park
center: stamp seven; stamp eight: At Tuolumne Pass, Yosemite National Park / 1930 [crossed out] / 1926; Dassonville Paper
upper right, blue ink: 1.
lower right, graphite: 1

22.* (PLATE 15)
Skier, Yosemite National Park, about 1929
15 x 20.1 cm (5 7/8 x 7 15/16 in.)
Recto: signed on sheet, lower right: Ansel E Adams

23. (PLATE 32)
Albert Bender, about 1928
19.8 x 15.1 cm (7 13/16 x 5 15/16 in.)
Recto: signed on sheet, lower right: Ansel E Adams
Verso: inscribed on mount, center, graphite: Albert Bender / 1928; stamp five; stamp six: ALBERT BENDER, San Francisco; 3" x 4" Original Print / Dassonville Paper
lower right, graphite: 1

24.*
Mary Austin, Santa Fe, New Mexico, about 1929
19.8 x 15.1 cm (7 13/16 x 5 15/16 in.)
Recto: signed on sheet, lower right: Ansel E Adams; inscribed on sheet, lower left, graphite: Mary Austin
Verso: mount, center: stamp five; stamp six: MARY AUSTIN – SANTA FE, NEW MEXICO. (1928–1929?); graphite: Mary Austin

25. (PLATE 42)
Indian Dance, San Ildefonso Pueblo, New Mexico, 1929
14.3 x 19.7 cm (5 5/8 x 7 3/4 in.)
Recto: signed on sheet, lower right: Ansel E Adams; inscribed on sheet, lower right, graphite: Dance at San Ildefonso
Verso: mount, upper left: label two [cut off], graphite: 1498
center: stamp five; stamp six: Chorus Group (Horizontal[)] / BUFFALO DANCE, TESUQUE ["TESUQUE" crossed out], San Ildefonso Pueblo, NEW MEXICO. (1928–1929?); Dassonville Paper / 9 x 12 cm Reflex Camera

26. (PLATE 35)
Dance Group, San Ildefonso Pueblo, New Mexico, 1929
19.7 x 14.3 cm (7 3/4 x 5 5/8 in.)
Recto: signed on sheet, lower right: Ansel E Adams; inscribed on sheet, lower left, graphite: San Ildefonso
Verso: mount center: stamp five; stamp six: San Ildephonso [*sic*] Pueblo, Dance Group (vertical) / (1928–1929?); 3" x 4" [crossed out] / 4 x 5 Original Print
upper right, blue ink: 10-1
lower right, graphite: 1

27. (PLATE 34)
Eagle Dance, Tesuque Pueblo, New Mexico, 1929
14.3 x 19.7 cm (5 5/8 x 7 3/4 in.)
Recto: signed on sheet, lower right: Ansel E Adams; inscribed on sheet, lower left, graphite: Eagle Dance
Verso: mount, upper left: Eagle Dance / San Ildefonso Pueblo NM
center: stamp five; stamp six: EAGLE DANCE SAN ILDEFONSO PUEBLO. N.M. (1928–1929?); 4 x 5 Original Print / Dassonville Paper
lower right, graphite: 1

28. (PLATE 43)
Pueblo Indian Passing Oven at Tesuque, New Mexico, 1929
19.7 x 14.3 cm (7 3/4 x 5 5/8 in.)
Recto: signed on sheet, lower right: Ansel E Adams; inscribed on sheet, lower left, graphite: At Tesuque
Verso: mount, upper left: label two [cut off], graphite: P. 140
top center: Pueblo Indian Passing Oven
center: stamp five; stamp six: PUEBLO WOMEN ["WOMEN" crossed out] Indian PASSING OVEN (NOT certain what Pueblo) Tesuque / (1928–1929?); Dassonville / Paper / 9 x 12 cm Reflex

GROUP F/64: THE 1930S

29. (PLATE 17)
Shipwreck Series #1, Steel and Stone, San Francisco, about 1932
20.4 x 15 cm (8 1/16 x 5 7/8 in.)
Recto: signed: Ansel Adams
Verso: inscribed on mount, center: Shipwreck Series #1 / Steel & Stone / San Francisco / Ansel Adams; stamp four [crossed out]; stamp five; stamp six: SHIPWRECK, STEEL AND STONE, SAN FRANCISCO / CA 1932; 4 x 5 Original Print.; EL label: 53; [14]; [36]
upper right: [36] [crossed out]
lower right, graphite: (11); *L* ; 52–1065 [?]; 9
lower left, graphite [cut off]: 212 [?]

30.*
Hulls, San Francisco, about 1933
18 x 23.2 cm (7 1/16 x 9 1/8 in.)
Recto: signed: Ansel Adams
Verso: inscribed on mount, upper left, graphite: 3959
center: label four, typed: HULLS; stamp five; stamp six: HULLS S.F. CA 1933; 8 x 10 Original Print / graphite: 2; EL label: 55
lower right, graphite: (13); *L*; 8 / 1
lower left, graphite: Z65

31.*
Anchors, San Francisco, 1931
16.5 x 22.1 cm (6½ x 8¹¹⁄₁₆ in.)
Recto: signed: Ansel Adams
Verso: inscribed on mount, upper left, blue ink: ③
top center, blue ink: Anchors / Ansel Adams 1932
center: stamp seven; stamp six: Anchors.
San Francisco California / CA 1932 / Pan. Film + #29
Filter; 8 x 10 Original Print
upper right: #11
lower right, graphite: 10 / 1
lower left, graphite: 1932 / Z69

32.*
Still Life, San Francisco, about 1932
49.2 x 36.8 cm (19⅜ x 14½ in.)
Recto: signed: Ansel Adams
Verso: inscribed on mount, upper left, graphite:
W. Lane
center: stamp seven; stamp eight: Arrangement
San Francisco / CA 1932; 8 x 10

33.*
Minerva, Sutro Gardens, San Francisco, 1933
20.2 x 15.1 cm (7¹⁵⁄₁₆ x 5¹⁵⁄₁₆ in.)
Recto: signed: Ansel Adams
Verso: inscribed on mount, upper left, graphite:
25 ⁰⁰
center: label four, typed: SUTRO GARDENS, graphite:
1933
upper right: #12
lower left: 33-5

34. (PLATE 22)
Sutro Gardens, San Francisco, 1933
23.6 x 16.5 cm (9⁵⁄₁₆ x 6½ in.)
Recto: signed: Ansel E Adams; inscribed on mount,
lower left, graphite: From Sutro Gardens
Verso: mount, upper left, graphite: Group – /f.64
top center: label three; graphite: From Sutro
Gardens, San Francisco
center: stamp five; stamp six: "Minerva" / From
Sutro Garden. S.F. 1933; 35; EL label: 68
lower right, graphite: 1

35. (PLATE 18)
Rocks, Baker Beach, San Francisco, about 1931
16.6 x 22.2 cm (6⁹⁄₁₆ x 8¾ in.)
Recto: signed: Ansel Adams
Verso: mount, center: stamp five; stamp six: Rocks
Baker's [*sic*] Beach / San Francisco / CA 1931;
9 x 12 cm Original Print
lower right, graphite: 79.486 / L / 9 / 1 / 10
lower left, graphite: 314

36. (PLATE 21)
The Golden Gate before the Bridge, San Francisco,
1932
16.6 x 22.9 cm (6⁹⁄₁₆ x 9 in.)
Recto: signed: Ansel Adams
Verso: inscribed on mount, upper left, blue ink: ㉑
top center: stamp seven
center: Early Photograph / The Golden Gate 1933 /
San Francisco / before the building of the Bridge;
stamp four; 8 x 10 view camera / 12" Dagor /
graphite: ⑥
upper right, graphite: 28
lower left, graphite: 86-2-B
face mat, lower right, graphite: 1
face mat, lower left, graphite: ⑥ [H]

37.
Pine Cone and Eucalyptus Leaves, San Francisco,
1932; print date: about 1963
19.3 x 24.1 cm (7⅝ x 9½ in.)
Recto: signed on mount, lower right, black ink:
Ansel Adams
Verso: inscribed on mount, upper left: Ⓛ
center: stamp five; stamp six: Pine Cone and
Eucalyptus Leaves, San Francisco / CA 1935; 1963⁺
Print / 4 x 5 Camera
lower right, graphite: 6

38. (PLATE 4)
Leaves, Mills College, Oakland, California, about
1931
26.5 x 30.3 cm (10⁷⁄₁₆ x 11¹⁵⁄₁₆ in.)
Recto: signed: Ansel Adams
Verso: mount, center: stamp seven; stamp eight, blue
ink: Leaves, Mills College / 1932
lower right, graphite: 3

39. (PLATE 19)
Rose and Driftwood, San Francisco, about 1932
22.9 x 28.9 cm (9 x 11⅜ in.)
Recto: signed: Ansel Adams
Verso: mount, center: stamp seven; Rose and
Driftwood / Ansel Adams / CA 1934 / Valuable Print
lower left, graphite: 20

40. (PLATE 10)
Fence near Tomales Bay, California, 1936
17 x 21.3 cm (6¹¹⁄₁₆ x 8⅜ in.)
Recto: signed: Ansel Adams
Verso: inscribed on mount, upper left, graphite:
25 ⁰⁰
center: stamp seven; stamp eight: near Bolinas,
California / 1933
lower right, graphite: 29

lower left, graphite: 1933 Near Bolinas Cal.;
graphite: 271
lower left, graphite: 5-C-179

41. (PLATE 23)
White Cross, San Rafael, California, about 1936
13.6 x 16.8 cm (5⅜ x 6⅝ in.)
Recto: signed on mount, lower right, black ink:
Ansel Adams
Verso: mount, center: stamp seven; stamp eight:
Cross, San Rafael, Calif / California / 1932;
4 x 5 View Camera / Protar lens
lower right, graphite: 15
lower left, graphite: 65- / #16

42.
Boards and Thistles, San Francisco, about 1932
23.2 x 17.3 cm (9⅛ x 6¹³⁄₁₆ in.)
Recto: signed: Ansel Adams
Verso: inscribed on mount, center: stamp four
["NEG." crossed out in red ink], red ink: 15 / Board
+ Thistles / San Francisco; CA 1933
upper right, blue ink: #11
lower left, graphite: 261-E; graphite: 8
face mat, lower left, graphite: 8

43. (PLATE 24)
Wrecking of the Lurline Baths, San Francisco, 1938
23.3 x 17.9 cm (9⁵⁄₁₆ x 7¹⁄₁₆ in.)
Recto: signed: Ansel Adams
Verso: inscribed on mount, upper left, graphite:
4014 / Ⓛ / blue ink: ㉖
center: stamp seven; label four, typed: Wrecking of
the Lurline Baths. S.F. / 1938; 8 x 10 Camera /
graphite: 35
lower left, graphite: 207

44.*
*Cemetery Statue and Oil Derricks, Long Beach,
California*, 1939
25.2 x 30.4 cm (9¹⁵⁄₁₆ x 11¹⁵⁄₁₆ in.)
Recto: signed on mount, lower right, black ink:
Ansel Adams
Verso: mount, center: stamp seven; stamp eight:
Long Beach Cemetery / CA 1941

45. (PLATE 25)
Discussion in Art, San Francisco, 1936
17.8 x 23 cm (7 x 9¹⁄₁₆ in.)
Recto: signed: Ansel Adams
Verso: inscribed on mount, upper left, blue ink: ㉘
[crossed out]
top center: stamp seven
center, blue ink: Discussion in art / Ansel Adams /

ANSEL ADAMS / Not For Sale; stamp four; CA 1935 / Contax Photograph; [12]
upper right: 2-3
lower right, graphite: 52.1063 / 2
lower left, graphite: 127-A

46. (PLATE 26)
Museum Storeroom, de Young Museum, San Francisco, about 1935
17.8 x 23 cm (7 x 9 1/16 in.)
Recto: signed: Ansel Adams
Verso: inscribed on mount, upper left, graphite: 3950; blue ink: (41) [crossed out in black ink]
center: stamp five; label four, typed: Museum Storeroom 1935; graphite: 32; (V) [crossed out in graphite]; graphite: 40 / #3; EL label: 453 / (19) [crossed out]; "Found" Subject / 8 x 10 Camera / [59]
lower right, graphite: (2) / 2 / 52.1070
lower left, blue-colored pencil: (82); graphite: Box 401

47. (PLATE 28)
Americana, Cigar Store Indian, Powell Street, San Francisco, 1933
19.7 x 15.2 cm (7 3/4 x 6 in.)
Recto: signed: Ansel Adams
Verso: mount, center: stamp seven; stamp eight: Wooden Indian, San Francisco – California / 1933
lower right, graphite: 30
lower left, graphite: 260

48.*
Political Sign, 1937
24.1 x 18.8 cm (9 1/2 x 7 3/8 in.)
Recto: signed: Ansel Adams
Verso: inscribed on mount, upper left, graphite: 3973; blue ink: (38)
center: label four ["San Francisco" crossed out], typed: TEXTURE [crossed out] 1937, blue ink: Political Sign; stamp five; stamp six: Political Sign – 1937; [8 x 10] Original Print; graphite: 40; [55] [crossed out]
upper right: #17
lower right, graphite: 9 / 2
lower left, graphite: 275

49.*
Scissors and Thread, San Francisco, about 1931
24.2 x 16.9 cm (9 1/2 x 6 5/8 in.)
Recto: signed: Ansel Adams / 1930
Verso: inscribed on mount, top center: (TOP)
center: stamp eleven [upside down]: Scissors and Thread / S.F. Ca. 1930

50. (PLATE 27)
Political Circus, San Francisco, 1932
23.7 x 18.6 cm (9 5/16 x 7 5/16 in.)
Recto: signed: Ansel Adams
Verso: inscribed on mount, upper left, graphite: 3954
center: label four, typed: Political Circus, San Francisco; graphite: 43; 1932 CA; 1932 / 8 x 10 / Camera 12" Dagor
lower right, graphite: 26
lower left, graphite: 276-B

51. (PLATE 29)
Date of My Birth, Movie Set, Los Angeles, 1940
11.7 x 16.5 cm (4 5/8 x 6 1/2 in.)
Recto: signed: Ansel Adams
Verso: inscribed on mount, center, graphite: "Date of my Birth" / Ansel Adams / 1940; stamp seven; stamp eight: "Date of Birth" / Movie Set, Los Angeles, Calif. / 1940; 5 x 7 Original Print
lower right, graphite: 21
lower left, graphite: 52-S
face mat, lower right, graphite: (21) / 3
face mat, bottom center, graphite: A

52.
Wooden Shutters, Columbia Farm Movie Lot, Los Angeles, about 1940
23.7 x 17.1 cm (9 5/16 x 6 1/4 in.)
Recto: signed: Ansel Adams
Verso: mount, center: stamp four ["NEG." crossed out in red ink], red ink: 32 / Shutters and Doors / Movie Lot.; Original Print. / CA 1940
lower right, graphite: 22
lower left, graphite: 282
face mount, lower right, graphite: 3 / 22

53. (PLATE 20)
Laurel Hill Cemetery, San Francisco, about 1936
34.2 x 24.1 cm (13 7/16 x 9 1/2 in.)
Recto: signed on mount, lower right, black ink: Ansel Adams
Verso: inscribed on mount, upper left, graphite: S.F. Cal / 1943
center: stamp eight: Laurel Hill Cemetery Detail / San Francisco Calif / CA 1936; [5 x 7] Original Print; stamp seven
lower right, graphite: 12
lower left, graphite: (23)

54. (PLATE 103)
Remains of Old Square Piano, Lundy, California, 1939
22.6 x 17 cm (8 7/8 x 6 11/16 in.)
Recto: signed: Ansel Adams

Verso: inscribed on mount, upper left, graphite: 4007
center: label four, typed: Remains of old Square Piano, LUNDY, 1939; 4 x 5 Camera / Original not toned [21]
upper right: #11
lower right, graphite: 23 / 2
lower left, graphite: 259

55. (PLATE 102)
Old Wall Paper in House at Lundy, California, 1939
32.3 x 23 cm (12 11/16 x 9 1/16 in.)
Recto: signed: Ansel Adams
Verso: inscribed on mount, upper left, blue ink: (45) [crossed out]
center: label four ["San Francisco" crossed out], typed: Old Wall Paper, in house at LUNDY, Calif. / 1939; stamp five
upper right: #11

56.*
Stove in Pennsylvania Farmyard, 1938
24.6 x 31.7 cm (9 11/16 x 12 1/2 in.)
Recto: signed: Ansel Adams
Verso: inscribed on mount, upper left, blue ink: (49)
center: label four, typed: Stove in Pennsylvania Farmyard., graphite: 1938
lower left, graphite: #18

57.*
Ruins, near Princeton, New Jersey, 1939
31.5 x 24.8 cm (12 3/8 x 9 3/4 in.)
Recto: signed: Ansel Adams
Verso: inscribed on mount, upper left, graphite: 3980
center: label four, typed: Ruins, near PRINCETON, New Jersey 1939; 5 x 7 Original Print
upper right: #14
lower right, graphite: L / 8 / [10]
lower left, graphite: 209

58.*
Houses in Rain, Mineral King, California, 1936
22.4 x 17.7 cm (8 13/16 x 6 15/16 in.)
Recto: signed: Ansel Adams
Verso: inscribed on mount, upper left, blue ink: (46)
center: stamp nine, red ink; blue ink: Houses in Rain / Mineral King, California / Ansel Adams; 1927 CA / or / 1932 CA / blue ink: [26]; Print 1933+ / 4 x 5 View Camera
upper right: #17
lower left, graphite: (47)-A / 1932–33; Mineral King vicinity

59.
Walbridge Ranch, Sonoma County, California, about 1938
23.7 x 18.7 cm ($9\frac{5}{16}$ x $7\frac{3}{8}$ in.)
Recto: signed on mount, lower right, black ink: Ansel Adams
Verso: mount, center: stamp five; Walbridge Ranch / Sonomo [*sic*] County / CA 1952 / 4 x 5
right center: E T Spencer, Architect
lower right, graphite: (5)
face mount, lower right, blue ink: (5)

60.
Westport, California, about 1936
30 x 39.8 cm ($11\frac{13}{16}$ x $15\frac{11}{16}$ in.)
Recto: signed: Ansel Adams
Verso: mount, center: stamp seven; stamp eight: West Port [*sic*], California / CA 1936 ["1936" in blue ink]; 8 x 10
lower right: #5

61. (PLATE 30)
Westport, California, about 1936
23.2 x 29 cm ($9\frac{1}{8}$ x $11\frac{7}{16}$ in.)
Recto: signed on mount, lower right, black ink: Ansel Adams
Verso: mount, center: stamp seven; stamp six: Westport, California / CA 1936; 8 x 10
lower right, graphite: 5

62. (PLATE 98)
Mr. Shepard at His Home, Independence, California, about 1936
23.2 x 16.8 cm ($9\frac{1}{8}$ x $6\frac{5}{8}$ in.)
Recto: signed: Ansel Adams
Verso: mount, center, stamp, purple ink: Visitatiepost Eindhoven. Invoerr. en Accijnzen; label five: Mr. Shepard at his home / Independence, California. / CA 1936
lower left, graphite: 129-C

63.*
Tomales Point, California, about 1936
19 x 23.7 cm ($7\frac{1}{2}$ x $9\frac{5}{16}$ in.)
Recto: signed on mount, lower right, black ink: Ansel Adams
Verso: inscribed on mount, upper left, green ink: (37)
center: stamp seven; Tomales Point / California / Ansel Adams / CA 1936 / ANSEL ADAMS / 131-24th Avenue / San Francisco 21 / Calif.
upper right: #14
lower left, graphite: O; stamp, red ink: OMAHA INTERNATIONAL SALON 194 / PKG 2 PRINT 2 / -210 [crossed out in green ink]

64.*
Old Wreck, Cape Cod, Massachusetts, about 1936
11.4 x 15.8 cm ($4\frac{1}{2}$ x $6\frac{1}{4}$ in.)
Recto: signed: Ansel Adams
Verso: mount, center: stamp five; stamp six: OLD WRECK CAPE COD. MASS. 1936 CA; stamp four [address crossed out in black ink and "NEG." crossed out in red ink], red ink: G 1 / Wreck Shore / Cape Cod Massachusetts; EL label: 163; Jewell? / 5 x 7 Linhoff Camera / Protar Lens / Novobrom paper
lower left, graphite: 2-S-A; W.L.
face mat, lower right, graphite: 2
face mat, lower left, graphite: #2H

65.
Cape Cod Architecture, Massachusetts, 1939
23.7 x 32.4 cm ($9\frac{5}{16}$ x $12\frac{3}{4}$ in.)
Recto: signed: Ansel Adams
Verso: inscribed on mount, upper left, graphite: 3987
center: label four, typed: CAPE COD ARCHITECTURE / 1939, black ink: 5 x 7; graphite: (14); Original Print
upper right, graphite: #17
lower right, graphite: 12 / 2 / 8 / *L*
lower left, graphite: (54)

YOSEMITE

66. (PLATE 16)
Clouds Rest from Mt. Watkins, Winter, Yosemite National Park, about 1929; print date: 1930–32
8.1 x 11.7 cm ($3\frac{3}{16}$ x $4\frac{5}{8}$ in.)
Recto: signed: Ansel Adams
Verso: inscribed on mount, upper left: (L)
top center: stamp seven
center: stamp eight: From near Mt. Watkins winter / Yosemite Nat. Park / 1929 CA / Printed 1930 to 1932
lower left, graphite: 32 / 74-S
face mat, lower right, graphite: 1
face mat, lower left, graphite: 32

67. (PLATE 91)
Thunderstorm over North Palisade, Sierra Nevada, California, 1933
23.6 x 17.2 cm ($9\frac{5}{16}$ x $6\frac{3}{4}$ in.)
Recto: signed: Ansel Adams
Verso: inscribed on mount, center: stamp four: 4-S-; North Palisade / Sierra Nevada / CA 1930
upper right: #9
lower right, graphite: 1
lower left: 362-11

68. (PLATE 74)
Grass and Reflections, Lyell Fork of the Merced River, Yosemite National Park, about 1943
18.9 x 23.9 cm ($7\frac{7}{16}$ x $9\frac{7}{16}$ in.)
Recto: signed on mount, lower right, black ink: Ansel Adams
Verso: inscribed on mount, upper left: 51
center: stamp five; stamp six: Grass and Reflections / In the Lyell Fork of the Merced River / YN.P. [*sic*] / CA 1935; EL label: 135
lower right, graphite: 679–490 / 2 / High S – Yos

69.*
General Sherman Tree, Sequoia National Park, California, 1938
23.8 x 18 cm ($9\frac{3}{8}$ x $7\frac{1}{16}$ in.)
Recto: signed: Ansel Adams
Verso: inscribed on mount, upper left: (L); graphite: SEQUOIA / GIGANTEA; blue ink: (54)
center: label four ["San Francisco" crossed out], typed: General Sherman Tree, SEQUOIA NAT. PARK / 1938; stamp five; stamp six: General Sherman Tree. / Sequoia National Park. Calif; graphite: (19) / 1-CAL-27; "Flemish-Gold" Toner / (Selenium) / 8 x 10 Camera
upper right: #15 [crossed out]; #6
lower left, graphite: 166-A

70. (PLATE 69)
Pool, Tuolumne Meadows, Yosemite National Park, about 1937
11.6 x 16.9 cm ($4\frac{9}{16}$ x $6\frac{5}{8}$ in.)
Recto: signed: Ansel Adams
Verso: mount, upper left, blue ink: (64) [crossed out]
center, graphite: Pool, Tuolumne Meadows / Yosemite Nat. Park / Ansel Adams; Calif CA 1938 1937?; stamp five; 5 x 7 Deardorf [*sic*] Camera
lower left, graphite: I-S-A

71. (PLATE 68)
Leaves on Pool, Sierra Nevada, California, about 1935
11.6 x 16 cm ($4\frac{9}{16}$ x $6\frac{5}{16}$ in.)
Recto: signed: Ansel Adams
Verso: mount, center: stamp five; stamp six: LEAVES ON POOL SIERRA NEVADA, CALIFORNIA. / Tuolumne Meadows / near Parsens [*sic*] Lodge; stamp four, red ink: 55 / Leaves on Pool. / Sierra Nevada; EL label: 149; 1935 / CA 5 x 7 Linhoff

72.
North Dome, from Glacier Point, Yosemite National Park, about 1937
19 x 23.5 cm ($7\frac{1}{2}$ x $9\frac{1}{4}$ in.)
Recto: signed on mount, lower right, black ink: Ansel Adams
Verso: inscribed on mount, upper left: 48
center: stamp six: Sentinel Rock, Y.V. [crossed out] / CA 1937; N.E. from Glacier Point / North Dome, etc. from Glaicer [*sic*] Point / Y.V.; stamp five
upper right, graphite: 12
lower right, graphite: 2
lower left, graphite: 29

73. (PLATE 73)
Trees, Illilouette Ridge, Yosemite National Park, about 1945
49.9 x 39 cm ($19\frac{5}{8}$ x $15\frac{3}{8}$ in.)
Recto: signed on mount, lower right, black ink: Ansel Adams
Verso: mount, center: stamp seven; stamp eight: Illouette [*sic*] Ridge, Yosemite National Park
lower right, graphite: *L*

74. (PLATE 90)
Lake near Muir Pass, Kings River Canyon, California, 1933
18.6 x 23.5 cm ($7\frac{5}{16}$ x $9\frac{1}{4}$ in.)
Recto: signed on mount, lower right, black ink: Ansel Adams
Verso: mount, center: EL label: 72; stamp five; stamp six: Lake near Muir Pass Sierra Nevada / CA 1930
lower right, graphite: 29 / 5 / High S. – Yos

75. (PLATE 72)
Dead Tree, Dog Lake, Sierra Nevada, California, about 1936
17.1 x 11.1 cm ($6\frac{3}{4}$ x $4\frac{3}{8}$ in.)
Recto: signed: Ansel Adams
Verso: inscribed on mount, upper left, blue ink: (63)
center, blue ink: Dead Tree / Sierra Nevada / California / Ansel Adams; stamp five; stamp six: DEAD TREE SIERRA NEVADA / CALIF / CA 1936
lower left, graphite: 27-S-A
face mat, lower right, graphite: (3)

76.
Merced River, Cliffs of Cathedral Rocks, Autumn, Yosemite National Park, 1939
39.6 x 50 cm ($15\frac{9}{16}$ x $19\frac{11}{16}$ in.)
Recto: signed: Ansel Adams
Verso: mount, center: stamp seven; stamp eight: Merced River, Cliffs of Cathedral Rocks, Trees - Autumn / Yosemite Valley / CA 1939; 8 x 10

77. (PLATE 66)
Pine Forest in Snow, Yosemite National Park, about 1932
23.9 x 18.8 cm ($9\frac{7}{16}$ x $7\frac{3}{8}$ in.)
Recto: signed: Ansel Adams
Verso: mount, center: stamp seven; Winter / Yosemite Valley / California / Ansel Adams; CA 1936; ANSEL ADAMS / 131-24 Avenue / San Francisco 21 / Calif
upper right: #7
lower right, graphite: 2
lower left, graphite: O; stamp, red ink: OMAHA INTERNATIONAL SALON 194 / PKG 2 PRINT 1 / 231-A

78. (PLATE 3)
Snow on Trees, Yosemite National Park, about 1930
20.9 x 14.3 cm ($8\frac{1}{4}$ x $5\frac{5}{8}$ in.)
Recto: signed: Ansel Adams
Verso: mount, center: label six, typed: YOSEMITE NATIONAL PARK / DETAIL: FOREST IN WINTER; stamp seven; stamp eight: Snow on Trees Yosemite Valley / CA 1940; 4 x 5 / Novobrom paper / graphite: 1930?
upper right: #7
lower right, graphite: 9 / 1
lower left, graphite: 223

79. (PLATE 75)
Rain, Yosemite Valley, California, about 1940
39.8 x 48.5 cm ($15\frac{11}{16}$ x $19\frac{1}{8}$ in.)
Recto: signed on mount, lower right, black ink: Ansel Adams
Verso: mount, center: stamp seven; stamp eight: Yosemite Valley California - Rain / CA 1940; 8 x 10

80.
Clearing Winter Storm, Yosemite National Park, about 1937
38.8 x 49.3 cm ($15\frac{1}{4}$ x $19\frac{7}{16}$ in.)
Recto: signed: Ansel Adams
Verso: inscribed on mount, upper left, graphite: 1937 / 1944? [erased]
center: stamp seven; stamp eight: Winter Storm / Yosemite Valley; 8 x 10

81. (PLATE 57)
Clearing Winter Storm, Yosemite National Park, about 1937
18.8 x 23.5 cm ($7\frac{3}{8}$ x $9\frac{1}{4}$ in.)
Recto: signed on mount, lower right, black ink: Ansel Adams
Verso: inscribed on mount, upper left, graphite: 372-C
center: stamp seven; "Flemish Gold" Toner / (Selenium) / 8 x 10 Camera; label five, typed: YOSEMITE VALLEY STORM / SLIGHT GOLD TONE, graphite: 1938
upper right: (L)
lower right: #15
lower left, graphite: (1)

82. (PLATE 58)
Grass and Burned Stump, Sierra Nevada, California, 1935
28.4 x 20.1 cm ($11\frac{3}{16}$ x $7\frac{15}{16}$ in.)
Recto: signed on mount, lower right, black ink: Ansel Adams
Verso: mount, center: stamp seven; stamp eight: Grass and Burned Stump. CA 1936 / CA 1936; 4 x 5
lower right, graphite: 31 / 2 / 6

83.
Indian Mortar Holes, Big Meadow, Yosemite National Park, about 1940
19 x 23.7 cm ($7\frac{1}{2}$ x $9\frac{5}{16}$ in.)
Recto: signed: Ansel Adams
Verso: mount, center: stamp five; stamp six: INDIAN POT HOLES BIG MEADOW, YOS VALLEY [crossed out] / Yosemite National Park / CA 1940; stamp four [crossed out in black ink and "NEG" crossed out in red ink], red ink: 37 / Indian Pot Holes; Big Meadow / Yosem Valley ["Valley" crossed out in black ink]; Nat Park; 8 x 10
lower right, graphite: 12
lower left, graphite: 13-S
face mat, lower right, graphite: 12 / 3

84.*
Early Morning, Merced River Canyon, Yosemite National Park, about 1950
39.4 x 49.7 cm ($15\frac{1}{2}$ x $19\frac{9}{16}$ in.)
Recto: signed: Ansel Adams
Verso: mount, center: stamp seven; stamp eight: Morning, Merced River Canyon / Yosemite National Park; 8 x 10 CA 1944 / water-bath Development

85.
White Stump, Dog Lake, Sierra Nevada, California, about 1936; print date: about 1963
33.4 x 22.3 cm ($13\frac{1}{8}$ x $8\frac{3}{4}$ in.)
Recto: signed on mount, lower right, black ink: Ansel Adams
Verso: mount, center: stamp five; stamp six: Stump. Sierra Nevada at Dog Lake 1936 CA / Print 1963$^{\pm}$; 5 x 7 Camera
upper right: 15
lower right, graphite: B
lower left, graphite: 26

86.*
El Capitan with Rain Clouds, Yosemite National Park, about 1936
16.5 x 11.5 cm (6½ x 4½ in.)
Recto: signed: Ansel Adams
Verso: inscribed on mount, upper left: 59
center: stamp five; stamp six: El Capitan. Rain Clouds / CA 1936
lower left, graphite: 373
face mat, lower left, graphite: 5V

87. (PLATE 70)
Edward Weston, Lake Tenaya, Yosemite National Park, 1937
24.1 x 19.2 cm (9½ x 7⁹⁄₁₆ in.)
Recto: signed: Ansel Adams
Verso: inscribed on mount, upper left: L
center: stamp seven; stamp eight: EDWARD WESTON, LAKE TENAYA, YOSEMITE NATIONAL PARK, 1937; 8 x 10 Camera
lower right, graphite: 2
lower left, graphite: 133

88. (PLATE 71)
Charis Weston, Sierra Nevada, California, 1937
24.1 x 17.4 cm (9½ x 6⅞ in.)
Recto: signed: Ansel Adams
Verso: mount, center: stamp seven; Charis Weston; Ansel Adams CA 1938 / graphite: (47)
lower right, graphite: 22 / 2
lower left, graphite: 1938 Charis Wilson Weston; graphite: 152

89. (PLATE 101)
Poplar Trees, Owens Valley, California, about 1936
34.4 x 24.3 cm (13⁹⁄₁₆ x 9⁹⁄₁₆ in.)
Recto: signed: Ansel Adams
Verso: mount, center: stamp seven; Poplar Trees / Owens Valley. / California / Ansel Adams / 8 x 10 CA. 1936
lower right, graphite: 2 / XI

90. (PLATE 100)
Windmill, Owens Valley, California, about 1935
22.2 x 14.4 cm (8¾ x 5¹¹⁄₁₆ in.)
Recto: signed: Ansel Adams
Verso: inscribed on mount, upper left: (L)
center: stamp seven; stamp eight: Windmill Owens Valley Calif. / 1935 CA; 5 x 7 Linhoff Camera
upper right: #5
lower right, graphite: 24
lower left, graphite: 255

91.*
Mount Williamson, Sierra Nevada, from Owens Valley, California, about 1939
16.6 x 23.9 cm (6⁹⁄₁₆ x 9⁷⁄₁₆ in.)
Recto: signed: Ansel Adams
Verso: inscribed on mount, upper left: (L)
center: stamp seven; MT. Williamson CA-1939-40 / Sierra Nevada / From Manzanar / Ansel Adams; [13.] [crossed out in graphite]; graphite: (19); negative damaged / Conviva [illeg.] Paper / Ansco "Flemish Gold" Toner / (Selenium) / split-tone / 8 x 10 View Camera
upper right: #9
lower right, graphite: 2
lower left, graphite: Mt. Williamson 194[4?] / 345B

92. (PLATE 67)
Lone Pine Peak, Sierra Nevada, California, 1948
38.8 x 49.1 cm (15¼ x 19⁹⁄₁₆ in.)
Recto: signed: Ansel Adams
Verso: mount, center: stamp seven; stamp eight: Lone Pine Peak Sierra Nevada / California / CA 1940; 8 x 10

93.*
Mount Williamson from Manzanar, Sierra Nevada, California, 1944
39.7 x 49.5 cm (15⅝ x 19½ in.)
Recto: signed: Ansel Adams
Verso: mount, center: stamp seven; stamp eight: Mount Williamson from Manzanar Calif / (Sierra Nevada) / 1944; 8 x 10

THE AMERICAN SOUTHWEST

94. (PLATE 31)
Interior, Penitente Morada, Northern New Mexico, about 1930
28.5 x 21.7 cm (11¼ x 8⁹⁄₁₆ in.)
Recto: signed: Ansel Adams
Verso: mount, center: stamp seven; stamp eight: Interior - Penetente [sic] Morada, Norther [sic] New Mexico / CA 1930
lower right, graphite: 6
lower left, graphite: 23

95.*
At Palm Springs, California, 1936
22.2 x 15.7 cm (8¾ x 6³⁄₁₆ in.)
Recto: signed: Ansel Adams
Verso: inscribed on mount, upper left, graphite: 20 ⁰⁰
center: At Palm Springs / California / Ansel Adams; stamp five; stamp six: AT PALM SPRINGS - CALIF. / NO NEGATIVE; blue ink: [52]; no negative / 1936
lower right, graphite: 9

96.*
Mexican Section, Palm Springs, California, about 1934
16.9 x 21.6 cm (6⅝ x 8½ in.)
Recto: signed: Ansel Adams
Verso: inscribed on mount, upper left: (L)
center: stamp seven; stamp eight: Mexican Section, Palm Springs Calif. / 1934 CA; 4 x 5 camera Print, about 1935+
upper right, graphite: Mexic[an] Palm Springs; #11
lower right, graphite: 1
lower left, graphite: 273

97. (PLATE 36)
White Cross and Church, Coyote, New Mexico, 1937
22.2 x 16.9 cm (8¾ x 6⅝ in.)
Recto: signed: Ansel Adams
Verso: mount, center: stamp five; stamp two; At / COYOTE / New Mexico / CA 1936
lower left, graphite: (35)

98. (PLATE 33)
The Enchanted Mesa, near Acoma Pueblo, New Mexico, 1937
26 x 29 cm (10¼ x 11⁷⁄₁₆ in.)
Recto: signed: Ansel Adams
Verso: inscribed on mount, upper left: (L)
center, graphite: Landscape- / Ghost Ranch [crossed out] / New Mexico / 1937 / For Albert Bender / From / Ansel Adams; stamp seven; The Enchanted Mesa / New Mexico near Acoma Pueblo / 4 x 5 View Camera
upper right: #10
lower right, graphite: 8 / Box 10 / 2
lower left: 324

99. (PLATE 38)
Adobe Church, Hernandez, New Mexico, 1937
16.1 x 22.3 cm (6⁵⁄₁₆ x 8¾ in.)
Recto: signed: Ansel Adams
Verso: inscribed on mount, upper left, graphite: 25 ⁰⁰
center: stamp two; Adobe Church, New Mexico / Hernandez-Facade / 1932 CA
upper right: #17
lower right, graphite: 27 / 1
lower left: 72-2

100. (PLATE 45)
Georgia O'Keeffe and Orville Cox, Canyon de Chelly National Monument, Arizona, 1937; print date: about 1955

17 x 24.1 cm (6¹¹⁄₁₆ x 9½ in.)
Recto: signed on mount, lower right, black ink:
Ansel Adams
Verso: inscribed on mount, upper left, blue ink: ⑥₁
center: stamp five; graphite: Georgia O'Keeffe /
Orville Cox / 1937; stamp six, graphite: Georgia
O'Keeffe; Georgia O'Keeffe / Orville Cox / 1937 /
Cañon de Chelle Nat. Monument / Arizona; EL
label: 450; blue ink: Not For Sale; <u>Valuable</u> / ⑥7 /
35 mm Zeiss Contax II / 50 mm Tessar; shown in
London / print about 1955⁺
upper right, blue ink: 12-4
lower left, graphite: 123

101. (PLATE 44)
Thunderstorm, Ghost Ranch, Chama River Valley,
Northern New Mexico, 1937; print date: about 1948
16.6 x 22.9 cm (6⁹⁄₁₆ x 9 in.)
Recto: signed: Ansel Adams
Verso: inscribed on mount, upper left, graphite:
20 ⁰⁰; Ⓛ
center: stamp seven; stamp eight: Thunderstorm,
New Mexico 1937 / Ghost Ranch; Print about
1948? / 5 x 7 Camera
lower right, graphite: 19 / 2
lower left, graphite: New Mexico, 1937 / 350

102. (PLATE 48)
Aspens, Dawn, Dolores River Canyon, Colorado,
1937
11.7 x 16 cm (4⅝ x 6⁵⁄₁₆ in.)
Recto: signed on mount, lower right, black ink:
Ansel Adams
Verso: mount, center: stamp seven; stamp eight:
ASPENS, Dawn, Colorado / CA 1938
upper right, blue ink: #6
lower left, graphite: 17 / 44-S
face mat, lower left, graphite: #17

103. (PLATE 47)
Saguaro Cactus, Sunrise, Arizona, 1942
24 x 17.8 cm (9⁷⁄₁₆ x 7 in.)
Recto: signed: Ansel Adams
Verso: inscribed on mount, upper left: Ⓛ
center: stamp seven; stamp eight: SAGUERO [*sic*]
Cactus. near Tucson, Arizona / 1948; 8 x 10 Camera
(For Portfolio I) 1948 Print
lower left, graphite: 3

104.*
Maynard Dixon, Artist, Tucson, Arizona, about
1945
26.3 x 33.7 cm (10⅜ x 13¼ in.)

Recto: signed: Ansel Adams
Verso: inscribed on mount, center: stamp eleven,
brown ink: MAYNARD DIXON, ARTIST / Tucson,
Arizona / graphite: ca. 1945
lower right, graphite: LANE

105. (PLATE 9)
White House Ruin, Canyon de Chelly National
Monument, Arizona, 1941
33.7 x 24.6 cm (13¼ x 9¹¹⁄₁₆ in.)
Recto: signed: Ansel Adams
Verso: inscribed on mount, upper left, blue ink: ㊸
center: label five, typed italics: *White House Ruin,*
Canon de Chelley [*sic*] / Nat. Mon. Arizona.
(U.S.D.I.) 1942 [touched up in blue ink]; Print about
<u>1943</u> / 5 x 7 Camera; graphite: ㉝ [crossed out] /
33 / OK; ③4 [crossed out in graphite]
upper right: #14
lower right, graphite: 4
lower left, graphite: 199-A

106.*
Flowers at Dusk, Canyon de Chelly National
Monument, Arizona, 1947
11.4 x 16.4 cm (4½ x 6⁷⁄₁₆ in.)
Recto: signed: Ansel Adams
Verso: inscribed on mount, top center, red ink: TOP
center; stamp five; stamp four [crossed out in red
ink]; Flowers at Dusk / Canyon de Chelle Nat
Monument / Arizona / CA 1942
lower left, graphite: 12-S
face mat, lower right, graphite: 3
face mat, lower left, graphite: <u>15</u>

107. (PLATE 46)
Rocks, Joshua Tree National Monument, California,
about 1942
19.1 x 23.9 cm (7½ x 9⁷⁄₁₆ in.)
Recto: signed on mount, lower right, black ink:
Ansel Adams
Verso: mount, center: stamp one; stamp six, blue ink:
IN JOSHUA TREE NAT'L MONUMENT (CALIF) / PRINT #9
USED IN PORTFOLIO II; graphite: #14; circa 1941
lower right, graphite: 5
lower left, graphite: 21

108. (PLATE 52)
From Zabriskie Point, Death Valley National
Monument, California, 1941
19.3 x 24.4 cm (7⅝ x 9⅝ in.)
Recto: signed: Ansel Adams
Verso: inscribed on mount, upper left, blue ink: ⑩
center: stamp five; From Zabriski [*sic*] Point / Death

Valley National Monument / San Francisco / Ansel
Adams; 1935 / CA / 8 x 10 / camera; blue ink: ③4
[crossed out in graphite]; Print about / 1940;
graphite: ㉚
lower left, graphite: ⑦
face mat, lower right, graphite: 2
face mat, lower left, graphite: 38 Ⓗ

109. (PLATE 39)
U.S. Potash Company, Carlsbad, New Mexico, 1941
26.1 x 32 cm (10¼ x 12⅝ in.)
Recto: signed: Ansel Adams
Verso: inscribed on mount, upper left: Ⓛ
center: stamp five; U.S. Potash Co. / Carlsbad N.M.;
stamp six: U.S. POTASH CO. CARLSBAD. NEW MEXICO.
CA 1938; 8 x 10 Camera / [8 x 10] Print; stamp two,
purple ink; EL label: 328
lower right, graphite: <u>10</u>

110. (PLATE 37)
Moonrise, Hernandez, New Mexico, 1941; print
date: 1965–75
53.6 x 73.3 cm (21⅛ x 28⅞ in.)
Recto: signed on mount, lower right, black ink:
Ansel Adams
Verso: mount, center: stamp five; stamp six; blue ink:
Moonrise over Hernandez (N.M.)

111.
Manly Beacon, Death Valley National Monument,
California, about 1948
18.9 x 24 cm (7⁷⁄₁₆ x 9⁷⁄₁₆ in.)
Recto: signed: Ansel Adams
Verso: mount, center: stamp five; stamp four [address
crossed out in black ink and "NEG." crossed out in
red ink], red ink: 27; red ink: Manly Beacon / Death
Valley; CA / 1944
lower left, graphite: 360-B
face mat, lower left, graphite: 16

112.*
Trailer Camp Children, Richmond, California, 1944
24.2 x 16 cm (9½ x 6⁵⁄₁₆ in.)
Recto: signed: Ansel Adams
Verso: inscribed on mount, upper left, blue ink:
㉕ [crossed out in graphite]
center: stamp five; stamp six: TRAILER CAMP CHIL-
DREN - RICHMOND, CALIF 1944; label five: Trailer
Camp Children, Richmond, California, Courtesy /
Fortune Magazine and Twice a Year / must not be
reproduced without permission; graphite: courtesy
Fortune Mag / and / "Twice a Year["] / 1944 / Value
$500 ⁰⁰ / Only Print extant; EL label: 325; graphite:

1.1952; 2" x 2" Zeiss Super Ikonta B; graphite: (11);
21 [crossed out in graphite]
lower left, blue ink: 162; graphite: 32

113. (PLATE 95)
Men and Dog, Hornitos Homecoming, California,
1938
22.1 x 15.6 cm (8¹¹⁄₁₆ x 6⅛ in.)
Recto: signed: Ansel Adams
Verso: inscribed on mount, center: label five, typed:
HORNITOS GROUP, MEN AND DOG / HORNITOS CALI-
FORNIA CONTAX, graphite: 1935, black ink: CA 1935;
Contax 35 mm Original Print
lower right, graphite: (1) / 1
lower left, graphite: 136

114. (PLATE 96)
Church and Fence, Hornitos, California, 1946
23.7 x 18.7 cm (9⁵⁄₁₆ x 7⅜ in.)
Recto: signed on mount, lower right, black ink:
Ansel Adams
Verso: inscribed on mount, upper left: (L)
center: stamp seven; stamp eight: Church and fence,
Hornitos California / From Portfolio I / 1940; Print
1947⁺ / 8 x 10 Camera
lower left, graphite: 9

115.* (PLATE 94)
Moment in a Crowd, Hornitos Homecoming,
California, 1938
15.6 x 19.5 cm (6⅛ x 7¹¹⁄₁₆ in.)
Recto: signed on mount, lower right, black ink:
Ansel Adams
Verso: mount, center: EL label: 326; stamp five;
stamp four [address crossed out]; Hornitas [sic]
Homecoming / Detail / HORNITAS [sic], California /
1935 / Contax Photograph Original Print /
35 mm / 17 / 1939 CA [crossed out]
lower right, graphite: 14
face mat, lower right, graphite: 1

116. (PLATE 93)
Residents, Hornitos, California, about 1935
35.1 x 27.1 cm (13¹³⁄₁₆ x 10¹¹⁄₁₆ in.)
Recto: signed: Ansel Adams
Verso: mount, center: stamp two; Residents /
Hornitos. Calif / "Old Timers" / Original Print
early / CA 1935
lower right, graphite: 1

117. (PLATE 97)
At Hornitos, California, about 1934
18.7 x 24 cm (7⅜ x 9⁷⁄₁₆ in.)
Recto: signed Ansel Adams
Verso: inscribed on mount, upper left: (L)
center: stamp seven; AT HORNITOS, California /
Ansel Adams / CA. 1934 / 8 x 10 Camera / "Gamma
Intoning" Development / 15
upper right: MA / 1940
lower right, printed label: EXHIBITED LAKE CHARLES
CAMERA CLUB, LAKE CHARLES, LOUISIANA; graphite:
(29)-B

118. (PLATE 92)
Old Church, Hornitos, California, 1943
18.4 x 23 cm (7¼ x 9¹⁄₁₆ in.)
Recto: signed: Ansel Adams
Verso: inscribed on mount, upper left, brown ink: 1.
center: stamp seven; stamp eight: 1943; Old Church,
Hornitos, California / [Calif. Mining Town] / Ansel
Adams
upper right: 42.
lower right, graphite: 3
lower left, graphite: (43)

119.* (PLATE 99)
Detail, Church, Chinese Camp, California, about
1944
24.1 x 19.2 cm (9½ x 7⁹⁄₁₆ in.)
Recto: signed: Ansel Adams
Verso: inscribed on mount, upper left: (L)
center: stamp seven; stamp four, graphite: 1-C-203;
Detail, Church, Chinese Camp, California CA. 1944
/ [1944] Print; graphite: Box #3
lower left, graphite: 274-A
face mat, lower left, graphite: 9 V

ALFRED STIEGLITZ AND NEW YORK

120.*
Century Apartments from Central Park, New York
City, about 1945
16.9 x 11.6 cm (6⅝ x 4⁹⁄₁₆ in.)
Recto: signed: Ansel Adams
Verso: mount, center: stamp seven; stamp eight;
stamp four ["NEG." crossed out in red ink], red ink:
62 / New York City; CA-1936 / 1935?
lower left, graphite: 17

121. (PLATE 1)
Alfred Stieglitz at An American Place, New York
City, about 1939; print date: 1973
34.2 x 25.8 cm (13⁷⁄₁₆ x 10³⁄₁₆ in.)

Recto: signed: Ansel Adams
Verso: mount, center: stamp seven; stamp eight:
Alfred Stieglitz at / An American Place; graphite:
PRINT 1973
lower right, graphite: 20

122. (PLATE 6)
O'Keeffe Sunflower Painting in Storeroom, An
American Place, New York City, 1939
31.6 x 25.2 cm (12⁷⁄₁₆ x 9¹⁵⁄₁₆ in.)
Recto: signed: Ansel Adams
Verso: mount, center: EL label: 424; stamp five;
stamp four [address crossed out]; O'Keeffe Painting
in Storeroom; 4 x 5 Camera / graphite: (62); CA 1936
/ Print 1940!
upper right: #12
lower left, graphite: 15 / 33-2-B

123. (PLATE 7)
O'Keeffe Painting and Reflections, An American
Place, New York City, about 1938
24.8 x 25 cm (9¾ x 9¹³⁄₁₆ in.)
Recto: signed: Ansel Adams
Verso: inscribed on mount, upper left: (L)
center: stamp five; stamp four [address crossed out];
O'Keeffe Painting, Reflections; blue ink: at / "An
American Place"; CA. 1938 / 4 x 5 Camera / Print
1940+?

124. (PLATE 2)
New York City from the Barbizon Plaza Hotel,
about 1940
32.2 x 24.5 cm (12¹¹⁄₁₆ x 9⅝ in.)
Recto: signed: Ansel Adams
Verso: mount, center: EL label: 162; stamp four
[crossed out]; brown ink: 3; 3; stamp five; brown
ink: New York City / 7 ; stamp four [crossed out];
stamp three [crossed out]; stamp two [touched up];
stamp six: NEW YORK CITY FROM BARBIZON-PLAZA
HOTEL / CA 1940; 4 x 5 / early Print
lower right, graphite: 3 / (1)
lower left, graphite: (62)

125.
R.C.A. Building, New York City, 1941
23.8 x 15.5 cm (9⅛ x 6⅛ in.)
Recto: signed on mount, lower right, black ink:
Ansel Adams
Verso: mount, center: stamp seven; stamp six:
R.C.A. Building / 1941
upper right: 17
lower left, graphite: 1941 R.C.A. Building N.Y. /
12 / 63

126.*
Trinity Church Yard, New York City, about 1936
11.7 x 16.6 cm (4⅛ x 6⁹⁄₁₆ in.)
Recto: signed: Ansel Adams
Verso: mount, center: EL label: 166; stamp five;
stamp six: TRINITY CHURCH YARD, NEW YORK CITY /
1936 CA; stamp four ["NEG." crossed out in red ink],
red ink: 47 / Cemetery / New York City; Trinity
Churchyard / 18 / 5 x 7 Deardorf [*sic*] Camera
lower left, graphite: 60-S
face mat, lower left, graphite: 9

127.
John Marin, Artist, Cliffside, New Jersey, 1949
33.8 x 22.2 cm (13⁵⁄₁₆ x 8¾ in.)
Recto: signed: Ansel Adams
Verso: mount, center: stamp seven; stamp eight: John
Marin, Artist / Cliffside, N.J. / CA 1950? / Contax /
35 mm
lower right, graphite: 3

128.* (PLATE 59)
Surf Sequence #1, 1940, printed 1973
26.2 x 32.2 cm (10⁵⁄₁₆ x 12¹¹⁄₁₆ in.)
Recto: signed: Ansel Adams; inscribed on mount,
lower left, graphite: 1.
Verso: mount, center: stamp seven; stamp eight: Surf
Sequence #1 / 4-C-217
lower right, graphite: 19
lower left, graphite: III
Gift of Saundra B. Lane in honor of Clifford S.
Ackley, 2002.880

129.* (PLATE 60)
Surf Sequence #2, 1940, printed 1973
26 x 32.2 cm (10¼ x 12¹¹⁄₁₆ in.)
Recto: signed: Ansel Adams; inscribed on mount,
lower left, graphite: 2.
Verso: mount, center: stamp seven; stamp eight:
Shipwreck Series [crossed out] / CORRECTION: Surf
Sequence #2 / 4-C-218
lower right, graphite: 15
lower left, graphite: V
Gift of Saundra B. Lane in honor of Clifford S.
Ackley, 2002.881

130.* (PLATE 61)
Surf Sequence #3, 1940, printed 1973
26.4 x 32.2 cm (10⅜ x 12¹¹⁄₁₆ in.)
Recto: signed: Ansel Adams; inscribed on mount,
lower left, graphite: 3
Verso: mount, center: stamp seven; stamp eight: Surf
Sequence #3 / 4-C-219

lower right, graphite: 16
lower left, graphite: IV
Gift of Saundra B. Lane in honor of Clifford S.
Ackley, 2002.882

131.* (PLATE 62)
Surf Sequence #4, 1940, printed 1973
26.2 x 32.2 cm (10⁵⁄₁₆ x 12¹¹⁄₁₆ in.)
Recto: signed: Ansel Adams; inscribed on mount,
lower left, graphite: 4
Verso: mount, center: stamp seven; stamp eight: Surf
Sequence #4 / 4-C-220
lower right, graphite: 18
lower left, graphite: II
Gift of Saundra B. Lane in honor of Clifford S.
Ackley, 2002.883

132.* (PLATE 63)
Surf Sequence #5, 1940, printed 1973
26.5 x 32.2 cm (10⁷⁄₁₆ x 12¹¹⁄₁₆ in.)
Recto: signed: Ansel Adams; inscribed on mount,
lower left, graphite: 5
Verso: mount, center: stamp seven; stamp eight: Surf
Sequence #5 / 4-C-221
lower right, graphite: 17
lower left, graphite: I
Gift of Saundra B. Lane in honor of Clifford S.
Ackley, 2002.884

THE NATIONAL PARKS

133.*
Grass, Water, and Sun, Alaska, 1948; print date:
1962
36.5 x 49.1 cm (14⅜ x 19⁵⁄₁₆ in.)
Recto: signed: Ansel Adams
Verso: inscribed on mount, upper left: Ⓛ
center: stamp four; Grass, Water, and Sun / Alaska /
1948 / Print 1962 / 8 x 10 Camera
lower right, graphite: L

134. (PLATE 54)
*Interglacial Forest #1, Glacier Bay National
Monument, Alaska*, about 1948
12.2 x 10.1 cm (4¹³⁄₁₆ x 4 in.)
Recto: signed on mount, lower right, black ink:
Ansel Adams
Verso: inscribed on mount, center: stamp four: 4-
NPS-164; Inter-Glacial Forest #1 / Glacier Bay,
Alaska; graphite: 112-R / 15-S-A; 1947
face mat, lower left, graphite: 14 / V

135.*
*Interglacial Forest #2, Glacier Bay National
Monument, Alaska*, about 1948
10.2 x 12.3 cm (4 x 4¹³⁄₁₆ in.)
Recto: signed on mount, lower right, black ink:
Ansel Adams
Verso: center: stamp four: 4-NPS-169; Inter-Glacial
Forest #2 / Glacier Bay, Alaska; graphite: 113-R;
1947
face mat, lower left, graphite: 13 / V

136. (PLATE 53)
*Interglacial Forest #3, Glacier Bay National
Monument, Alaska*, about 1948
12.2 x 10.1 cm (4¹³⁄₁₆ x 4 in.)
Recto: signed on mount, lower right, black ink:
Ansel Adams
Verso: center: stamp four: 4-NPS-166; Inter-Glacial
Forest #3 / Glacier Bay, Alaska; graphite: 111-R / 16-
S-A; 1947
face mat, lower left, graphite: 12 / V

137.
Rocks, Glacier Bay National Monument, Alaska,
1948
12.2 x 9.7 cm (4¹³⁄₁₆ x 3¹³⁄₁₆ in.)
Recto: signed: Ansel Adams
Verso: inscribed on mount, upper left: Ⓛ
center: stamp four, red ink: 56; Rocks, Glacier Bay
N. Mon. / Alaska.; 1948 / 4 x 5 Camera
lower left, graphite: 10-S-A / 4
face mat, lower left, graphite: 4

138.*
Trailside, near Juneau, Alaska, about 1948; print
date: 1972
30.9 x 23.6 cm (12¹⁄₁₆ x 9⁵⁄₁₆ in.)
Recto: signed: Ansel Adams
Verso: mount, center: stamp seven; stamp eight:
Trailside, Alaska near Juneau / 1947; 3" x 4";
graphite: PRINT 1972
lower right, graphite: 18

139.
Mount McKinley and Wonder Lake, Alaska, 1948
39.8 x 49.4 cm (15¹¹⁄₁₆ x 19⁷⁄₁₆ in.)
Recto: signed: Ansel Adams
Verso: mount, center: stamp seven; stamp eight:
Mount McKinley from Wonder Lake Alaska / 1947;
8 x 10

140.*
Indian Gravestone Carving, near Juneau, Alaska,
about 1948
25.6 x 33 cm (10¹/₁₆ x 13 in.)
Recto: signed on mount, lower right, black ink:
Ansel Adams
Verso: mount, center: stamp five; stamp six:
Indian Gravestone carving, Alaska (near Juneau) /
CA 1947
lower right, graphite: 18

141.
*Moth and Ancient Wood, Interglacial Forest, Glacier
Bay National Monument, Alaska,* 1948
20.5 x 17 cm (8¹/₁₆ x 6¹¹/₁₆ in.)
Recto: signed: Ansel Adams
Verso: center: stamp four, red ink: 21; red ink: Moth
& Ancient Wood / Glacier Bay Nat. Mon. / Alaska;
1948? / 4 x 5 Camera / in Portfolio One; graphite:
⑦²
upper right, blue ink: #6
lower right, graphite: A
lower left graphite: 10 / 19-S
face mat, lower left, graphite: 10

142.*
Cliff Palace, Mesa Verde National Park, Colorado,
1941
19.1 x 23.8 cm (7½ x 9⅜ in.)
Recto: signed on mount, lower right, black ink:
Ansel Adams
Verso: mount, center: stamp seven; stamp eight: Cliff
Palace, Mesa Verde Nat. Park, Colorado / CA 1947;
Ⓤ Ⓢ / Adams-US-1-NPS-30
lower right, graphite: 14
lower left, graphite: 203
face mat, lower right, graphite: 14

143.*
*The Tetons and Snake River, Grand Teton National
Park, Wyoming,* 1942
Sight: 47.1 x 61.2 cm (18⁹/₁₆ x 24⅛ in.)
Recto: signed on mount, lower right, black ink:
Ansel Adams
Verso: mount, upper left, typed MoMA loan label
center: stamp five; stamp six: The Tetons And Snake
River / 1-NP-105; stamp four [address crossed out];
Teton Range - Snake River / Wyoming
exhibition mount, upper left, blue ink: 63.1221
upper right, typed MoMA loan label: ANSEL ADAMS /
THE TETONS, AND SNAKE RIVER, / WYOMING. 1941 /
63.1221 / 1

144.*
*Ferns, Near Kilauea Crater, Hawaii National Park,
Hawaii,* about 1948
39.5 x 49 cm (15⁹/₁₆ x 19⁵/₁₆ in.)
Recto: signed: Ansel Adams
Verso: mount, center: stamp seven; stamp eight:
Ferns Hawaii National Park Hawaii, Hawaii /
CA 1948; 4 x 5
lower right, graphite: 1

145.*
Canyon de Chelly National Monument, Arizona,
1942; print date: about 1967
37.6 x 47.5 cm (14¹³/₁₆ x 18¹¹/₁₆ in.)
Recto: signed on mount, lower right, black ink:
Ansel Adams
Verso: inscribed on mount, upper left: Ⓛ
center: stamp five; stamp six: Cañon de Chelly Nat
Monument, Arizona 1942; 8 x 10 Camera / print
1967⁺
lower right, graphite: L

146. (PLATE 55)
*From Hurricane Hill, Olympic National Park,
Washington,* 1948
17.9 x 23.5 cm (7¹/₁₆ x 9¼ in.)
Recto: signed on mount, lower right, black ink:
Ansel Adams
Verso: mount, center: stamp seven; stamp eight: in
Olympic National Park, Washington / CA 1942
lower right, graphite: 3 / 26

147. (PLATE 56)
*Dawn, Autumn, Great Smoky Mountains National
Park, Tennessee,* 1948
30.5 x 21.8 cm (12 x 8⁹/₁₆ in.)
Recto: signed on mount, lower right, black ink:
Ansel Adams
Verso: mount, center: stamp seven; stamp four
["NEG." crossed out in red ink], red ink: 17 /
Autumn. Great Smoky Mts. Nat. Park / Tenn. USA;
CA 1941
upper right: #6
lower left, graphite: 165 / 14

148.
*Lake McDonald, Evening, Glacier National Park,
Montana,* 1942
18.8 x 24 cm (7⅜ x 9⁷/₁₆ in.)
Recto: signed: Ansel Adams
Verso: inscribed on mount, upper left: Ⓛ
center: stamp five; stamp six: Lake McDonald

Glacier Nat'l Park CA. 1942 / [CA. 1942] Print ⁺;
8 x 10 Camera
upper right, graphite: MA
lower left, graphite: Glacier Nat Park 1942 / 331

149. (PLATE 40)
Salt Flats near Wendover, Utah, about 1941
19.1 x 24.3 cm (7½ x 9⁹/₁₆ in.)
Recto: signed: Ansel Adams
Verso: mount, center: stamp seven; stamp eight: Salt
Flats near Wendover, Utah / CA 1948
upper right: #8
lower right, graphite: 79.489
lower left, graphite: 327-B / 13

150. (PLATE 50)
*Old Faithful Geyser, Yellowstone National Park,
Wyoming,* 1942
32.1 x 23 cm (12⅛ x 9¹/₁₆ in.)
Recto: signed: Ansel Adams
Verso: mount, center: stamp seven; stamp eight: Old
Faithful Geyser / Yellowstone National Park
Wyoming / 1941 CA; Original Print; blue ink:
ADAMS-U.S.-3-N.P.S.-32
lower right, graphite: 1 / 3

151.
*Old Faithful Geyser, Yellowstone National Park,
Wyoming,* 1942
32.2 x 22.7 cm (12¹¹/₁₆ x 8¹⁵/₁₆ in.)
Recto: signed on mount, lower right, black ink:
Ansel Adams
Verso: inscribed on mount, upper left: Ⓘ
center, graphite: Old Faithful Geyser / Yellowstone
National Park / Courtesy U.S.D.i [sic] Personal Print /
Ansel Adams; stamp five; stamp six: OLD FAITFUL
[sic] GEYSER YELLOWSTONE NAT'L PARK. / U.S.D.i. [sic] /
CA 1941; graphite: ⑦⁶ [crossed out in
black ink]

152.* (PLATE 51)
*Old Faithful Geyser, Yellowstone National Park,
Wyoming,* 1942
24.6 x 17.5 cm (9¹¹/₁₆ x 6⅞ in.)
Recto: signed: Ansel Adams
Verso: inscribed on mount, center: stamp eleven: Old
Faithful / Yellowstone National Park
bottom center, graphite: 3176

153. (Frontispiece)
Self-Portrait, Monument Valley, Utah, 1958
34.8 x 23.3 cm (13¹¹⁄₁₆ x 9⁳⁄₁₆ in.)
Recto: signed: Ansel Adams
Verso: mount, center: stamp seven; stamp eight: Self
portrait, Monument Valley, Utah / 1958
lower right, graphite: 31

154. (PLATE 65)
Gerry Sharpe, Ouray, Colorado, 1958
24.1 x 18.4 cm (9½ x 7¼ in.)
Recto: signed on mount, lower right, black ink:
Ansel Adams
Verso: mount, center: stamp five; stamp six: Gerry
Sharpe, Ouray, California ["California" crossed out]
Colorado; CA 1958 (+) / [CA 1958 (+)] Print / 8 x
10 Camera / 445
lower left, graphite: 28

155. (PLATE 104)
Grass and Pool screen, about 1948
Each panel: 167.8 x 51.4 cm (66¹⁄₁₆ x 20¼ in.)

156.* (PLATE 41)
*The Nave from the Sanctuary, Mission San Xavier
del Bac, Tucson, Arizona*, about 1952
47.7 x 38 cm (18¾ x 14¹⁵⁄₁₆ in.)
Recto: signed on mount, lower right, black ink:
Ansel Adams
Verso: mount, center: stamp seven; stamp eight: The
Nave from the Sanctuary, Mission San Xavier Del
Bac / Tucson, Arizona / CA 1952; 8 x 10
lower right, graphite: 1

157.*
*Our Lady of Sorrows, East Chapel, Mission San
Xavier del Bac, Tucson, Arizona*, about 1952
47.9 x 37.4 cm (18⅞ x 14¼ in.)
Recto: signed on mount, lower right, black ink:
Ansel Adams
Verso: mount, center: stamp seven; stamp eight: Our
Lady of Sorrows, East Chapel, Mission San Xavier
del Bac / Tucson, Arizona / CA 1952; 8 x 10

158.*
*Statue of St. Francis, Mission San Xavier del Bac,
Tucson, Arizona*, about 1953
18.9 x 16.2 cm (7⁷⁄₁₆ x 6⅜ in.)
Recto: signed: Ansel Adams

Verso: mount, center: stamp five; stamp six: DETAIL,
STATUE OF ST. FRANCIS / MISSION SAN XAVIER DEL
BAC. / ARIZONA.; stamp four [address crossed out];
Detail of Statue of St. Francis / at Mission San
Xavier del Bac / Tucson, Arizona / CA 1953
lower right, graphite: 10-A

159. (PLATE 79)
Freeway Interchange, Los Angeles, 1967
37.2 x 34.8 cm (14⅝ x 13¹¹⁄₁₆ in.)
Recto: signed: Ansel Adams
Verso: mount, center: stamp seven; stamp eight:
Freeway Interchange. Los Angeles Calif. / University
of California and McGraw-Hill Book Company /
1967; Hasselblad from about 1000 feet / 120 mm
lens
lower right, graphite: 1

160. (PLATE 78)
*Housing Development, San Bruno Mountains, San
Francisco*, about 1966
24.4 x 32 cm (9⅝ x 12⅝ in.)
Recto: signed on mount, lower right, black ink:
Ansel Adams
Verso: mount, center: stamp seven; stamp eight:
Housing Development, San Francisco / San Bruno
Mountains / CA 1966?; Hasselblad
lower right, graphite: L / (17)

161.*
*Television Antenna, Moon, Haleakala, Maui,
Hawaii*, about 1952
49.1 x 36.2 cm (19⁵⁄₁₆ x 14¼ in.)
Recto: signed on mount, lower right, black ink:
Ansel Adams
Verso: mount, center: stamp seven; stamp eight:
Television Antenna, Moon, Haleakala, Maui Hawaii
/ First Nat Bank of Hawaii / CA 1952; Hasselblad /
250 mm
lower right, graphite: 1

162.*
Rails and Jet Trails, Roseville, California, about
1953
33.8 x 25.5 cm (13⁵⁄₁₆ x 10¹⁄₁₆ in.)
Recto: signed on mount, lower right, black ink:
Ansel Adams
Verso: mount, center: stamp seven; stamp four
["NEG." crossed out in red ink], red ink: 15; red ink:
Rails and Jet Trails / Roseville, California; CA 1953
upper right: #5
lower left, graphite: 20 / 250-A

163.*
Fence and Barn, Near Alturas, Northern California,
about 1960
17.8 x 24.1 cm (7 x 9½ in.)
Recto: signed on mount, lower right, black ink:
Ansel Adams
Verso: mount, center: stamp seven; stamp eight: Barn
Northern California (Near Alturas) / CA 1960; 8 x 10
lower right, graphite: 11

164.*
*Stream, Buttermilk County, Owens Valley,
California*, about 1948
33.1 x 24.2 cm (13¹⁄₁₆ x 9½ in.)
Recto: signed on mount, lower right, black ink:
Ansel Adams
Verso: mount, center: stamp seven; stamp eight:
Stream. Buttermilk County Owens Valley California /
CA 1948; 5 x 7
lower right, graphite: (5) / XI

165. (PLATE 80)
Crosses, Mono Lake Cemetery, California, about
1960
24.8 x 31.2 cm (9¾ x 12⁵⁄₁₆ in.)
Recto: signed: Ansel Adams
Verso: mount, center: stamp seven; stamp eight:
Crosses Mono Lake Cemetery California / CA 1960;
8 x 10
upper right, blue ink: #6
lower right, graphite: L / XI / (8)
lower left, blue ink: 283-4; graphite: (Graveyard of
Basque sheepherders)

166.*
Dunes, Oceano, California, 1963
27.5 x 30.1 cm (10¹³⁄₁₆ x 11⅞ in.)
Recto: signed on mount, lower right, black ink:
Ansel Adams
Verso: mount, center: stamp seven; stamp eight:
Dunes, Oceano, Calif / CA 1960; Hasselblad
lower right, graphite: 16

167. (PLATE 64)
Dunes, Oceano, California, about 1950
25.8 x 26.2 cm (10³⁄₁₆ x 10⁵⁄₁₆ in.)
Recto: signed on mount, lower right, black ink:
Ansel Adams
Verso: mount, center: stamp five; stamp six: Dunes,
Oceano Calif CA. 1960
lower right, graphite: 11

168. (PLATE 81)
Spiritual America, Horns and Belfry, Foothills, Sierra Nevada, California, about 1966
34.4 x 25.3 cm (13⁹/₁₆ x 9¹⁵/₁₆ in.)
Recto: signed: Ansel Adams
Verso: mount, center: stamp seven; stamp eight: "Spiritual America["] Horns and Belfrey [*sic*] / Foothills, Sierra Nevada / CA 1966; Hasselblad
lower right, graphite: 21

169.
Northern California Coast, near Elk, California, 1964
26.5 x 32.3 cm (10⁷/₁₆ x 12¹¹/₁₆ in.)
Recto: signed on mount, lower right, black ink: Ansel Adams
Verso: mount, center: stamp five; stamp six: At Elk, CALIFORNIA (North Coast) CA 1959 / [CA 1959] Print; 8 x 10 Camera; .9
lower left, graphite: 23

170.*
Coast, North of Bodega Bay, California, about 1960
26.3 x 34.5 cm (10⅛ x 13⁹/₁₆ in.)
Recto: signed on mount, lower right, black ink: Ansel Adams
Verso: mount, center: stamp seven; stamp eight: Coast—North of Bodega Bay / California / CA 1960; 5 x 7
lower right, graphite: 25

171.*
Upper Yosemite Fall, Yosemite National Park, about 1960
34.5 x 26.4 cm (13⁹/₁₆ x 10⅜ in.)
Recto: signed on mount, lower right, black ink: Ansel Adams
Verso: inscribed on mount, upper left: 40.
center: stamp five; stamp six: Upper Yosemite Fall, Winter, Yosemite Valley / Upper Yosemite Fall Winter Y.V. CA 1960; Hasselblad Camera
lower right, graphite: 17 / 79.491

172.
Glacier-Scored Rocks, Tenaya Lake, Yosemite National Park, about 1969
27.5 x 33.7 cm (10¹³/₁₆ x 13¼ in.)
Recto: signed: Ansel Adams
Verso: mount, center: stamp seven; stamp eight: Glacier-Scored Rocks Tenaya Lake / Yosemite National Park / CA 1969
lower right, graphite: 32

173.*
Winter, Badger Pass, Yosemite National Park, about 1957
18.8 x 23.9 cm (7⅜ x 9⁷/₁₆ in.)
Recto: signed on mount, lower right, black ink: Ansel Adams
Verso: inscribed on mount, upper left: (L)
center: stamp five; stamp six: WINTER, BADGER PASS, YOSEMITE CA 1957 / Print [CA 1957]; 8 x 10 Camera
lower right, graphite: (3)

174.*
Ice on Merced River, Yosemite National Park, about 1942; print date: about 1963
19 x 24 cm (7½ x 9⁷/₁₆ in.)
Recto: signed on mount, lower right, black ink: Ansel Adams
Verso: inscribed on mount, upper left: 44.; (L)
center: stamp five; stamp six: Ice on Merced River / y.v. CA 1960 Print 1963⁺; 8 x 10 Camera
upper right: #16
lower right, graphite: (1)
lower left: ? 11-21

175. (PLATE 77)
Sodium Sulphite Crystals, 1962
44.2 x 33.6 cm (17⅜ x 13¼ in.)
Recto: signed on mount, lower right, black ink: Ansel Adams
Verso: inscribed on mount, top center: Sodium Sulphite Crystals / Type 55 P/N neg / Polaroid
center: EL label: 278; stamp five; stamp six: SODIUM SULFITE [*sic*] CRYSTALS; stamp ten

176. (PLATE 76)
Wall Writing, Hornitos, California, about 1960
48.8 x 38.3 cm (19³/₁₆ x 15¹/₁₆ in.)
Recto: signed on mount, lower right, black ink: Ansel Adams
Verso: inscribed on mount, upper left: (L)
center: stamp five; stamp six: WALL WRITING, HORNITOS Calif 1960⁺; Print 1964⁺ / 8 x 10 Camera
lower right: L

177.*
Silverton, Colorado, 1951
19.3 x 24.1 cm (7⅝ x 9½ in.)
Recto: signed: Ansel Adams
Verso: inscribed on mount, upper left: (L)
center: stamp four [crossed out]; stamp five; stamp six: Silverton, Colorado / CA 1956 / [1956] Print +;

Silverton, Colorado / 8 x 10 Camera / 10" Kodak wide Field Lens
upper right: #17
lower left, graphite: 16; graphite: (69)-A

178.
Church and Road, Bodega, California, about 1953
34.8 x 24.5 cm (13¹¹/₁₆ x 9⅝ in.)
Recto: signed: Ansel Adams
Verso: mount, center: stamp seven; stamp eight: Church and Road Bodega, Calif. / CA 1953; 4 x 5
lower right, graphite: 27

179. (PLATE 49)
Aspens, Northern New Mexico, 1958
48.9 x 38.1 cm (19¼ x 15 in.)
Recto: signed on mount, lower right, black ink: Ansel Adams
Verso: mount, center: stamp seven; stamp eight: ASPENS, NEW MEXICO
upper right: L
lower right, graphite: *L*

CHRONOLOGY

1902
Ansel Easton Adams, the only child of Olive Bray and Charles Hitchcock Adams, is born on February 20 at 114 Maple Street, San Francisco. Charles Adams works for Washington Mills, a lumber company founded by his father, William James Adams.

1903
The family home is completed at 129 Twenty-fourth Avenue, along the dunes overlooking the Golden Gate. Adams resides there, or in the house built next to it, for nearly sixty years.

1904
Virginia Rose Best is born January 18.

1906
A powerful earthquake strikes San Francisco on April 18, followed by a fire that burns out of control for three days. The Adams family's home survives with little damage, but four-year-old Ansel suffers a broken nose in an aftershock.

1907
Grandfather Adams dies and the family lumber business fails. Ansel's father spends the rest of his life trying to repay business debts.

1908
An inquisitive and gifted child, Adams is sent to public school, but the experience is not a success. Grandfather Bray and Aunt Mary Bray come to live with the family.

1911
Briefly attends the Rochambeau School, having been previously tutored at home by his father and Aunt Mary.

1914
Adams' father takes Ansel out of school again and tutors him at home. He also makes arrangements for him to study ancient Greek and take piano lessons. Over the next fifteen years, music becomes a larger and larger part of his studies.

1915
In lieu of conventional schooling, his father buys him a season pass to the Panama-Pacific Exposition and Adams visits nearly every day.

1916
Persuades his parents to take a family vacation in Yosemite National Park. Adams takes pictures there using his first camera and develops a deep interest in both photography and the park. On returning to San Francisco, he studies with photofinisher Frank Dittman. He returns to Yosemite every year for the rest of his life, becoming a dedicated mountaineer and environmentalist.

1917
Receives grammar school diploma from Kate M. Wilkins Private School, San Francisco. Though largely self-taught in photography, he works that summer and next at Frank Dittman's commercial photofinishing business.

1918
Learns the basics of the photographic darkroom during his second summer at Dittman's photofinishing business in San Francisco.

1919
After several seasons of hiking, exploration, and photography in Yosemite, Adams joins the Sierra Club and applies for a job as summer custodian of the club's Yosemite headquarters.

1920
Spends the first of four summers as custodian of the Sierra Club's headquarters in Yosemite. During this period, Adams photographs intensively while exploring the High Sierra, the upper elevations of the Sierra Nevada surrounding Yosemite Valley. His first published photograph appears in the *Sierra Club Bulletin*. He continues piano training with professional ambitions, studying with Frederick Zech.

1921
Finds a piano to practice on during his second summer in Yosemite at Best's Studio, a Yosemite concession selling paintings, photographs, books, and gifts. Meets Harry Best's daughter, Virginia. Takes first high-country trip into the Sierra with Francis "Uncle Frank" Holman and Mistletoe, the burro.

1922
Publishes first illustrated article, on the Lyell Fork of the Merced River, in the *Sierra Club Bulletin*.

1923
Makes earliest fully realized photograph, *Banner Peak and Thousand Island Lake*, during a clearing storm. Takes first trip with Sierra Club into the High Sierra. Cedric Wright, who becomes his best friend, introduces him to the philosophy of Elbert Hubbard and Edward Carpenter.

1925
Decides to become a concert pianist and, with his father's help, purchases a Mason and Hamlin grand piano. Explores Kings River Canyon with Professor Joseph N. LeConte's family. On his return to San Francisco at the end of the summer, Adams breaks up with Virginia, convinced that marriage is incompatible with the musical career he seeks.

1926
Takes first trip to Carmel with Albert Bender, who becomes his most important early patron, and meets Robinson Jeffers there. Explores Kings River Canyon again with the LeConte family.

1927
Makes the photograph *Monolith—The Face of Half Dome*, which he considers his first photographic "visualization" (see page 17). He increasingly thinks of photography, rather than music, as his life's work. Publishes a portfolio of eighteen images, *Parmelian Prints of the High Sierras* (San Francisco: Jean Chambers Moore). One hundred portfolios are printed and sell for fifty dollars apiece. Ansel and Virginia renew their relationship. Travels with Bender in Carmel, California, and Santa Fe and Taos, New Mexico, where Adams meets authors Mary Austin, Witter Bynner, and others.

1928

On January 2, marries Virginia Best in Yosemite. Adams' first one-man exhibition is held at the Sierra Club, San Francisco. William Colby, executive director of the club, invites Adams to be the official photographer of their outing to Jasper and Mount Robson Parks in the Canadian Rockies. Adams meets photographer Edward Weston at Bender's.

1929

Travels to Santa Fe and Taos working on a book with Mary Austin. Photographs at Taos Pueblo in northern New Mexico and meets Georgia O'Keeffe and John Marin at Mabel Dodge Luhan's estate. In Yosemite, writes lyrics, selects music, and acts a leading role for the Bracebridge Dinner, a Christmas production that becomes an annual event.

1930s

Photographs Kings River and Kern River in the Sierra Nevada. He prints Farm Security Administration photographer Dorothea Lange's photographs while she is out in the field.

1930

Meets Paul Strand in Taos and after seeing his negatives is inspired to commit to a full-time career in photography. Builds home and studio at 131 Twenty-fourth Avenue, San Francisco, adjoining his parents' home. Takes a ski trip into the High Sierra in midwinter. Publishes *Taos Pueblo*, containing twelve original photographs with text by Mary Austin. Begins taking on commercial photography assignments; one of the first is a catalogue for Gump's, the San Francisco specialty store. Continues doing commercial work into the early 1970s.

1931

Writes a photography column for the *Fortnightly*, reviewing Eugène Atget, Edward Weston, and Imogen Cunningham exhibitions at San Francisco's M. H. de Young Memorial Museum. The Smithsonian Institution in Washington, D.C., mounts a solo exhibition of sixty of Adams' photographs, entitled "Pictorial Photographs of the Sierra Nevada Mountains by Ansel Adams."

1932

Has first important one-man show at the de Young Museum. With Edward Weston, Willard Van Dyke, Imogen Cunningham, Sonya Noskowiak, and Henry Swift, founds Group f/64, which is dedicated to exhibiting and exploring the expressive potential of straight, or "pure," photography.

1933

Meets Alfred Stieglitz at his gallery An American Place in New York City. Son Michael is born. In September, opens Ansel Adams Gallery at 166 Geary Street, San Francisco. Has first New York exhibition at Alma Reed's Delphic Studios. The San Francisco Museum of Art gives Adams a one-man exhibition.

1934

Writes first series of technical articles, "An Exposition of My Photographic Technique," in *Camera Craft* magazine (January–May). Gives up his gallery in order to spend more time making photographs. Is elected to the board of directors of the Sierra Club (and serves continuously until his resignation in 1971). Writes "The New Photography," in *Modern Photography, 1934–35* yearbook (London and New York: Studio Publications, 1935).

1935

Daughter Anne is born. Publishes how-to book, *Making a Photograph* (Studio Publications), which remains in print for nearly two decades. Starts experimenting with the 35mm camera and printing photo murals.

1936

In January, attends a conference on the national parks held in Washington, D.C., to lobby on behalf of the Sierra Club for the establishment of Kings Canyon as a national park. Shows his photographs of the Sierra Nevada to lawmakers and Secretary of the Interior Harold Ickes. Moves to Berkeley, where he and Virginia live for several months in a Bernard Maybeck–designed home. Virginia inherits Best's Studio after her father's death. That autumn, Alfred Stieglitz hosts a one-man exhibition of Adams' work at An American Place in New York, and Katharine Kuh Gallery gives him a one-man show in Chicago. In December, Adams is hospitalized with a chest infection and mononucleosis.

1937

Ansel and Virginia move to Yosemite in the spring, where they take over the proprietorship of Best's Studio. In June, a fire in his darkroom destroys one-third of his early negatives. Adams continues to work and maintain his professional studio in San Francisco. He takes photography treks with Edward Weston through the High Sierra and with Georgia O'Keeffe and David McAlpin in the Southwest. His photographs are included in the first historical survey of the medium at the Museum of Modern Art, New York (MoMA). Hires Rondal Partridge as photographic assistant through 1940. The University of California, San Francisco, hosts a one-man show by Adams.

1938

Leads O'Keeffe and McAlpin on a trip through Yosemite and the High Sierra. Photographs with Edward Weston in the arid Owens Valley between the Sierra Nevada and the Inyo and White Mountains. Adams' book *Sierra Nevada: The John Muir Trail* is published (Berkeley, CA: Archetype Press). He sends a copy to the Department of the Interior, and it is shown to President Franklin D. Roosevelt. Roosevelt keeps the book for the White House, and Adams sends Interior Secretary Ickes another copy.

1939

Meets Beaumont and Nancy Newhall in New York. Has a major exhibition at the San Francisco Museum of Art.

1940s–50s

George Waters at Kodak hires Adams, along with Edward Weston, Paul Strand, and Charles Sheeler, to shoot advertising photographs with Kodak film.

1940

Teaches the U.S. Camera Yosemite Photographic Forum, his first workshop in Yosemite, with Edward Weston. With Beaumont Newhall and McAlpin, he helps to found the Department of Photography at MoMA, the world's first museum department of photography. Adams curates and edits the catalogue for "A Pageant of Photography," held at the Palace of Fine Arts, at the Golden Gate Exposition, San Francisco. He shoots his celebrated *Surf Sequence* on an outing with Beaumont and Nancy Newhall. Beaumont Newhall and Adams cocurate the first photography exhibition at MoMA. Many years after Adams' lobbying trip to Washington, D.C., Congress finally passes a bill making Kings Canyon a national park.

1941

Adams is appointed photomuralist for the Department of the Interior. Makes what will become his best-known photograph, *Moonrise, Hernandez, New Mexico*, on November 1. Publishes the children's book *Michael and Anne in Yosemite Valley* with text by Virginia Adams (Studio Publications). In March, Albert Bender, his friend and patron, dies. Adams makes his own version of Timothy O'Sullivan's 1873 photograph of the ancient ruins at Canyon de Chelly, Arizona.

1942

The Department of the Interior photomural project lapses during World War II. Adams works with Dorothea Lange for the Office of War Information. Curates "Photographs of the Civil War and American Frontier" at MoMA. With colleague Fred Archer, codifies his Zone System technique of exposure and development control while teaching at the Art Center School in Los Angeles.

1943

Begins a photo-essay on the plight of loyal Japanese Americans evacuated and interned after Pearl Harbor. He photographs at Manzanar Relocation Center, Owens Valley, California, at his own expense, refusing government funding.

1944

Gives a lecture series on photography at MoMA. His book *Born Free and Equal* is published by U.S. Camera, and the related exhibition "Manzanar" is held at MoMA.

1945

Ted Spencer, president of the San Francisco Art Association, invites Adams to set up a department of photography at the California School of Fine Arts (CSFA). In February, Adams collaborates with Dorothea Lange to photograph the wartime shipyards in Richmond, California, for *Fortune*.

1946

Receives John Simon Guggenheim Memorial Foundation Fellowship to photograph the national parks and monuments (renewed in 1948). Hires Minor White to teach with him at CSFA and leaves full-time teaching the following year.

1947

Does extensive photography in America's national parks and makes his first photographic trip to Hawaii.

1948

His Guggenheim Fellowship is renewed. The Sierra Club issues *Portfolio I*, featuring twelve original prints in an edition of seventy-five. Adams also publishes the first two volumes of his Basic Photo Series—*Camera and Lens* (New York: Morgan & Morgan) and *The Negative* (Morgan & Morgan)—as well as *Yosemite and the High Sierra*, edited by Charlotte E. Mauk, with selected words of John Muir (Boston: Houghton Mifflin).

1949

Becomes consultant to the newly founded Polaroid Corporation, thanks to his friendship with Edwin Land. Publishes *My Camera in Yosemite Valley* (Houghton Mifflin).

1950s

Adams and Dorothea Lange work together on magazine assignments—one on the Mormons of Utah for *Life*, and another for *Fortune* on agriculture in the San Joaquin Valley.

1950

Adams' mother, Olive, dies. The Sierra Club issues *Portfolio II: The National Parks and Monuments*, with fifteen photographs in an edition of 105. He publishes his third volume of Basic Photo Series, *The Print* (Morgan & Morgan), as well as *My Camera in the National Parks* (Houghton Mifflin) and a reprint of the 1903 book *The Land of Little Rain*, with text by Mary Austin and photographs by Adams (Houghton Mifflin). Adams goes to Hawaii on an assignment for Kodak. He begins his association with Victor Hasselblad and the Hasselblad camera system.

1951

His father, Charles, dies. He hires Pirkle Jones, who had previously developed negatives for him when he was on extended trips, as his photographic assistant through 1953.

1952

Publishes Basic Photo Series 4: *Natural-Light Photography* (Morgan & Morgan). Has an exhibition at the George Eastman House, Rochester. Helps

found *Aperture*, a groundbreaking journal of creative photography, with the Newhalls, Minor White, and others. In June and July, Adams and Nancy Newhall collaborate on a series of articles for *Arizona Highways*, a magazine that showcases photographs of nature. Virginia and Ansel Adams start a company called 5 Associates with three friends. The company produces high-quality photographic postcards and notecards, which are sold at Best's Studio.

1953

The November 2 issue of *Time* magazine features photography. It includes mention of Adams, whose color photograph of Mono Lake is reproduced.

1954

Publishes *Death Valley* (Palo Alto: 5 Associates), *Mission San Xavier del Bac* (5 Associates), and *The Pageant of History and the Panorama of Today in Northern California* (San Francisco: American Trust). Nancy Newhall contributes the text for all three books. *Life* magazine publishes an article by Daniel Dixon featuring photographs by Adams and Dorothea Lange on the Mormons in Utah.

1955

The Ansel Adams Yosemite Workshop begins as an annual event each June. Nancy Newhall and Adams curate an exhibition called "This Is the American Earth," held at the LeConte Memorial Lodge in Yosemite before traveling throughout the United States. A book of the same title is published in 1960 (San Francisco: Sierra Club); along with Rachel Carson's *Silent Spring* (1962), it is influential in inspiring environmental activism.

1956

Publishes Basic Photo Series 5: *Artificial-Light Photography* (Morgan & Morgan). Don Worth becomes his photographic assistant through 1960, and Gerry Sharpe works on special projects through the early 1960s.

1957

The film *Ansel Adams: Photographer* is produced by Larry Dawson and directed by David Meyers, with script by Nancy Newhall and narration by Beaumont Newhall. Adams takes a major photographic expedition to Hawaii; work continues in 1958, resulting in a book, *The Islands of Hawaii*, with text by Edward Joesting (Honolulu: Bishop National Bank of Hawaii).

1958

Tries to resign from the Sierra Club during the battle to widen the Tioga Road near Tenaya Lake in Yosemite. In the end, he loses his battle and believes the region is done irreparable harm. His resignation is not accepted. He has a rubber stamp made that reads "Remember Tenaya!!" and uses it on all his correspondence. He receives his third Guggenheim Fellowship for creative work.

1959

Publishes *Yosemite Valley*, edited by Nancy Newhall (5 Associates). He moderates a series of five films for public television, *Photography: The Incisive Art* (directed by Robert Katz and produced by N. E. T.). The series is rebroadcast over the next forty years, attracting millions of viewers.

1960s

Adams and the Sierra Club fight to get Pacific Gas & Electric to move the site of its nuclear power plant from Nipomo Dunes to Diablo Canyon in California. The site is moved, but deep political rifts are created within the Sierra Club.

1960

The Sierra Club issues *Portfolio III: Yosemite Valley*, containing sixteen photographs in an edition of 208. The Sierra Club publishes Adams' *This Is the American Earth*, with text by Nancy Newhall.

1961

Adams is granted an honorary doctorate of fine arts degree from the University of California, and subsequently receives honorary degrees from numerous other institutions, including Yale and Harvard. Lacking a high school diploma, he is pleased and proud to be recognized by "higher academia."

1962

Builds a home and studio overlooking the Pacific Ocean in Carmel Highlands, California. Moves from Yosemite to new Carmel home. Publishes *Death Valley and the Creek Called Furnace*, with text by Edwin Corle (Los Angeles: Ward Ritchie) and *These We Inherit: The Parklands of America* (Sierra Club).

1963

"The Eloquent Light," a retrospective exhibition featuring Adams' prints from 1923 to 1963, is shown at the de Young Museum. Adams receives the Sierra Club's John Muir Award. The Sierra Club issues *Portfolio IV: What Majestic Word*, in memory of Russell Varian, with fifteen photographs in an edition of 260. The first volume of a biography, *Ansel Adams: The Eloquent Light* with text by Nancy Newhall, is published (Sierra Club); the second volume is never completed. Liliane De Cock becomes Adams' photographic assistant through 1971. He produces the *Polaroid Land Photography Manual*.

1964

Publishes *An Introduction to Hawaii*, with text by Edward Joesting (5 Associates). He is commissioned by Clark Kerr, president of the University of California, to undertake, with Nancy Newhall, a book celebrating the university's centennial in 1968.

1965

Meets with President Lyndon B. Johnson to discuss environmental issues. At President Johnson's request, Adams and Nancy Newhall produce a book called *A More Beautiful America*, which uses Adams' photographs and text from Johnson's speeches. Adams leads and wins a battle to prevent Humble Oil Company from building a refinery at Moss Landing in California. He is invited, as the representative for the Sierra Club and the Foundation for Environmental Design, to witness the signing of the Arts and Humanities Act at the White House. He goes to the Tetons with Nancy Newhall to work on a new book.

1966

Cole Weston leases an art gallery space to Adams, who starts an organization called Friends of Photography in Carmel. Adams is invited to the All-University Faculty Conference at the University of California, Davis, where he presents a resolution to establish a department of photography.

1967

Becomes president and, later, chairman of the board of trustees of the Friends of Photography, Carmel. Publishes *Fiat Lux: The University of California*, with text by Nancy Newhall (New York: McGraw Hill). Commissioned by the university, Adams spends three years on the massive project, making six thousand photographs of the myriad campuses and people of the university. It is the largest "commercial" project of his career.

1968

Secretary of the Interior Stewart Udall awards Adams the Conservation Service Award, the Interior Department's highest civilian honor.

1969

Adams leads the painful and public fight to oust the Sierra Club's executive director and his former protégé, David Brower, as a result of Brower's unwillingness to follow the board of directors' policies.

1970

Receives the Chubb Fellowship from Yale University. Parasol Press issues *Portfolio V*, with ten 16 x 20 inch prints in an edition of 110. Adams publishes *The Tetons and the Yellowstone*, with text by Nancy Newhall (5 Associates) and a revised edition of Basic Photo Series 1: *Camera and Lens* (Morgan & Morgan). He rebuilds his Yosemite darkroom into a laboratory for teaching and plans additional workshops in Yosemite.

1971

After thirty-seven years of service (from 1934 to 1971), David Brower resigns as director of the Sierra Club. Adams hires William A. Turnage as his business manager (until 1977). Adams becomes more involved with the Wilderness Society, because of its focus on wilderness issues and his friendship with Turnage, who is serving as its executive director.

1972

Adams has a retrospective exhibition, "Recollected Moments," at the San Francisco Museum of Modern Art (SFMoMA); the show is sent by the U.S. Information Agency (USIA) to Europe and South America. He publishes a monograph, *Ansel Adams*, edited by Liliane De Cock (Morgan & Morgan). Best's Studio is renamed the Ansel Adams Gallery. Ted Orland becomes his photographic assistant until 1974.

1973

Adams begins his association with Little, Brown and Company, which becomes his sole authorized publisher.

1974

Takes his first trip to Europe and attends the Photography Festival in Arles, France. A major exhibition underwritten by his longtime friend David McAlpin, "Photographs by Ansel Adams," is initiated by the Metropolitan Museum of Art and later travels to Europe and Russia, through 1977. Parasol Press issues *Portfolio VI*, with ten prints in an edition of 110. Adams publishes *Singular Images* (Morgan &

Morgan) and *Images, 1923–1974* (Boston: New York Graphic Society [NYGS]). Andrea Gray becomes his executive assistant until 1980, and Alan Ross becomes his photographic assistant until 1979. In the spring, McAlpin organizes an exhibition at MoMA to display Adams' lesser-known work in portraiture. On July 7, Nancy Newhall dies.

1975

On January 28, President Gerald Ford requests a print of *Clearing Winter Storm*; Adams presents him with the print, as well as his outline of *A New Initiative for the National Parks*. Adams helps to found the Center for Creative Photography (CCP) at the University of Arizona, Tucson, where his archive is established. The Ansel Adams Publishing Rights Trust (AAPRT) is established. Adams stops taking individual print orders, effective at the end of the year, but the three thousand photographs requested by December 31 take him three years to print.

1976

Parasol Press issues *Portfolio VII*, with twelve images in an edition of 115. Adams returns to the Arles Photography Festival and photographs in Scotland, Switzerland, and France. He is elected Honorary Fellow of the Royal Photographic Society of Great Britain. He publishes *Photographs of the Southwest* (NYGS). Lectures in London, Tucson, Los Angeles, and San Diego. Attends the opening of an exhibition of his work at the Victoria and Albert Museum, London.

1977

Publishes *The Portfolios of Ansel Adams* (NYGS) and a facsimile reprint of the book *Taos Pueblo* (NYGS). With Virginia, he endows a curatorial fellowship at MoMA in honor of Beaumont and Nancy Newhall. The exhibition "Photographs of the Southwest, 1928–1968" is organized and circulated by the CCP. Adams begins a complete revision of his technical books, with the collaboration of Robert Baker.

1978

The Friends of Photography mounts an exhibition entitled "Ansel Adams: 50 Years of Portraits," with a catalogue by James Alinder (Carmel: Friends of Photography). Adams publishes *Polaroid Land Photography* (NYGS). He is elected honorary vice president of the Sierra Club.

1979

On September 3, Adams is the subject of a *Time* magazine cover story. The dramatic increase in sales of Adams' prints at auction and through photography dealers leads to a growing public interest in collecting photography. Adams' prints account for nearly half of the total dollar value of photography sales in the United States during the year. A major retrospective exhibition curated by John Szarkowski, "Ansel Adams and the West," is held at MoMA and then circulated in the United States. Adams publishes *Yosemite and the Range of Light* (NYGS). He begins printing his Museum Set, seventy-five prints representative of his life's work. He also starts writing his autobiography with Mary Alinder, who is employed as his chief of staff. John Sexton becomes his photographic assistant through 1982. Adams is invited to make official photographs of President Jimmy Carter and Vice President Walter Mondale for the National Portrait Gallery, the first time photographs rather than paintings are used for this purpose.

1980

On June 9, Adams receives the Presidential Medal of Freedom, the nation's highest civilian honor, from President Carter. Later that year, Carter signs the Alaska Lands Act, the last great wilderness preservation effort, in which Adams plays a key role. An exhibition, "Ansel Adams: Photographs of the American West," is organized by the Friends of Photography for the U.S. International Communications Agency (USICA) and circulated through 1983 in India, the Middle East, and Africa.

1981

Adams holds a final workshop in Yosemite, then transfers the workshop location to Carmel under the administration of the Friends of Photography. A biographical film, *Ansel Adams: Photographer*, is co-produced by Andrea Gray and John Huszar for FilmAmerica. A mural-size print of *Moonrise, Hernandez, New Mexico* sells for $71,500, a record price for a photograph.

1982

The exhibition "The Unknown Ansel Adams" is curated by Jim Alinder for the Friends of Photography in Carmel. Chris Rainier becomes Adams' photographic assistant until 1985.

1983

Adams publishes *Examples: The Making of 40 Photographs* (NYGS). He is the subject of an extensive interview in the May issue of *Playboy* magazine, in which he expresses his opposition to Ronald Reagan's policies. On June 30, he meets with President Reagan to discuss environmental concerns.

1984

Adams dies of heart failure in Monterey, California, on April 22, Easter Sunday, at the age of eighty-two. California senators Alan Cranston and Pete Wilson sponsor legislation to create an Ansel Adams Wilderness Area between Yosemite National Park and the John Muir Wilderness Area, which is approved by Congress. A memorial book, *Ansel Adams, 1902–1984*, is published by the Friends of Photography.

1985

Mount Ansel Adams, an 11,760-foot peak located at the head of the Lyell Fork of the Merced River on the southeast boundary of Yosemite National Park, is officially named on the first anniversary of Adams' death.

ENDNOTES

Unless otherwise noted, all quoted letters are in The Lane Collection.

ANSEL ADAMS:
SEEKING A CENTER FOR PHOTOGRAPHY

1. Adams to William H. Lane, October 7, 1974.

2. Ansel Adams, with Mary Street Alinder, *Ansel Adams: An Autobiography* (Boston: Little Brown, 1985), 371.

3. See Ruth Cowing, "Ansel Adams, 1902–1984," *Afterimage* 12 (Summer 1984): 6; and Stephen Robert Frankel, "Looking in Neglected Corners while Awaiting the Next Superstar," *Art News* 80 (April 1981): 98–99.

4. David L. Jacobs, "Blindness and Insight," *Afterimage* 13 (May 1986): 8.

5. Alfred Stieglitz was the self-proclaimed leader of the American pictorialist movement at the turn of the century. In 1902 he founded the movement's so-called Photo-Secession Group, which included photographers Edward Steichen, Gertrude Käsebier, Clarence H. White, and others. One of the goals of the pictorialists was to distance their work from that of the newly ubiquitous Kodak snapshooters of the day by emphasizing its handcrafted, one-of-a-kind aspects. The mostly amateur practitioners often chose aesthetic or symbolist subject matter, which they then printed on matte, textured papers and/or manipulated to give their photographs the appearance of fine prints or drawings. During the 1910s, Stieglitz became disillusioned with the excesses of pictorialism, and, under the influence of European modernism, African art, and the work of young photographers such as Paul Strand, he was converted to straight photography, with its sharp-focus, inherently photographic images of everyday subjects.

6. Andrea Gray [Stillman], *Ansel Adams: An American Place, 1936* (Tucson: Center for Creative Photography, University of Arizona, 1982), 13.

7. Tom Cooper and Paul Hill, "Interview: Ansel Adams," *Camera* (English edition) 55 (January 1976): 27.

8. In a letter to Paul Strand, written after his 1933 trip to New York, Adams wrote: "I am perplexed, amazed, and touched at the impact of [Stieglitz's] force on my own spirit. I would not believe before I met him that a man could be so psychically and emotionally powerful." Quoted in [Stillman], *Ansel Adams: An American Place*, 14.

9. Adams to Stieglitz, November 29, 1936, Yale Collection of American Literature, Beinecke Rare Book and Manuscript Library, Yale University.

10. Adams, *Autobiography*, 126: "Rather than say Stieglitz influenced me in my work, I would say he revealed me to myself."

11. Adams to Patsy English, November 21, 1936, quoted in [Stillman], *Ansel Adams: An American Place*, 24.

12. For an in-depth account of this exhibition, see [Stillman], *Ansel Adams: An American Place*. Although Stieglitz's earlier gallery "291" had begun primarily as a photography gallery, by the time he showed Adams' work at An American Place in late 1936, it had been four years since he had exhibited another photographer's work, in that case, his earlier protégé Paul Strand; see Mary Street Alinder, *Ansel Adams: A Biography* (New York: Henry Holt, 1996), 118.

13. Stieglitz apparently sold at least nine of Adams' prints over the course of the show, including *The White Tombstone* (about 1936), which went to David McAlpin for the then-unheard-of price of one hundred dollars. The *New York Times'* Howard DeVree, who had also reviewed Adams' 1933 show at Alma Reed's gallery, wrote (November 8, 1936): "A large selection of photographic work by Ansel Adams is being sponsored by Alfred Stieglitz till Nov. 20 at An American Place—and that is perhaps sufficient commentary on the caliber of the exhibition." Quoted in [Stillman], *Ansel Adams: An American Place*, 31.

14. Adams to Stieglitz, November 29, 1936, Beinecke, Yale University.

15. Adams to Stieglitz, December 22, 1936, Beinecke, Yale University.

16. Ansel Adams, "A Personal Credo," in Edwin Land, David H. McAlpin, Jon Holmes, and Ansel Adams, *Ansel Adams: Singular Images* (Boston: Little, Brown, 1974), unpaginated.

17. Alma Reed also exhibited contemporary and Latin American art, including the work of José Clemente Orozco, whom Adams photographed on Reed's porch in 1933. In addition, she gave László Moholy-Nagy his first one-man exhibition in the United States and showed the work of Edward Weston in 1930 and again in 1932.

18. Alinder, *Ansel Adams: A Biography*, 113.

19. Howard DeVree, "Other Shows," *New York Times*, November 19, 1933, quoted in Adams, *Autobiography*, 125.

20. Cooper and Hill, "Interview: Ansel Adams," 27; Adams discussed the fact that he was at the same time doing "portraits and advertising work" and went on to say: "One of my main jobs was doing catalogues for the [deYoung] Art Museum. Photographs of works of art. I also sold a few prints. I did assignments for 'Life,' 'Fortune' chiefly, and a lot of publicity for Yosemite Park." Only late in life was Adams able to live solely on his earnings from the sale of his personal work, and, as a result, over the years he had to do his share of photographing what he described as "table settings, copies of paintings, clothing catalogues, architecture, an automobile, a horse, a dog, people, reports, businesses, [and] wineries"; quoted in Victoria and David Sheff, "Playboy Interview: Ansel Adams," *Playboy* 30, no. 5 (April 1983): 82.

21. Adams to Stieglitz, June 22, 1933, Beinecke, Yale University.

22. [Stillman], *Ansel Adams: An American Place*, 15.

23. Adams to Stieglitz, October 9, 1933, Beinecke, Yale University.

24. Adams to Stieglitz, June 22, 1933, Beinecke, Yale University.

25. Stieglitz to Adams, June 28, 1933, Beinecke, Yale University.

26. Adams to Strand, September 12, 1933, quoted in Ansel Adams, *Ansel Adams: Letters and Images, 1916–1984*, ed. Mary Street Alinder and Andrea Gray Stillman (Boston: Little, Brown, 1988), 57.

27. Adams to Reed, June 22, 1933, 1933–34 exhibition file, Ansel Adams Archive (AAA), Center for Creative Photography (CCP), University of Arizona, Tucson.

28. Adams to Stieglitz, September 19, 1933, Beinecke, Yale University: "there is a starved group of intelligent people here who have sorely missed the most important phases of contemporary art. They cannot come to New York, for several reasons—time and money. Most of the galleries here have played "safe" economically, and have been totally devoid of imagination and a conception of a larger purpose. We have seen thousands of things brought here just to sell, and we are frankly tired of it. . . . If it were not for the large group of people here that hungers for something real and alive, I know I would take the attitude and content of the galleries as a barometer as far as the art situation was concerned. But I know it is otherwise; and I know that if the groups here can be given a chance this city will assume a very different complexion than it now has in the art world. . . . As for me and my generation—we are young and it will do us good to battle a little. I begin to understand what you have been up against; the Crusaders sought something mystically unattainable and bled and died in glorified destruction—but your spiritual Crusade has been more fortunate; Marin, O'Keeffe, Stieglitz exist—the struggle has been worth while."

29. Adams to Stieglitz, May 20, 1934, Beinecke, Yale University. Stieglitz replied to Adams (June 9, 1934, Beinecke, Yale University): "I frequently wondered how long you could manage a Gallery and photograph at the same time. Your letter therefore didn't come as a surprise.—Of course the experience is invaluable."

30. Adams to Stieglitz, July 6, 1933, Beinecke, Yale University.

31. Several of Adams' West Coast contemporaries were in the "Film und Foto" exhibition, including eighteen-year-old Brett Weston, whose father was one of the organizers of the American section of the show.

32. Adams wrote a series of *Fortnightly* reviews of exhibitions held at the de Young Museum in San Francisco, on Eugène Atget (November 6, 1931), Edward Weston (December 18, 1931), and Imogen Cunningham (February 12, 1932). He also penned a number of technical articles for *Camera Craft*, including "An Exposition of My Photographic Technique" (January 1934), "Landscape" (February 1934), "Portraiture" (March 1934), "Applied Photography" (April 1934), and "Winter Photography" (January 1935).

33. Anne Hammond, *Ansel Adams: Divine Performance* (New Haven: Yale University Press, 2002), 72–73.

34. Ansel Adams, "The New Photography," in C. Geoffrey Holme, ed., *Modern Photography, 1934–35: The Studio Annual of Camera Art* (London and New York: Studio Limited, 1935), 9–18.

35. Adams, "The New Photography," 12. Willard Van Dyke, "Group f/64," *Scribner's Magazine* (March 1938): 55, quoted in Anne Hammond, "Ansel Adams and Objectivism: Making a Photograph with Group f/64," *History of Photography* 22, no. 2 (Summer 1998): 175n101.

36. Ansel Adams, *Conversations with Ansel Adams*, oral history interviews conducted by Ruth Teiser and Catherine Harroun, Brancroft Library Regional Oral History Office, in 1972, 1974, and 1975 (Berkeley: Regents of the University of California, 1978), 129. Adams described this as "the first book of any consequence in the instructional sense," and he went on to state: "I think my contribution, if there is one . . . is that, as far as I know, I'm the first one that codified technique in relation to aesthetics," 137.

37. John Szarkowski, *Ansel Adams at 100* (Boston: Little, Brown, 2001), 35.

38. As late as April 18, 1938, Adams was still echoing this idea in a letter to Stieglitz when he wrote: "If you have not given me the awareness of anything but a standard, I would be eternally grateful. It is up to me, and to the others that have so greatly benefited through your influence to pass on the message. The woods are thicker these days, but we will get through somehow." Beinecke, Yale University.

39. The Basic Photo series consists of five books: *Camera and Lens* (1948), *The Negative* (1948), *The Print* (1950), *Natural Light Photography* (1952), and *Artificial Light Photography* (1956);

and the new and revised Ansel Adams Photography series (with Robert Baker) includes *The Camera* (1980), *The Negative* (1981), and *The Print* (1983).

40. For an insightful discussion of Weston's and Adams' differing thoughts on personal expression and the final print, see Hammond, "Ansel Adams and Objectivism," 175.

41. Thanks in part to books on him—like Heinrich Schwarz, *David Octavius Hill: Master of Photography* (New York: Viking, 1931)—Hill had become something of a "poster child" for the straight photography movement by the 1930s. Alvin Langdon Coburn reprinted a number of Hill's photographs from his original negatives, and these prints then appeared in the subsequent exhibitions at the Albright, MoMA, and the "Pageant of Photography." See also Adams' own piece on the "Pageant of Photography" show, "Photo Pageant," *Art Digest* (July 1, 1940): 14, in which he describes Hill's photographs as representing "the earliest, and as yet unequalled, important creative work with the camera."

42. Adams to Stieglitz, May 16, 1935, Beinecke, Yale University.

43. Ansel Adams, *Making a Photograph: An Introduction to Photography* (London: Studio Limited, 1935), 14.

44. Adams to McAlpin, February 14, 1939, AAA, CCP.

45. Newhall to Adams, July 13, 1960, quoted in Adams, *Letters and Images, 1916–1984*, 264.

46. Beaumont Newhall, "Review of *Making a Photograph: An Introduction to Photography* by Ansel Adams," *American Magazine of Art* 28, no. 8 (August 1935): 508, 512; Adams, *Autobiography*, 193.

47. Stieglitz to Adams, May 13, 1935, Beinecke, Yale University.

48. Adams to Stieglitz, May 16, 1935, Beinecke, Yale University.

49. Adams, *Autobiography*, 196; and Adams, *Conversations*, 395: "Boy, that was an awful hard job, but it was a contribution, and that's what brought, for the first time, photography in many of its approaches, to the attention of the people in the West. . . . It was a very good show. It did bring to San Francisco, at least, an awareness of photography it had never had before." See also Ansel Adams, "The Pageant of Photography," *Camera Craft* 47, no. 9 (September 1940): 437–45.

50. Adams to Stieglitz, April 13, 1940, Beinecke, Yale University; Adams claimed to have "panned" the 1939 exhibition and "bemoaned the fact that there was no decent photographic show there."

51. Adams, *Conversations*, 387.

52. Adams to McAlpin, September 9, 1940, AAA, CCP; looking back on the undertaking from the perspective of a few months, Adams recalled it as being very hard work: "Not to boast—but it was a real job!!"

53. Adams, *Autobiography*, 196.

54. Adams, *Conversations*, 395–98; Adams to McAlpin, September 9, 1940, AAA, CCP: "I figured it out—if all the photographic exhibits were given at one time (you see, two galleries change every two weeks, one every three weeks), it would require nearly thirty galleries of about 100 feet of wall space to carry it."

55. Adams to Stieglitz, April 13, 1940, Beinecke, Yale University; Adams went on to reassure his mentor that he would "choose an empty gallery rather than a poorly filled one."

56. The men listed under the heading of contemporary California photographers included Will Connell, Fred Archer, and Edgar Bissantz; and the women, Imogen Cunningham, Sonya Noskowiak, and Alma Lavenson.

57. Adams, "Photo Pageant," 15; Tom White, "Pictures at Pacific Fair: Photographers May Find Many Subjects and Numerous Camera Exhibitions," *New York Times*, June 30, 1940, 125; the anonymous preview, "A Pageant of Photography: Palace of Fine Arts, Golden Gate International Exposition," in *Camera Craft* 47, no. 6 (June 1940): 295, went on to say: "Because of [Adams'] persistent efforts, Photography will this year occupy its rightful place among the art exhibits at the San Francisco Fair. Last year photography had no place among the art exhibits at either fair, but this year, in San Francisco at least, it comes into its own. Advance plans indicate that the Pageant of Photography will rank among the finest photographic exhibits ever held." Adams must have been especially pleased that photography at the 1940 fair was no longer marginalized, as it had been at the Panama Pacific International Exposition of 1915, which as a thirteen-year-old he had attended almost daily, thanks to his father's purchase of a yearlong pass for him in lieu of normal schooling; there it was shown in the industry and technology building rather than with the other fine arts.

58. McAlpin to Adams, April 22, 1940, AAA, CCP.

59. Adams to McAlpin, May 14, 1940, AAA, CCP.

60. Adams to Stieglitz, May 27, 1940, Beinecke, Yale University.

61. Adams, *Conversations*, 114.

62. Adams, "Introduction," *A Pageant of Photography* (San Francisco: Golden Gate International Exposition, 1940), unpaginated [5].

63. Adams to Stieglitz, May 23, 1940, Beinecke, Yale University.

64. See Anne Hammond's chapter "Objective Photography," in *Ansel Adams: Divine Performance*, 58–79.

65. Adams, "Introduction," *A Pageant of Photography*, [5, 7].

66. Adams, *A Pageant of Photography*, [6]. Assembling this material for the "Pageant of Photography" show may, in turn, have inspired Adams' MoMA exhibition, "Photographs of the Civil War and the American Frontier," which he cocurated with Beaumont Newhall in 1942. See also Rebecca Senf, "Ansel Adams in the American Southwest," in this volume, p. 53, for a discussion of his "re-photographing" O'Sullivan's famous image in 1941.

67. Stieglitz to Adams, May 20, 1940, Beinecke, Yale University: "You know, dear Adams, I do not cave in readily. And I do not intend to cave in if I can help it now. But I do want you to feel that I am with you in what you are endeavoring to do even though I seem not to be helping you concretely. You undoubtedly have arranged a grand show."

68. The dedication reads: "To Alfred Stieglitz, who has devoted his strength and spirit to the advancement of photography." The portrait of Stieglitz by Cunningham was made six years earlier, in 1934; in it, Stieglitz already has the look of an elder statesman, and in the catalogue he appears opposite a similarly dour portrait of Abraham Lincoln by Alexander Gardner.

69. Adams to McAlpin, May 14, 1940, AAA, CCP; earlier in the same letter, Adams wrote in a similar vein: "Wife, two kids, old folks. My photography is the means of support. I can't be aloof—I would starve to death if I operated as Stieglitz does."

70. *Monolith* is misdated 1928, *Golden Gate* is misdated 1935, and *Family Portrait*, which refers to the group portrait of the Tresidder family taken at the Ahwahnee Hotel in Yosemite, is misdated 1937. The portrait cannot date from that year, because it was

featured in Adams' American Place exhibition in 1936. The subject of the folding screen is described in the catalogue simply as "wheels," and the decorative overmantel, "horn and wheel." Neither is known to survive, but the screen image is almost certainly the photograph of wooden wagon wheels reproduced as the opening illustration in Adams' essay "Photo-Murals," in *U.S. Camera* 1, no. 12 (November 1940): 52.

71. Quoted in Adams, *Autobiography*, 198.

72. Adams, *Conversations*, 391–92. He describes the device as having been a stereoscopic polarizing viewing apparatus created in collaboration with Edwin Land of Polaroid, in which one could examine 11 x 14 (positive) transparencies of works of art by Clarence Kennedy.

73. Adams to Stieglitz, May 27, 1940, Beinecke, Yale University.

74. Adams, *Autobiography*, 309–10; Adams also often mentioned how important his 1930 meeting in Taos with painter John Marin had been and how the older man's generous conversations about art with the budding photographer later inspired Adams to "pass it on" to others.

75. Ansel Adams, "Workshop Idea in Photography," *Aperture* 9, no. 4 (1961): 162.

76. Adams, *Autobiography*, 309. Adams wrote in his "Editorial" in the *Journal of Aesthetics and Art Criticism* 39, no. 3 (Spring 1981), 247: "Photography has been notoriously weak in the whole area of teaching. The individual isn't brought out. And, if the individuality of the student is stressed, he is not often given the technique to manage it."

77. Adams to McAlpin, July 5, 1940: "The photographic Forum in Yosemite proved very successful from a teaching point of view, and encourages me along the lines of pedagogic enterprise. But I am fully aware that, whatever I do, I must not put myself in the position of neglecting my own creative work."

78. In his autobiography he wrote that he began there in 1940, but most other sources agree that his tenure at the Art Center lasted from the late fall of 1942 through March 1943; Adams apparently returned for another stint of only a few weeks in August 1945.

79. The Art Center "Faculty" Web site, under www.artcenter.edu (accessed on March 13, 2005).

80. Adams to Nancy Newhall, n.d. [1943], quoted in Adams, *Letters and Images, 1916–1984*, 143.

81. Adams, *Autobiography*, 313–15.

82. For a detailed discussion of this subject, see Ira Latour, "Ansel Adams, the Zone System and the California School of Fine Arts," *History of Photography* 22, no. 2 (Summer 1998): 147–54; and Ira Latour, "The Grove of Akademus," *Photo Metro* 14 (December 1996): 42–43.

83. Adams to McAlpin, November 17, 1942, AAA, CCP; in a letter to Stieglitz (August 22, 1943), Adams reiterated this idea: "I have pulled endless strings to get into some useful branch of the service—but all to no avail. I am good at teaching, have a simplified technical approach that I know would be useful to the military" (Beinecke, Yale University).

84. Adams to Nancy Newhall, September 18, 1945, quoted in Latour, "Ansel Adams, the Zone System," 148.

85. Latour, "Ansel Adams, the Zone System," 148.

86. Deborah Klochko, "The Legacy of Minor White: California School of Fine Arts, the Exhibition *Perceptions*," in Susan Herzig and Paul Hertzmann, *Ten Photographers*, 1946–54 (San Francisco: Paul M. Hertzmann, 2004), 41. Klochko quotes from the minutes of the September 1934 CSFA board meeting: "Mr. Ansel Adams instructor, two periods a week, salary $60.00 a month. Camera and apparatus to be supplied by Mr. Adams and the students, the Association to allow $200.00 to furnish a dark-room and installation. The suggestion was laid on the table for further consideration."

87. Adams to Nancy Newhall, October 4, 1945, quoted in Latour, "Ansel Adams, the Zone System," 147.

88. Susan Landauer, *The San Francisco School of Abstract Expressionism* (Berkeley: University of California Press, 1996), 35–37. Adams described some of the difficulties of teaching photography in an art school setting, in *Conversations* (108): "We had a wonderful department. . . . But whenever we tried to get a gallery to do something with our work, the painters were there first. Maybe the artists weren't really afraid of us. They were just *jealous* of time, space, and money"; and in his *Autobiography* (317): "The painters, sculptors, printmakers, and ceramicists arose in wrath and protest; photography is *not* an art, they claimed, and had no place in an art school."

89. According to Sandra Phillips, in her introduction to Szarkowski, *Ansel Adams at 100* (12), the Columbia Foundation funds were given with the proviso that Adams be the one to head the CSFA program.

90. Adams, *Autobiography*, 316–17.

91. Minor White, "A Unique Experience in Teaching Photography," *Aperture* 4, no. 4 (1956): 151, 156.

92. Adams to McAlpin, September 18, 1945, AAA, CCP.

93. See Van Deren Coke, "The Art of Photography in College Teaching," *College Art Journal* 19, no. 4 (Summer 1960): 333–34; and Adams to McAlpin, September 18, 1945: "Every school in the country is somewhat of a racket insofar as they skip basic things and teach a lot of people to be 'shutter parrots,' falsely convincing them that with only a year or so of not too careful training they can become 'professionals'" (AAA, CCP).

94. In his letter to McAlpin, September 18, 1945, Adams wrote, explaining his proposed curriculum: "The plan I have visualized is to establish a photography department wherein basic photography will be stressed, chiefly from the expressive point of view. Professional applications will not be touched until the second or third year."

95. See Alinder, *Ansel Adams: A Biography*, 208; and "The Columbia Foundation Grant for the Establishment of the Photography Department, California School of Fine Arts," Report to the President, San Francisco Art Association, March 25, 1948, AAA, CCP.

96. Adams to Nancy Newhall, September 2, 1945, quoted in Latour, "Ansel Adams, the Zone System," 148. He also wrote to David McAlpin (September 18, 1945) that he was relieved to be leaving the Art Center once again, but that he was glad to have had "a chance to prove some teaching theories" during his short tenure there.

97. Adams to McAlpin, September 18, 1945; and Adams, "Report on the Proposed Department of Photography, California School of Fine Arts," to the Board of Trustees, May 1945, CSFA file, AAA, CCP. San Francisco was named as the first conference site of the United Nations in the spring of 1945, and many hoped that this international attention would help propel the city into the forefront of American culture as well as politics; see also Latour, "Ansel Adams, the Zone System," 151.

98. Latour, "Ansel Adams, the Zone System," 149–51. Sandra Phillips, in Szarkowski, *Ansel Adams at 100* (11–12), discusses the move toward collecting photography under Grace Morley at the San Francisco Museum during this period, and in his letter to McAlpin, September 18, 1945, Adams

recounts some of his aspirations for the school's program: "If this department of photography at the California School of Fine Arts comes to pass, it might be a nucleus for constructive endeavor in several directions. The school is affiliated with the University of California and degrees could be given in photography. . . . While such extreme academic development is not necessary to creative work, it would do a tremendous amount to awaken the public to [the] potential and dignity of photography."

99. Adams, "The Profession of Photography," *Aperture* 1, no. 3 (1952): 11.

100. Adams, *Conversations*, 455: "I'm very fond of Minor: he's really a remarkable person. I get mad at him, in a genteel way, and he gets mad at me ditto, but it's kind of an affectionate madness."

101. Minor White, "A Unique Experience in Teaching Photography," 150, 151.

102. In 1976 Adams recalled: "I worked like a dog, but we had a good staff. I was supposed to teach three mornings a week and ended up teaching 8 days a week! You have to admit teaching is not casual! We turned out some very fine people." See Cooper and Hill, "Interview," 38.

103. See Sandra Phillips in Szarkowski, *Ansel Adams at 100*, 9. As early as 1934, Adams had applied to the Guggenheim for support to research and write a book on the history of photography and its relationship to the development of American art, but he had been turned down (a full three years before Edward Weston had applied for and received the first Guggenheim granted to a photographer and Beaumont Newhall had written the first real history of the medium). His second application, that same year, was for a project entitled "A Photographic Record of the 'Pioneer' Architecture of the Pacific Coast," and it too was turned down. Alinder, *Ansel Adams: A Biography*, 208.

104. See Rebecca Senf, "Ansel Adams in the American Southwest," in this volume, for a discussion of Adams' national parks mural project and its continuation during his Guggenheim grant (66–70).

105. Quoted in Adams, *Autobiography*, 317.

106. Adams to McAlpin, "Saturday night" (probably August 1945), AAA, CCP.

107. The idea of naming the University of Arizona program the Center for Creative Photography is particularly telling, in light of a letter Adams wrote to McAlpin regarding what ultimately might happen to Stieglitz's work at the time of his death: "I do have a feeling that Beaumont and Nancy, and our small group will in some way combine our energies

towards a very active center for creative photography." Adams to McAlpin, "Saturday night" (probably August 1945, AAA, CCP).

ANSEL ADAMS IN THE AMERICAN SOUTHWEST

I am indebted to the research of many Adams scholars who have preceded me, but I want to give special thanks to Anne Hammond, Jonathan Spaulding, and Mary Street Alinder. In addition, I offer my deep appreciation to Kate Palmer, who graciously read this manuscript and offered insightful comments.

1. The epigraph is from Nancy Newhall, *Ansel Adams: The Eloquent Light* (Millerton, NY: Aperture, 1980), 60.

2. Ansel Adams, *Ansel Adams: An Autobiography* (Boston: Little, Brown, 1985), 329, and Ansel Adams, *Photographs of the Southwest* (Boston: New York Graphic Society, 1976), viii.

3. Adams, *Photographs of the Southwest*, viii.

4. Ansel Adams to Virginia Adams, [November 1928], quoted in Ansel Adams, *The Grand Canyon and the Southwest* (Boston: Little, Brown, 2000), 91. In the same letter, Adams mentioned that Mary Austin had offered to sell them a "good size lot" near her home, on which they could build "a handsome adobe house" for about two thousand dollars, an indication that Adams' desire to live in New Mexico dates from the late 1920s. Adams' comment about no one doing "pictorial photography on a large scale" referred not to the pictorialist style but to the more generic use of the term signifying creative photography, and by "large scale," Adams meant in great number, not large prints.

5. Paula Richardson Fleming and Judith Luskey, *The North American Indians in Early Photographs* (London: Calmann and King, 1986), 214, 220. Edward S. Curtis, *The North American Indian: The Complete Portfolios* (Cologne: Taschen, 1997), 5.

6. Martha Sandweiss, *Laura Gilpin: An Enduring Grace* (Fort Worth, TX: Amon Carter Museum, 1986), 36–50, and Laura Gilpin, *Laura Gilpin Retrospective: An Exhibition of Photographs by Laura Gilpin Done between 1910 and 1974* (Santa Fe: Museum of Fine Arts, Museum of New Mexico, 1974), 6.

7. Adams, *Autobiography*, 87.

8. In writing about Bertha Pope, Ansel Adams and Nancy Newhall variously referred to her as Bertha Pope, Bertha Pope Damon, and Bertha Damon. She was married to Arthur Upham Pope around 1905, but was divorced from him by 1920, when he married Phyllis Ackerman. In 1922 she edited *The Letters of Ambrose Bierce* as Bertha Clark Pope, and by 1938 she had published her reminiscences, *Grandma Called It Carnal*, as Bertha Clark Damon.

9. Adams, *Autobiography*, 89.

10. After his initial childhood visit to Yosemite with his family in 1916, Adams returned to the valley every year of his life, including for many extended stays and periods of residence.

11. Adams, *Autobiography*, 87.

12. Mary Street Alinder, *Ansel Adams: A Biography* (New York: Henry Holt, 1996), 68.

13. Van Deren Coke, *Taos and Santa Fe: The Artist's Environment, 1882–1942* (Albuquerque: University of New Mexico Press, 1963), 9. Painters such as Bert G. Phillips and Ernest L. Blumenschein were early year-round settlers in northern New Mexico, and other artists such as Robert Henri, Marsden Hartley, and John Sloan came for shorter durations.

14. Adams to Bender, [November 1928], quoted in Adams, *Grand Canyon*, 93.

15. Adams to Applegate, n.d., Ansel Adams Archive (AAA), Center for Creative Photography (CCP), at the University of Arizona, in Tucson.

16. Adams to Applegate, February 27, 1929, Mary Austin Collection, Huntington Library, San Marino, California. All items from the Huntington Library are reproduced by permission of the Huntington Library, San Marino, California.

17. Applegate to Adams, August 30, 1929, AAA, CCP.

18. Austin to Adams, April 9, 1930, AAA, CCP.

19. Adams to Austin, August 28, 1929, Mary Austin Collection, Huntington Library.

20. Theresa Salazar, "Ansel Adams and Spanish Colonial Arts," *History of Photography* 22, no. 2 (Summer 1998): 164, 166. In her thorough and illuminating article on this project, Salazar discussed in great detail the ways in which Adams approached these photographic subjects, as well as his concern for print quality, were they ever to be reproduced.

21. Salazar, "Ansel Adams and Spanish Colonial Arts," 162–63.

22. Ibid., 163.

23. Ibid.

24. Adams to Harold Jones, November 17, 1967, AAA, CCP.

25. Applegate to Adams, December 1, 1929, and October 15, 1930, AAA, CCP; "Southwestern American Colonial Interior and Fabrics," *Ladies' Home Journal* (December 1930): 58. Neither Adams nor Applegate is credited anywhere in *Ladies' Home Journal*, as Applegate sent the story and photographs under the name of Spanish Arts. Applegate also mentioned working on an article in *Survey Graphic* magazine, but no payment appears to have been sent (Applegate to Adams, September 9, 1929, and December 1, 1929, AAA, CCP).

26. Bainbridge Bunting, *John Gaw Meem: Southwestern Architect* (Albuquerque: University of New Mexico Press, 1983), illustrations on 40, 42–43, 49, 75–76, 79, 132–33, 142. Laura Gilpin also did architectural photography for Meem.

27. Anne Hammond, "Ansel Adams and Mary Austin, Taos Pueblo (1930)," *History of Photography* 23, no. 4 (Winter 1999): 384.

28. Ficke to Adams, May 10, 1928, AAA, CCP; seven prints are listed in the Parmelian Print Log, AAA, CCP. One print of an Adams portrait of Ficke (88.10.3) can be found in the Art Collection at the Huntington Library.

29. Ansel Adams to Virginia Adams, April 4, 1928, quoted in Adams, *Grand Canyon*, 89; Ansel Adams to Virginia Adams, [November 1928], quoted in Adams, *Grand Canyon*, 94.

30. Adams to Austin, July 10, 1929, Mary Austin Collection, Huntington Library.

31. Ibid.

32. Six vintage prints of Indian dance subjects (88.10.4, 88.10.5, 88.10.6, 88.10.7, 88.10.15, 88.10.18) are in the Art Collection at the Huntington Library, and three vintage prints exist in The Lane Collection.

33. Ansel Adams, *Conversations with Ansel Adams*, oral history interviews conducted by Ruth Teiser and Catherine Harroun, Brancroft Library Regional Oral History Office, in 1972, 1974, and 1975 (Berkeley: Regents of the University of California, 1978), 189.

34. Leah Dilworth, *Imagining Indians in the Southwest: Persistent Visions of a Primitive Past* (Washington, DC: Smithsonian Institution Press, 1996), 17.

35. Ibid., 91–92.

36. Ibid., 17–18; and Keith L. Bryant Jr., "The Origins and Development of the Santa Fe Railway Collection of Western Art," in *Standing Rainbows: Railroad Promotion of Art, the West and Its Native People* (Topeka, KS: Kansas State Historical Society, 1981), unpaginated [2, 4]. The restaurants were part of the Fred Harvey Company and not owned by the ATSF, but the two companies operated in close cooperation.

37. Dilworth, *Imagining Indians*, 18.

38. Adams to Bender, [November 1928], quoted in Adams, *Grand Canyon*, 93.

39. Adams to Austin, August 21 [1929?], Mary Austin Collection, Huntington Library.

40. The Section of Photography was established in 1896 within the Division of Graphic Arts, which, in the late 1920s, was part of the Department of Arts and Industries. Olmstead was the curator of the photography section from 1920 to 1946. James A. Steed, "Finding Aids to Official Records of the Smithsonian Institution, Record Unit 206, National Museum of History and Technology, Division of Graphic Arts and Photography, Records, 1882–1969," Smithsonian Institution Archives, http://www.si.edu/archives/archives/findingaids/FARU0206.htm (accessed December 22, 2004).

41. Bryant to Olmstead, November 19, 1930, AAA, CCP.

42. Olmstead to Adams, November 20, 1930, AAA, CCP.

43. Adams to Olmstead, November 26, 1930, AAA, CCP.

44. The checklist for a large exhibition held at Mills College from January 29 to March 1, 1933, features a section titled "New Mexico Series," and although it includes four photographs referred to as "New Mexican Colonial Types" and many architectural views made in 1928 and 1929, no Indian dance pictures are listed at all. It would appear that these photographs were first exhibited again in Nancy Newhall's massive Adams retrospective in 1963, "Ansel Adams: The Eloquent Light," where three dance pictures appeared in her "1923–1930 Pictorialism" section. See the files on Mills College and "Eloquent Light" exhibitions, AAA, CCP. For Adams, straight photography meant the Group f/64 style: unmanipulated, large-format negatives, made with sharp focus and great depth of field, and then printed on glossy papers to retain the exquisite detail and texture such negatives could produce.

45. Anne Hammond, *Ansel Adams: Divine Performance* (New Haven: Yale University Press, 2002), 16.

46. Albert Sperisen, "The Book Club Library and Recent Acquisitions," *The Book Club of California Quarterly News-letter* 34, no. 3 (Summer 1969): 61. Referring to the process of sensitizing the printing paper for the photographic illustrations in *Taos*, this book collectors' newsletter reads, "this production was the first of its kind in fine bookmaking. Economically, this *tour de force* could never again be duplicated."

47. Hammond, "Ansel Adams and Mary Austin," 384.

48. After marrying Tony Lujan, Mabel Dodge decided to spell her last name with an *h*, rather than a *j*, to aid her friends with the correct pronunciation. Adams, *Autobiography,* 90–91.

49. Hammond, "Ansel Adams and Mary Austin," 386.

50. Adams to Austin, February 23, 1930, Mary Austin Collection, Huntington Library. Adams had also sold his earlier fine art portfolio *Parmelian Prints of the High Sierras* by subscription. This method, where an announcement of the pending publication was sent to prospective buyers, helped ensure that all the limited-edition copies were bought. It also sometimes allowed for the publisher (or, in this case, Adams) to collect some of the money ahead of the printing, to offset the expenses incurred.

51. Adams to Austin, April 4, 1930, Mary Austin Collection, Huntington Library.

52. Austin to Adams, April 9, 1930, AAA, CCP.

53. Adams to Austin, April 4, 1930, Mary Austin Collection, Huntington Library.

54. Austin to Adams, March 13, 1931, AAA, CCP.

55. Adams, *Conversations*, 188, 199.

56. Adams, *Autobiography*, 109.

57. For a discussion of Strand's impact on Adams, see William A. Turnage, "An Introduction," in Adams, *Grand Canyon*, 7–8. See also Alinder, *Ansel Adams: A Biography*, 75–76.

58. Adams to Stieglitz, September 10, 1938, quoted in Ansel Adams, *Ansel Adams: Letters and Images, 1916–1984*, ed. Mary Street Alinder and Andrea Gray Stillman (Boston: Little, Brown, 1988), 108.

59. Laurie Lisle, *Portrait of an Artist: A Biography of Georgia O'Keeffe* (Albuquerque: University of New Mexico, 1986), 177.

60. Regarding late-night parties, see Ansel Adams, *Conversations*, 162–63. For discussion of visiting New Mexico towns with Applegate, see Ansel Adams to Virginia Adams, November 1929, quoted in Adams, *Grand Canyon*, 91. For mention of Indian dances with Ella Young, see Adams to Bender, March 30, 1929, quoted in Adams, *Grand Canyon*, 98.

61. Adams, *Autobiography*, 309–10.

62. Lisle, *Portrait of an Artist*, 180.

63. Ibid., 185.

64. Ibid., 218–20.

65. Adams to McAlpin, August 12, 1937, AAA, CCP.

66. Adams to Patsy English, AAA, CCP, cited in Alinder, *Ansel Adams: A Biography*, 145n37.

67. Adams, *Autobiography*, 224–25. Based on related photographs from the O'Keeffe-Adams trip in the Sarah Sage McAlpin Collection, additional Lane Collection photographs can be identified as having been made in New Mexico during Adams' 1937 sojourn, including *Adobe Church, Hernandez, New Mexico*; *White Cross and Church, Coyote, New Mexico*; and *The Enchanted Mesa, near Acoma Pueblo, New Mexico*.

68. Adams to Stieglitz, September 21, 1937, quoted in Adams, *Letters and Images, 1916–1984*, 98.

69. Jim Keogh, "Fitchburg Exhibit Captures Ansel Adams on the Road," *Princeton News*, http://princeton.thelandmark.com/story.php3?story=4381 (accessed November 30, 2004).

70. Printed sources that discuss Adams and O'Keeffe's southwestern travels are not in agreement on the various stops along their route. Stephen Jareckie's exhibition checklist for "Adams and O'Keeffe on the Road," Fitchburg Art Museum, September 29, 2002–January 12, 2003, lists photographs Adams made during the road trip, including those at the Laguna Pueblo; Inscription Rock; Walpi Mesa (Hopi Nation); Ganado, Arizona (Navajo Nation); Monument Valley; Canyon de Chelly; the Grand Canyon; and Silverton and Dolores River Valley in Colorado. Based on their inclusion in other printed sources and their proximity to places where Adams photographed, Zuni Pueblo, Ouray, Colorado, and Mesa Verde have also been listed with the itinerary.

71. Alinder, *Ansel Adams: A Biography*, 145.

72. Adams to Stieglitz, September 21, 1937, quoted in Adams, *Grand Canyon*, 107–8.

73. Ansel Adams, *Examples: The Making of 40 Photographs* (Boston: Little, Brown, 1983), 156–57.

74. Adams to McAlpin, October 16, 1937, AAA, CCP.

75. Adams to McAlpin, November 25, 1937, AAA, CCP.

76. Jonathan Spaulding, *Ansel Adams and the American Landscape: A Biography* (Berkeley: University of California Press, 1995), 130–31. For further discussion on the Kings River Canyon and issues concerning its status under the National Park or Forest Services, see Tom Turner, *Sierra Club: 100 Years of Protecting Nature* (New York: Harry N. Abrams, 1991), 123–25.

77. See Karen Haas's text "Japanese-style Folding Screens" in this volume (p. 141).

78. Demaray to Adams, January 10, 1939, quoted in Spaulding, *Ansel Adams and the American Landscape*, 169.

79. The current Department of Interior building was dedicated by President Franklin D. Roosevelt on April 16, 1936. Robert M. Utley and Barry Mackintosh, The Department of Everything Else: Twentieth Century Headliners and Highlights, National Park Service, http://www.cr.nps.gov/history/online_books /utley-mackintosh/interior13.htm (accessed December 17, 2004).

80. Alice Gray, *Ansel Adams: The National Park Service Photographs* (New York: Abbeville Press, 1995), 7.

81. Ibid., 7–8.

82. Document entitled "Statement of Time Devoted to Photo Mural Project Department of Interior," AAA, CCP.

83. The precise date that Farquhar gave the album to Adams is contested. In her *Divine Performance*, Anne Hammond mentioned 1932, whereas Mary Street Alinder, in her *Biography*, wrote that Adams had only recently received the album when he lent it to MoMA in 1937. Hammond, *Divine Performance*, 160n10; Alinder, *Ansel Adams: A Biography*, 138. Regarding the makeup of the Wheeler album, see George M. Wheeler, *Wheeler's Photographic Survey of the American West, 1871–1873* (New York: Dover Publications, 1983), v. The photographs made during the 1871 and 1873 seasons were by Timothy O'Sullivan, and those from the 1872 season were by William Bell.

84. Adams to Newhall, 1937. Published in Ansel Adams' "Appreciation," in Beaumont Newhall and Nancy Newhall, *T. H. O'Sullivan: Photographer* (New York: George Eastman House, 1966), unpaginated.

85. In 1941 Adams donated the Wheeler album to MoMA's photography department, which he helped found in 1940.

86. Adams, *Conversations*, 144.

87. Adams, *Examples*, 129.

88. Adams, *Letters and Images, 1916–1984*, 132.

89. Ansel Adams, *Camera and Lens* (New York: Morgan and Lester, 1948), 18; Ansel Adams, *These We Inherit: The Parklands of America* (San Francisco: Sierra Club, 1962), number 36; Adams, *Photographs of the Southwest*, 31; and Adams, *Examples*, 128.

90. Andrea Gray [Stillman], *Ansel Adams: An American Place, 1936* (Tucson, AZ: Center for Creative Photography, 1982), 20.

91. Sean Callahan, "Countdown to Moonrise," *American Photographer* 5, no. 1 (January 1981): 30–31.

92. Alinder, *Ansel Adams: A Biography*, 199–200.

93. Adams to Assistant Secretary E. K. Burlew, December 28, 1941, quoted in Gray, *National Park Service Photographs*, 11.

94. Ansel Adams, *My Camera in the National Parks* (Yosemite National Park: Virginia Adams; Boston: Houghton Mifflin, 1950).

95. Adams, "A Personal Statement," in *My Camera in the National Parks*, unpaginated.

96. Adams' first publication in the pages of *Arizona Highways* occurred when Raymond Carlson printed one of his color photographs of Monument Valley as a two-page spread in the March 1946 issue. Richard Maack, "Out of the Dust: Rarely Seen Photographs by Ansel Adams," *Arizona Highways* 81, no. 4 (April 2005): 9.

97. Adams to Carlson, November 8, 1951, AAA, CCP.

98. Color was of special significance to Carlson, as *Arizona Highways* was making its mark in the publishing world with its full-color photographic spreads. As current *Arizona Highways* photo editor Richard Maack wrote, "By 1946, *Arizona Highways* had a growing reputation for its work in published color photography, particularly photographs of the spectacular Arizona landscape. In December of that year, *Arizona Highways* made publishing history by producing the nation's first all-color consumer magazine." Maack, "Out of the Dust," 11.

99. Adams to Carlson, November 8, 1951, AAA, CCP.

100. Carlson to Adams, November 16, 1951, AAA, CCP.

101. Adams to Carlson, November 8, 1951, AAA, CCP.

102. Ansel Adams and Nancy Newhall, "Canyon de Chelly National Monument, Arizona," *Arizona Highways* 28, no. 6 (June 1952): 18–27.

103. Ansel Adams and Nancy Newhall, "Sunset Crater National Monument," *Arizona Highways* 28, no. 7 (July 1952): 2–5, 34–35; Ansel Adams and Nancy Newhall, "The Shell of Tumacacori," *Arizona Highways* 28, no. 11 (November 1952): 4–13.

104. Ansel Adams and Nancy Newhall, "Death Valley," *Arizona Highways* 29, no. 10 (October 1953): 16–35; Ansel Adams and Nancy Newhall, "Organ Pipe Cactus National Monument," *Arizona Highways* 30, no. 1 (January 1954): 8–17; Ansel Adams and Nancy Newhall, "Mission San Xavier del Bac," *Arizona Highways* 30, no. 4 (April 1954): 12–35.

105. Ansel Adams and Nancy Newhall, "Mary Austin's Country," *Arizona Highways* 44, no. 4 (April 1968): 2–9.

106. Ansel Adams and Nancy Newhall, *Mission San Xavier del Bac* (San Francisco: 5 Associates, 1954), and Ansel Adams and Nancy Newhall, *Death Valley* (San Francisco: 5 Associates, 1954).

107. Raymond Carlson, "Up and Down Country," *Arizona Highways* 28, no. 6 (June 1952): 1.

108. Adams and Newhall, "Canyon de Chelly National Monument," 24.

109. Adams, *Photographs of the Southwest*, 8.

110. It appears that Adams made at least four trips to Death Valley, including his first trip for the national parks project in 1941; two in 1947—one on his own early in the year and then another with Nancy and Beaumont Newhall in May and June; and a return trip in 1948, when he made his famous *Sand Dunes, Sunrise, Death Valley*. Adams, *Autobiography*, 246–47, and Alinder, *Ansel Adams: A Biography*, 212–14. A number of variations of *Manly Beacon, Death Valley National Monument*, have been published as circa 1952; however, close scrutiny reveals that they are all related to a vertical image published by Adams in 1950 in his book *My Camera in the National Parks*. The numbering of the related negatives by Adams as 1-NPS-xxx suggests that this group was actually made during one of his 1947 or 1948 trips while working on the Guggenheim Fellowship.

111. Karen E. Quinn and Theodore E. Stebbins Jr., *Weston's Westons: California and the West* (Boston: Museum of Fine Arts, Boston, in association with Bulfinch Press/Little, Brown, 1994), 23.

112. Adams, *Autobiography*, 246.

113. Adams to White, [1947], quoted in Adams, *Letters and Images, 1916 to 1984*, 180.

114. Adams and Newhall, "Death Valley," 33.

115. Ibid., 35.

116. Ibid., 16.

117. Carlson to Adams, October 22, 1952, AAA, CCP.

118. Adams to Carlson, November 21, 1952, AAA, CCP.

119. Raymond Carlson, "Mission in the Sun," *Arizona Highways* 30, no. 4 (April 1954): 1.

120. Adams to Chinn, November 21, 1952, AAA, CCP.

121. Ibid.

122. Chinn to Adams and Newhall, March 23, 1954, AAA, CCP.

123. Adams and Newhall, "Mission San Xavier del Bac," 13.

124. Adams, *Photographs of the Southwest*, vii.

125. Ibid.

126. See Karen Haas's essay "'A Great Day for Photography'" in this volume for more about The Lane Collection and the critical part that Ansel and Virginia Adams played in its formation (p. 91).

127. Adams, *Photographs of the Southwest*, ix.

A GREAT DAY FOR PHOTOGRAPHY

1. Sheeler to Lane, October 25, 1954.

2. Adams to Lane, October 25, 1954.

3. Lane to Adams, November 2, 1954.

4. Ansel Adams, *Conversations with Ansel Adams*, oral history interviews conducted by Ruth Teiser and Catherine Harroun, Bancroft Library Regional Oral History Office, in 1972, 1974, and 1975 (Berkeley: Regents of the University of California, 1978), 537.

5. Adams to Lane, August 12, 1967: "I deeply appreciate—more than you know—the great interest you have expressed in my work."

6. Adams to Lane, September 1, 1967.

7. Lane to Adams, November 9, 1968.

8. Adams to Lane, November 5, 1967.

9. Lane to Adams, June 1, 1968.

10. Lane to Adams, May 17, 1968.

11. Lane to Adams, December 5, 1967.

12. Lane to Adams, December 12, 1967.

13. Adams to Lane, October 7, 1974.

14. Lane to Adams, August 25, 1976.

15. Adams to Lane, September 26, 1979, Ansel Adams Archive (AAA), Center for Creative Photography (CCP), Tucson, Arizona.

16. Lane to Adams, November 12, 1981.

THE SIERRA CLUB OUTING ALBUMS, 1920–1945

1. Anne Hammond, "Ansel Adams and the High Mountain Experience," *History of Photography* 23, no. 1 (Spring 1999): 89.

2. The Bancroft's Sierra Club albums all share the number prefix 1971.031. The Ansel Adams albums are given the suffixes 1920:01-ALB, 1923:01-ALB, 1925:03-ALB, 1927:01-ffALB, 1928:04a-ffALB and 1928:04b-ffALB, 1929:03-ffALB, 1929:05-ALB, 1930:02-ffALB, 1931:01-ffALB, 1932:02-ffALB, 1933:01-ffALB, 1934:01-ffALB, 1935:01-ffALB, 1936:01-ffALB, and 1945:01-ALB.

3. Frederick Turner, "Introduction: The American Land and the History of Hope," in *Sierra Club: 100 Years of Protecting Nature*, by Tom Turner (New York: Harry N. Abrams, 1991), 23. Yosemite Park was created in 1864 but was governed by the state of California rather than the federal government. The surrounding High Sierra were made a national park in 1890, but at that point the Yosemite Valley and Mariposa Grove were still in state possession. Even when the state ceded these areas to the federal government, there was no National Park Service to manage Yosemite, or any of the parks, until 1916, hence the need for a watchdog group to protect the area's wilderness interests.

4. Tom Turner, *Sierra Club*, 47–48.

5. Bancroft Library, University of California, Berkeley, album 1971.031.1923:01-ALB. "Plain" meant that the negative was printed directly to retain the original sharp focus; "soft-focus" meant the image was intentionally blurred slightly when the negative was printed.

6. "Photographic Exhibit," *Sierra Club Bulletin* 13, no. 4 (August 1928): 124–25.

7. Ansel Adams, *Ansel Adams: An Autobiography* (Boston: Little, Brown, 1985), 142.

8. *Milestone Mountain* appeared in both 1927 and 1932. *Mount Winchell* appeared in both 1930 and 1933.

9. The portfolio sold for fifty dollars, a stunning price at the time. Albert Bender, Adams' first major patron, subsidized the project by purchasing ten portfolios and soliciting friends to buy additional copies. Adams was embarrassed by both the abandonment of the term *photograph* and the misspelling in the title—"Sierra" is already plural and does not require a final *s*. The edition, originally intended to number one hundred, plus ten artist's proofs, was never completely sold out, and the copy that is now in The Lane Collection was still in Adams' possession in the 1960s.

10. Adams to Bender, July 25, 1927, quoted in Adams, *Autobiography*, 140–41.

11. Walter L. Huber, "The Sierra Club in the Land of the Athabaska," *Sierra Club Bulletin* 14, no. 1 (February 1929): 8.

12. Ibid., 8–9.

13. Mary Street Alinder, *Ansel Adams: A Biography* (New York: Henry Holt, 1996), 40–41.

14. Always concerned with fine workmanship, Adams even specified which firm he would use for the portfolio's title page (the San Francisco fine book printers Johnck and Seeger) and who would make the portfolio cases (bookbinder Hazel Dreis).

15. Ansel Adams, *Examples: The Making of 40 Photographs* (Boston: Little, Brown, 1983), 11. In this account of *Frozen Lake and Cliffs*, Adams used Alfred Stieglitz's term "equivalent," meaning an abstracted image that captures the photographer's emotions at the moment of making the image, thus becoming the visual equivalent of that fleeting experience. John Szarkowski seemed to have appreciated the strenuous and challenging nature of the Sierra Club outings when he wrote of *Frozen Lake and Cliffs*, "This is not a landscape for picnics, or for nature appreciation, but for the testing of souls." John Szarkowski, "Kaweah Gap and Its Variants," in *Ansel Adams, 1902–1984*, ed. James Alinder (Carmel, CA: Friends of Photography, 1984), 14.

16. Ethel Boulware, "Afoot with the Sierra Club in 1933," *Sierra Club Bulletin* 19, no. 3 (June 1934): 9.

1. "Hornitos," *Sierra Foothill Magazine*, http://www.sierrafoothillmagazine.com/hornitos.html (accessed January 9, 2005).

2. Sierra College, On the Road: Hornitos, http://www.sierracollege.edu/events/thecenter/ontheroad/ontheroad_hornitos.html (accessed January 31, 2005).

3. Susan Ehrens, "Alma Lavenson: An Enduring Vision," in *Alma Lavenson: Photographs* (Berkeley: Wildwood Arts, 1990), 7, 9.

4. Ansel Adams, "Exploring the Commonplace," *U.S. Camera* 7, no. 4 (May 1944): 34.

5. Alma R. Lavenson, "Virginia City: Photographing a 'Ghost Town,'" *U.S. Camera* 1, no. 10 (June/July 1940): 65–66.

6. Ibid., 66.

7. Ibid., 65.

8. The 1930s date for the potential *Life* magazine spread comes from the presence of a large group of 35 mm negatives of the Hornitos "homecoming," found in the Ansel Adams Archive (AAA) at the Center for Creative Photography (CCP). An examination of the images suggests a date of 1938 for the group, based on a dated license plate. For a discussion of the popularity of ghost towns, especially their place in the American conception of the mythical West, see Dydia Delyser, "'Good, by God, We're Going to Bodie!': Ghost Towns and the American West," in *Western Places, American Myths: How We Think about the West*, ed. Gary J. Hausladen (Reno: University of Nevada Press, 2002), 273–95. Delyser traces the term "ghost town," which seems to have first been used between 1910 and 1920, and points to the increased automobile tourism of the 1920s as a period of intensified interest in these abandoned mining towns (273, 278, 282).

9. Mike Conway, "Adams' Photos Provide a Gateway to Yosemite," *Merced Sun-Star* (July 25, 1983): 6.

10. Maloney modeled the *U.S. Camera Annual* on examples such as the German *Deutsche Lichtbild* and the French *Fotografie*.

11. The first series of articles comprised "Photography of Architecture," *U.S. Camera* 1, no. 7 (1940): 56–59, 62–63; "An Approach to a Practical Technique," *U.S. Camera* 1, no. 9 (April/May 1940): 81, 90, 91; "Discussion of Filters," *U.S. Camera* 1, no. 11 (October 1940): 54, 56, 57; "Photo-Murals," *U.S. Camera* 1, no. 12 (November 1940): 52–53, 61–62, 71–72; "New York: On the 'Just Right' Conditions for a Picture," *U.S. Camera* 1, no. 13 (December 1940): 74; and "Practical Hints on Lenses," *U.S. Camera* 1, no. 15 (1941): 54, 61.

12. Ansel Adams, "Exploring the Commonplace," *U.S. Camera* 7, no. 4 (May 1944): 33–35, 53; "People," *U.S. Camera* 7, no. 5 (June 1944): 24–26, 52; "Manzanar," *U.S. Camera* 7, no. 8 (November 1944): 16–17, 59; and "Christmas Trees," *U.S. Camera* 7, no. 9 (December 1944): 16–17.

13. Adams, *Autobiography*, 258.

14. Ansel Adams, *Born Free and Equal: Photographs of the Loyal Japanese-Americans at Manzanar Relocation Center, Inyo County, California* (New York: U.S. Camera, 1944).

15. Adams, *Autobiography*, 263.

16. See Karen Haas's "Ansel Adams: Seeking a Center for Photography" in this volume for additional discussion of Adams' teaching (p. 11).

17. Adams, "People," 24.

18. Ibid., 25.

19. Ibid., 52.

20. Ibid.

21. Adams' essay "The Expanding Photographic Universe" in *Miniature Camera Work* (New York: Morgan and Lester, 1938) includes a reproduction of the bearded gentleman entitled *Old Timer*, cropped at the top and left side to emphasize the man's focused attention on the newspaper he holds. Adams also planned to use *Residents, Hornitos* to illustrate his unpublished manuscript "Geometric Approach to Composition," now in the AAA, CCP, making specific reference to the linear elements of his composition of the two men.

22. Several of Edward Weston's images of Hornitos are found in The Lane Collection, including two variations of graffiti entitled *Wall Scrawls, Hornitos* (Weston's negative numbers are ML40-H-1 and ML40-H-5); his view of the cemetery, *Hornitos, Motherlode* (ML40-H-2); a detail of Saint Catherine's, *Church Door, Hornitos* (ML40-H-6); and two images of a brick wall with flaking plaster, *Hornitos, Motherlode* (ML40-H-3 and ML40-H-4).

1. Quoted in Nancy Newhall, *Ansel Adams: The Eloquent Light* (San Francisco: Sierra Club, 1963), 129.

2. Andrea Gray [Stillman], *Ansel Adams: An American Place* (Tucson: Center for Creative Photography, 1982), unpaginated, pl. 33. Another version of this screen, made in the early- to mid-1950s, was in the artist's own collection. Its beautifully glowing highlights belied the fact that the original photograph was taken in subdued light without a very accurate meter. Adams later described it as underexposed and always one of his more challenging negatives to print.

3. Ansel Adams, with Mary Street Alinder, *Ansel Adams: An Autobiography* (London: Thames and Hudson, 1985), 130–32.

4. Ansel Adams, *The Print: Contact Printing and Enlarging* (Hastings-on-Hudson: Morgan and Morgan, 1967), 105 and 111.

5. In my research on the screens, I am greatly indebted to Adams scholar Andrea Stillman and to Leslie Calmes, archivist at the Center for Creative Photography. The numbers most often quoted are twelve or thirteen, although there is still disagreement over what those dozen or so screens were and where they are today.

6. For example, one of Adams' three-paneled screens depicting foliage was described as having been in the 1952 group exhibition at MoMA, "Diogenes with a Camera II" (perhaps the *Leaves, Mills College* screen owned by the artist [see n. 2]); see MoMA press release (November 1952), housed at Getty Research Institute, Newhall Collection, box 82, folder 2. Adams' 1937 show at the University of California was also said to include "general subjects and large screens"; see Adams to McAlpin, December 14, 1937. Two of his screens, *Fresh Snow* (in the collection of Ted and Jeannette Spencer) and *Sonoma County Hills/Oak Tree, Rain* (in the Skirball collection), appeared in the "Eloquent Light" exhibition organized by Nancy Newhall in 1963; *Fresh Snow* was also featured in John Szarkowski's "Ansel Adams and the West" show at MoMA in 1979.

7. The dimensions of the various screens differ, from about 5 feet to 6 feet high and approximately 8 feet to 10 feet long. The size of the individual panels was to some extent limited by the size of the rolls of

paper (40 inches wide) that were available to Adams at the time. Jiuan-jiuan Chen, conservator at the George Eastman House, has done research on the various varnishes and lacquers Adams used on his folding screens.

8. See Alice Gray, *Ansel Adams: The National Park Service Photographs* (New York: Abbeville, 1995), 10, in which she quotes Adams as saying: "Photomurals, because of the obvious limitations of the medium of photography, must be simpler—either purely decorative (like the screen in Secretary Ickes's office) or forcefully interpretive. I do not believe in mere big scenic enlargements, which are usually shallow in content and become tiresome in time."

9. Udall to Adams, January 31, 1961. Adams to Udall, August 4, 1967, Ansel Adams Archive (AAA), Center for Creative Photography (CCP).

10. This replacement screen is the same subject as the one Adams made in late 1947 or early 1948 for his architect friend Ted Spencer and Spencer's wife, Jeannette. Today the Spencers' screen is in the collection of the Stanford University Art Museum, having been donated by New York collector Peter Steil in 1982.

11. Adams to Udall, February 18, 1968; Udall to Adams, March 26, 1968, AAA, CCP. Unfortunately, an April 15, 1985, letter from National Gallery of Art curator of American art Nicolai Cikovsky to Adams' assistant Mary Street Alinder describes the Department of the Interior's *Fresh Snow* screen as too badly damaged to conserve (AAA, CCP).

12. Ansel Adams, "Photo-Murals," *U.S. Camera* 1, no. 12 (November 1940): 52–53, 61–62, 71–72. See also my discussion of Adams' mural-size prints for "A Pageant of Photography" on p. 27 of this volume.

13. This photograph may have been taken at Meyer's Ranch in Yosemite, a site that Adams and his friend Edward Weston visited together in September 1940. Weston's very similar pictures of wooden wagon wheels in a field, made during that trip, may well have been inspired by this late 1930s image by Adams. According to Michael Komanecky, Virginia Fabbri Butera, and Janet W. Adams, *The Folding Image: Screens by Western Artists of the Nineteenth and Twentieth Centuries* (New Haven: Yale University Art Gallery, 1984), 269n4, Adams recalled that they left this screen behind when he and Virginia moved from their San Francisco house to Carmel Highlands in 1962. The choice of wagon wheels is an unusual one for the artist, as all his other known screens depict either close-ups of nature or landscapes, but it is interesting to note that wagon wheels have historically been a popular subject in Japanese scrolls, screens, and lacquerware.

14. Although Adams did make four-part screens—and one example even had five sections—he claimed that the three-panel screen was the "most satisfactory form." See Adams, "Photo-Murals," 53.

15. Adams, "Photo-Murals," 53. Adams goes on to suggest that a small-scale model be made of a screen before an enlargement is produced, as "one of the most severe problems in dividing any composition into sections is to retain compositional value in each section."

16. Nancy Newhall, "Ansel Adams: Photographer and Reality," 1951, unpublished biography, chapter 5: "Extensions of an Idea: Art and Audience," 55–65, Getty Research Institute, Newhall Collection, box 251.

17. For an overview of the history of both Asian and Western screens, see Komanecky, Butera, and Adams, *The Folding Image*. One of the basic differences between Adams' screens and Japanese examples is that most of Adams' are three-paneled and Japanese screens are nearly always made up of two, four, or six panels.

18. Komanecky, Butera, and Adams, *Folding Image*, 269n10.

19. Christie's New York, *Photographs*, Thursday, October 4, 2001, lot 130.

20. Adams, in his book *The Print* (1983), describes having made three screens for close friends in 1948—Betty and George Marshall (now in the collection of George Eastman House, Rochester, New York), Ted and Jeannette Spencer (Stanford University Art Museum collection), and David McAlpin—but in an undated letter to Nancy Newhall, written in December 1947, he describes the three screens as finished. This probably meant that the photographs had been printed but not yet mounted. A letter dated June 7, 1948, from Nancy Newhall to Adams, supports this idea: "Betty's screen is beautiful!!! The tones are exquisite. Crazy to see Dave's. Too bad they've both been having troubles getting them mounted. The lack of the right aluminum channeling seems the real crux" (AAA, CCP).

21. See McAlpin's essay "Photographic Experience with Ansel Adams," in Edwin Land, David H. McAlpin, Jon Holmes, and Ansel Adams, *Ansel Adams: Singular Images* (Boston: Little, Brown, 1974), unpaginated. In it McAlpin describes the subject of his screen as pine needles floating on the water's surface, but they are clearly blades of grass. The *Grass and Pool* image was also included in Adams' *Portfolio III* (1960).

22. This image, which is simply titled *Leaves, Owens Valley, California* (about 1937), was mistakenly identified as representing palm fronds; it is reproduced in Adams, *Natural-Light Photography* (Hastings-on-Hudson: Morgan and Morgan, 1952), 4, and a picture of the screen in situ in Beaumont Newhall's office, about 1971, appears in Newhall's autobiography, *Focus: Memoirs of a Life in Photography* (Boston: Bulfinch Press, 1993), 228.

23. Adams to Beaumont Newhall, March 3, 1950, George Eastman House Archives.

24. "I have a brainstorm: I made a grand screen (3-panel) for the Pasadena exhibit. It is the best one yet—same pattern as Betty's but much more brilliant. . . . I thought this screen had been sold but the client backed out at the last minute. . . . How would you like me to send the screen to George Eastman House? On a loan basis—until somebody ups and buys it?" (ibid.). A decade later, on March 8, 1960, Adams donated the screen to the Eastman House. Newhall began as curator at the Eastman House in 1948, was named director in 1958, and retired in 1971.

25. Adams' photograph *Oak Tree, Rain* is often mistakenly dated 1960, which cannot be the case, as it appears on the screen made for the Skirballs in 1951.

26. See Komanecky, Butera, and Adams, *Folding Image*, 266. Adams wrote to Nancy Newhall on April 22, 1951: "Skirball screen installed yesterday with great success! . . . Best one yet."

27. The Mudds' screen came to the CCP in 1999 and was acquired in 2000.

28. Ansel Adams, *Conversations with Ansel Adams*, oral history interviews conducted by Ruth Teiser and Catherine Harroun, Brancroft Library Regional Oral History Office, in 1972, 1974, and 1975 (Berkeley: Regents of the University of California, 1978), 501. Adams credits the third Guggenheim, like "A Pageant of Photography" in 1940, with inspiring him to produce more "big screens" and "panel pictures" during this period. Bill and Saundra Lane visited the "Eloquent Light" exhibition in San Francisco in 1963, and again in a reduced version at the Museum of Fine Arts, Boston, in 1967; their excitement at seeing it explains, in part, the relatively large number of works they eventually purchased from the show.

SUGGESTED READING

Adams, Ansel. *The American Wilderness*. Edited by Andrea Gray Stillman. Introduction by William A. Turnage. Boston: Little, Brown, 1990.

————. *Ansel Adams*. Edited by Liliane De Cock. Hastings-on-Hudson, NY: Morgan and Morgan, 1972.

————. *Ansel Adams: California*. Edited by Andrea Gray Stillman. Introduction by Page Stegner. Boston: Little, Brown, 1997.

————. *Ansel Adams in Color*. Edited by Harry M. Callahan, with John P. Schaefer and Andrea Gray Stillman. Introduction by James L. Enyeart. Boston: Little, Brown, 1993.

————. *Ansel Adams: Letters and Images, 1916–1984*. Edited by Mary Street Alinder and Andrea Gray Stillman. Foreword by Wallace Stegner. Boston: Little, Brown, 1988.

————. *Ansel Adams, 1902–1984*. Edited by James Alinder. Carmel, CA: Friends of Photography, 1984.

————. *Examples: The Making of 40 Photographs*. Boston: Little, Brown, 1983.

————. *The Grand Canyon and the Southwest*. Edited by Andrea Gray Stillman. Introduction by William A. Turnage. Boston: Little, Brown, 2000.

————. *Our National Parks*. Edited by Andrea Gray Stillman and William A. Turnage. Boston: Little, Brown, 1992.

————. *Photographs of the Southwest: Selected Photographs Made from 1928 to 1968 in Arizona, California, Colorado, New Mexico, Texas, and Utah*. Boston: New York Graphic Society, 1976.

————. *Trees*. New York: Bulfinch, 2004.

————. *Yosemite and the High Sierra*. Edited by Andrea Gray Stillman. Introduction by John Szarkowski. Boston: Little, Brown, 1994.

————. *Yosemite and the Range of Light*. Boston: New York Graphic Society, 1979.

Adams, Ansel, with Mary Street Alinder. *Ansel Adams: An Autobiography*. Boston: Little, Brown, 1985.

Alinder, James. *Ansel Adams: Classic Images*. Boston: Little, Brown, 1986.

Alinder, Mary Street. *Ansel Adams: A Biography*. New York: Henry Holt, 1996.

Hammond, Anne. *Ansel Adams: Divine Performance*. New Haven, CT: Yale University Press, 2002.

Kemmerer, Allison. *Reinventing the West: The Photographs of Ansel Adams and Robert Adams*. Andover, MA: Addison Gallery of American Art, Phillips Academy, 2001.

Newhall, Nancy Wynne. *Ansel Adams: The Eloquent Light, His Photographs, and the Classic Biography*. Millerton, NY: Aperture, 1980.

Peeler, David P. *The Illuminating Mind in American Photography: Stieglitz, Strand, Weston, Adams*. Rochester, NY: University of Rochester Press, 2001.

Quinn, Karen E., and Theodore E. Stebbins Jr. *Ansel Adams: The Early Years*. Boston: Museum of Fine Arts, Boston, 1991.

Read, Michael, ed. *Ansel Adams, New Light: Essays on His Legacy and Legend*. San Francisco: Friends of Photography, 1993.

Spaulding, Jonathan. *Ansel Adams and the American Landscape: A Biography*. Berkeley: University of California Press, 1995.

[Stillman], Andrea Gray. *Ansel Adams: An American Place, 1936*. Tucson: Center for Creative Photography, University of Arizona, 1982.

Szarkowski, John. *Ansel Adams at 100*. Boston: Little, Brown, 2001.